To Bob & Jan:

I have so many pleasant memories of the earlier days of Continental, especially of your smiling face in the office, Jan. We shared in the best of airline operations and flying, that's for sure. I hope that you enjoy "Stardust Falling".

Wes Oss
1-24-08

STARDUST FALLING

BY

RET. CAPT. WES COSS

Copyright 2007

ISBN#978-0-9779243-0-1

Written by Wesley G. Coss
Published by Wesley G. Coss

Edited by Jaculine Harrier-Coss, Gerald A. Coss
and Wm. von Schulz

Book name and cover design by Annette R. Coss

Photography Layout by Gerald A. Coss and
Jody Coss Hillside Studio Staff of Freeport, Il.

Printed by:
A-1 Printing & Graphics, Inc.
22873 Lockness Ave.
Torrance, CA 90501
www.a1prints.com

www.stardustfalling.com
stardustfallingbook@yahoo.com
PO Box 6133 Denver, CO 80206-0133

DEDICATION

First and foremost, I want to dedicate this book to the brave men and women of the French Resistance. To those French Patriots that I have named, and to the many that forever remain nameless yet are deeply embedded in my memory, they are sincerely thanked, appreciated, and loved. Without their help I would surely have spent the remainder of WWII in a POW camp. These people are my heroes and always will be. They knew the cost of freedom and were willing to pay the price to be FREE.

Also, I would like to honor the crew of "Stardust," and the memory of S/Sgt. Edward Madigan, whose life was lost in the crash of "Stardust" on Jan 27th 1944.

I would also like to mention the men of the 99th Bomb Group and their Historical Society, and the Air Forces Escape and Evasion Society (AFEES), whose members have been shot down, evaded capture, and escaped the enemy to find FREEDOM again.

To ALL those who share the love of flying. I salute you!

Ret. Capt. Wes Coss

STARDUST FALLING

"all I ever wanted to do was fly…"

INTRODUCTION

If it were the carefree sixties, Fonzie would be loudly reving his motorcycle and Potsie would be readying his souped up jalopy while the neighbors shook their heads at the noise created by this disrespectful generation. It was the forties, however, and neighbors were more concerned about the rationing of gas and tires and sugar, and about sending their sons to war.

On a sultry, hot August day, even before the noon "whistle" blew, a huge Boeing B-17 "Flying Fortress" passed over the water tower and proceeded southwest out of sight. Within minutes, it returned loud and low overhead thrilling the town's youngsters, and while amusing many, others considered the antics wasteful as homegrown Lt. Wesley Coss roared down Main Street from west to east. All four powerful engines made a prolonged rumble as the pilot showed off *his* town to *his* crew. The airplane then made a turn to the north and came back over the village lower and slower than before. At the south edge of the small town, the throttles were pushed forward and the graceful bird made its exit in a shallow climb to head back from this practice mission to its Tennessee base.

A late afternoon walk through the village by the pilot's father, the local barber, soothed some angry locals as he paid some for the broken cups and dishes. That evening, he scolded his son by phone saying that he might be reported for the escapade and could be reprimanded. What could they do, thought Wes, "send me to combat?" To combat he went, not as a reprimand for rattling a few windows and dishes, but to dutifully fly for his country.

Barely out of their teens, boys no longer had time for adolescent pranks and quickly became men. Some lived to tell their stories, far too many did not. Lt. Wesley Coss not only survived, but thankfully shares the following account.   JHC

STARDUST FALLING
By
Ret. Capt. WES COSS

CONTENTS

ONE:
    Growing Up In Paw Paw   1

TWO:
    Learning To Fly   15

THREE:
    Royal Canadian Air Force   37

FOUR:
    U.S. Army Air Corps. Roswell & B17 Combat Training   69

FIVE:
    North Africa And Italy   105

SIX:
    Combat In Italy   141

SEVEN:
    Goodbye Stardust   175

EIGHT: The Maquis And Marcel	201
NINE: Aix-en-Provence	223
TEN: Perpignon	243
ELEVEN: Crossing The Pyrenees	259
TWELVE: Spain	287
THIRTEEN: Madrid And Gibraltar	319
FOURTEEN: England	339
FIFTEEN: Home At Last	365
EPILOGUE	373
POSTSCRIPT	385

CHAPTER 1

GROWING UP IN PAW PAW

In the sleepy pre-dawn hours, Doctor W. M. Avery was called to preside over the delivery of Art and Anna Coss' first-born child. The good doctor arrived at the home of Alf and Leaf Burnett, parents of Anna Coss, in time to attend to the delivery. At that time, they lived in the house on the east end of Main Street later known as the Gehlfuss house.

Recalling the tales I heard over the ensuing years, I will elaborate on supposition from this point forward. Doc Avery put his big finger in my small mouth to clear the mucus and promptly turned me upside down. Holding me by the heels, he smacked me firmly on the butt. I let out a squall that could be heard up and down the entire length of the one-block long main street in this small and close-knit town. It seems we are all destined to enter this world in such an undignified manner. Here I was, here I am -- HELLO WORLD!

My father, and his father before him, owned the barber shop on the main street of this small farming town in northern Illinois of Paw Paw. It was named after a grove of "paw paw trees," a mile or so southeast of town, bearing fruit similar to that of a small dark banana. My father, Art Coss, was most excited that they had a son as their firstborn child. After visiting with his wife and their new baby for a time, Art walked the half-block to the barbershop to help his father with the regular morning shave customers. On entering the shop he announced, "It's a boy." Grandpa Leander A. (Lee) Coss was happy for his son but didn't miss a stroke as he shaved the gentleman in his barber chair. Having raised seven children and previously welcomed several grand-children made this all-important event "no big deal." Still, Grandpa Lee broke out a fresh box of cigars for Art and all of the day's customers. For Alf and Leaf Burnett, however, it was somewhat more of a *big deal* as this was only their second grandchild and their very first grandson. Anna's younger sister and brother, Olive and Alfred, who were still living at home with their parents, were quite excited to meet and greet their new nephew.

Olive, couldn't wait to get on the telephone to tell their other sister Mabel about the new baby boy. Mabel and her husband, Cloyd lived on a farm several miles outside of this small town. Cloyd professed that he still had a day of farm work to complete, but Mabel wasn't about to wait until evening to go into town to see the baby. So, her husband obligingly ceased what he was doing, cranked up their Model "T" Ford, showed her how to shift gears with the foot pedals and how to control her speed, and sent her merrily on her way to town. Cloyd failed, however, to show her how to *stop* the Model "T." Mable proceeded carefully into town and tried to park in front of her parents' home. When she attempted to stop the car, it jumped the curb, crossed the lawn, and hit the porch with a force hard enough to dislodge one of the ornate wooden columns that supported the porch roof. Fortunately, this stopped the Model "T" and she hurriedly dashed into the house and flew up the stairs to see her first nephew.

Art Coss was on his way back to his in-laws' home just in time to see the car strike the porch. He joined his father-in-law in assessing the damage to the porch and helped him push the Model "T" back out onto the street where it really belonged. Thankfully, there was no apparent damage to the car but the porch was definitely a different story, needing lots of repair. Seems they don't make cars now the way they did in the old days. A bumper was a bumper then and it certainly served its purpose on that day when a mere "house" met a formidable "T."

All of the above is hearsay of course. The one fact that I know for sure is that Doc Avery did the honors at my delivery, and I have heard the tale of my Aunt Mabel running the "Model T" into the porch many, many times.

By the time I was nearing two, my first sister Audrey arrived. My Aunt Mabel and Uncle Cloyd then took every opportunity to take me to the farm with them to spend the night. I enjoyed everything on the farm except the chickens. An incident had happened where a rooster attacked me from the back and knocked me down and pecked and flailed me furiously. From that day to this I will not touch anything with feathers. Chickens, in my mind, are for eating and furnishing eggs for breakfast only, but are not to be tolerated in *any* other form!

I spent my first four or five years in this type of setting. I was at home with my family most of the time, but I did spend time on the farm whenever the opportunity arose. About this time, my second sibling Norma arrived. I was too young to remember her birth, but I do recall when they brought "the baby" home. With three children my parents were indeed busy.

At about seven years old, the "great depression" hit with a force that is hard to describe. As a small child I knew that it was bad, as this was all of the talk between my family and their friends. So many men were out of work and then all of the banks in the country closed. Everyone's savings accounts were frozen. Months later when the banks reopened, the depositors were allowed to take possession of *half* of their money. The bank owed the account-holder the remainder plus interest. I had about $70 in the savings account that my parents had started for me. When we were able to do so, we took the allowable $35 out of the account and with part of that money they bought a Shetland pony mare for me. Her name was "Cricket." The

3

STARDUST FALLING

pony was pastured on my aunt and uncle's farm and I spent many happy and imaginative days riding the pony bareback.

Shetland ponies are not always noted as friendly and "Cricket" was not exactly overjoyed with me. As I grew older, I learned to deal with her orneriness and could assert some amount of control over her. I often rode her across my uncle's farm to meet another farm-boy, Roger Tarr, at a creek that was about halfway between the two farms. We had great fun swimming and fishing in this shallow creek. I was probably about 10 at this time. I spent part of each summer on the farm and the rest in my home in Paw Paw. Each summer day that I was at home usually meant a baseball game. We would play "work up" baseball most of the time because we couldn't field one team, let alone two.

Work up baseball allowed each of us to field every position. The batter remained at bat as long as he got a hit. Running the bases meant running from home plate to first base and back. This meant that only a two-base hit counted. When you got a hit, you could then have another turn at bat before you went out to the field and to the bottom of the rotation.

All of my young friends had their own fielder's glove, and several owned a baseball. I always had the bat, as my Dad was the manager of the local *baseball town team* and I got all of the cracked and broken bats. I was fortunate that my grandfather, Alf Burnett, was quite skilled at gluing them back together. With a wood screw in the right place and wrapped with black friction tape, they were just as good as new.

My friends varied in age from a couple of years older to two or more years younger. This was a small town and there weren't that many boys my age to play with. A few of my friends that were regulars at our daily baseball game or other fun (mischief, some called it) were Tommy Boyle, who lived across from my grand-parents' home, and Kermit Knetsch, who lived on the opposite corner from my

GROWING UP IN PAW PAW

house. My cousins Bill Town and Marv Coss were regulars, as was Bob Avery. We always welcomed *anyone* who wanted to play ball with us. It mattered not if the newcomer could catch the ball as he could always pick it up when it stopped rolling and throw it back in to us.

On one nice summer's day when I was about 13 and my neighbor and friend Tommy Boyle was probably 11, he decided that we would see if we could ride his brother's motorcycle. We joyfully took his brother's old Henderson out of the family garage to see if we could get it started. We pushed the heavy bike down the short slope from his garage and finally, successfully got it running. Tom said he knew how to ride it and started off around the baseball outfield at a good clip. Eventually he stopped and told me to get on the bike. He showed me how to shift gears and control the speed, and I made a couple of circuits around the field. We soon decided that we had better return the bike to its normal parking place before our joy riding was detected.

Growing up was fun, school was easy, and if it hadn't been for the depression, it would have been idyllic. We were all poor and our parents worked very hard to keep food on the table and clothes on our back. Most of the people in town relied on their trees and gardens for their fruits and vegetables. We had three gardens that we kept planted and tilled so that my mother could can and preserve enough food to see us through the winter. We had schoolteachers living with us during the school year. The teachers paid room and board by the month, providing my parents with an income for the nine months of the school year. This also meant having to put a lot more food on the table than for just a family of five.

The barber business was very slow. There was not enough business for one barber, let alone two. Often farmers would bring eggs or butter or dressed chickens to barter for the family haircuts. Nearly everyone shaved themselves now, dull razor or not. The only exceptions to this were the local banker, the doctor, and a couple of other businessmen who thought it necessary to keep up the *appearance of prosperity*. Shaves were 15 cents and a haircut was two bits. I never thought about the fact that we were poor, as almost everyone else in our community was in the same situation; so being *poor* was never a conscious factor.

When I was eleven my only brother, Jerry, was born. I remember being able to see him at the noon recess of our school. I was happy to finally have a brother. The thought didn't cross my mind at that time that with us being 11 years apart in age, we probably would never actually be playmates. When he was six, I recall taking the little guy by the hand and proudly walking him to school. He was in first grade and I was a senior in high school and had already been flying airplanes solo for over a year. His eyes would light up with admiration, making me feel great to be his big brother!

The depression persisted but we never lacked food, as a matter of fact, my mother put good, nourishing meals on the table three times a day. Everyone was cash-poor. Even the farmers that owned substantial farms in the area were land-rich but cash-poor. Money had to be paid for coal to heat our house and the barbershop. There was the expense of the schoolbooks that always created a small crisis at the start of each school year. Then there was the question of whether there was enough money to buy tennis shoes for me so that I could go out for basketball practice in the fall of the year. Our mother made most of the girls' clothes.

I had a neighbor who lived across the street from our home who was in the business of fixing small electrical appliances in his home. His business was very slow, so in his spare time he built model airplanes as a hobby. He was quite good at this and I spent many happy hours watching him craft his models out of balsa wood and thin paper. He would then meticulously paint them to perfection. He made a large model of a "Ford Tri-motor" airplane that was so perfect in detail that it was displayed at the Chicago World's Fair.

I would watch my neighbor Roy Winterton by the hour on days and evenings when I could not play outdoors. He had several stacks of aviation magazines in his front room workshop and I would sit on the floor and look at the various airplanes in the magazines for hours on end. Under Roy's expert eye, I made several model airplanes of my own and was quite proud of my work.

When I was about 14 years old, I cut out an advertisement for a Piper J-3 Cub airplane. I filled out the coupon and put my age as 18. I soon received a nice brochure from Piper with a large and beautiful picture of a yellow J-3 Cub. The letter that accompanied the brochure said that a local Piper representative would "contact me soon." I just wanted the picture; I hadn't really counted on someone actually coming to talk with me! I was afraid of what my parents' reaction would be if a Piper dealer did try to contact me.

About a month later, on a sunny Saturday morning, a bright yellow J-3 Cub circled low over our town several times as if the pilot was looking for a place to land. I was sure that it was the Piper dealer, and I knew that if he landed and was looking for me, I was in d-e-e-p trouble. I was relieved when the airplane finally headed off in another direction. This was in 1937 and I imagine that the aircraft dealer, if it was indeed the Piper dealer, took one look at the poor little farming village and had his doubts that any 18 year old living there would have enough money to afford to buy a J-3 Cub.

By the time I was 13 or 14, I spent part of the summer months working on my Uncle Cloyd and Aunt Mabel's farm. I learned to hitch the horses to the corn plow and to drive the horses pulling a two-row corn plow. I helped with all of the chores - milking the cows, feeding the pigs. There was one duty that I detested most of all, which was to go to the hen house and gather the eggs. I wouldn't pull the hens off the nest to collect the eggs under them with my hands.

Instead, I would use a two-by-four board and gently pry the hen off the fruit of her labor, *quickly* snatching the eggs that the hen had been forced to abandon.

On the farm I did have a chance to drive the tractor, with my uncle beside me. I learned how to use the clutch to shift gears and I thoroughly enjoyed being able to drive the old tractor. I was afraid to even suggest that I might drive their car. My grandfather, Alf Burnett, would take me to the farm that he and grandma owned and rented out to my Uncle Alfred. I would help my grandfather in whatever he was doing around the farm, and sometimes he would let me drive his Chevrolet across the field and through a gate that he was holding open for me. Since we didn't own an automobile, I had no opportunity to try my driving skills on an actual road. Getting around town and out to my uncle's farm was always accomplished by getting on my bike and pedaling away. We never looked on this as exercise; it was just the normal way to get from one place to the other - cheap, handy, and the only set of "wheels" that I had.

In our small farming community there were only three sports. Baseball all summer, and then when it got too cold to catch or hit the baseball it was inside the school gymnasium for basketball all winter. The third sport was year-round and it was the activity of "boys chasing girls and girls chasing boys." This "sport" didn't, in any way, conflict with the two other activities of course.

By the time I was 15, I was working on the farm for my uncle when he needed me. In mid-summer, I had the opportunity to join a group of young men that went to work for a seed corn company detasseling hybrid seed corn. The area around Waterman, Illinois, was the location of this enterprise. Waterman was located about 20 miles northeast of my hometown and we were able to carpool to and from work. I think that my share of the ride came to about 75 cents a week. I was able to work at detasseling for three or four weeks that summer of 1938. This work was most welcome as it provided perhaps $50 or more to our larder, which meant that we could afford a new pair of corduroy pants for me to start the school year and the assurance that I would have tennis shoes for basketball that winter.

That '38 summer, I was also starting to take an interest in girls and had the occasion to get acquainted with a girl from the neighboring town of Shabbona, Illinois. Her mother and my mother were good friends and the young lady visited her grandparents, Mr. & Mrs. Schreck, who lived in Paw Paw. Her grandfather made horseshoes and shod horses, traveling from farm to farm as the need arose. She was close to my sister Audrey's age and they spent a great deal of time together. I was attracted to her and apparently she was interested in me. We sat on the porch steps talking most evenings that balmy summer. Her name was Dionne Firkins, and she was to play a large part in my young life.

School started the day after Labor Day and it was back to the grind of *education*. I was still more interested in building model-airplanes and spent a lot of time watching Roy Winterton at his model-building activities. School was sometimes interesting and sometimes exceedingly boring. I had favorite subjects of course, and those that I thoroughly detested, just like any other teenager. I was particularly fond of history. I would read the entire classroom textbook in the first couple of days of the school year. It was easy to remember the unfolding story of man's historical adventures with all of its twists and turns, and I devoured chapter after chapter.

It was in the fall of 1938 when I was a freshman in high school that disaster struck. A group of young guys, including myself, were looking for some mischief to get into when we decided to raid Mr. Roberts' muskmelon (cantaloupe) patch. We were busy picking the ripe melons when Mr. Roberts rose up out of his nearby berry patch and fired his shotgun at the sky. We took off, melons flying everywhere. I headed toward the high grass parallel to the road east out of town. This particular grassy area had one last fire hydrant almost completely obscured by the high weeds. I hit the hydrant with my left leg, going full speed. I took a real header and lay in the weeds for a while wondering if I had broken my leg above the left knee. I got up and started limping home. I was in great pain but made it, much to my short-lived relief.

I mistakenly told my mother the truth about this adventure. I said that we were swiping muskmelons and that Mr. Roberts had shot at us. She had utterly no sympathy for me, but did put some cold towels on the swollen leg and told me how disgusted she was with me. She sent me straight upstairs to bed. In the morning, I was in worse pain and told her that I couldn't possibly go to school. She insisted that I would indeed make it to school and I began hobbling the block and a half toward the school building. About halfway there, I fainted from the pain and was carried back home. The doctor was called, and after his inspection, he said that I had a severely torn tendon and muscle and would have to stay in bed until I could get around on crutches.

My basketball season had to sadly be cancelled, but after a couple of weeks I was able to get around. During the Christmas holiday, Dionne and I were able to see each other and being on crutches didn't seem to interfere with our spending time together.

I turned 16 on May first of 1939 and as soon as the school semester was finished, I started to work on the farm helping my Uncle Cloyd. I was looking forward to again working at Waterman detasseling seed corn when that work began. In mid-summer, the corn was shoulder high and the corn tassels were growing fast. The act of detasseling corn consisted of pulling the young tassels out of each stalk before they had a chance to pollinate their neighbors. Six rows would be denuded of their tassels and then two rows would be left with its tassels intact. By this method, the hybrid seed corn was created.

As in the year before, I had procured a ride to and from the facility and started work with great excitement and energy. Our team consisted mainly of young boys around my own age, and we joked

GROWING UP IN PAW PAW

around a lot and were a carefree and careless group. We were warned by one of the company foremen at noon of the first day that we were playing around too much and were leaving far too many tassels unpicked. He cautioned us that if we didn't straighten up and get down to business, we would be fired. This was a sobering thought and for the rest of that day, we did a far better job.

The second day on the job, however, we all got careless and were again leaving too many tassels. The foreman, who was my cousin Bernard Coss, came through the field behind us and stopped us at the end of our row. He said, "You are all fired. Go back to the office and pick up your pay for the day and a half that you have worked."

Frankly I was devastated; I knew that my parents were counting on me to again earn money to start my junior year at high school, and I knew for certain that I would be in big trouble when I went home that night.

On the day before and on this morning as we were working in the field, I had watched a cream-colored Taylorcraft airplane as it was flying around the Waterman Airport. The airport was about a half-mile north of the field that we were working that fateful morning. I was quite interested in the airplane and this may well have contributed to my missing some of my tassels.

After we were fired from the job, we had no transportation back to the plant and most of the guys headed directly across the field back to the facility. I elected to walk the short distance north to the airport, knowing I had to spend the rest of the day waiting for my ride home. The other carpool members were not working on the crew that was fired and I thought that I might as well spend the time at the airport.

When I arrived at the airfield, I saw several airplanes on the flight line and a couple more in the hanger. I spotted the cream-colored Taylorcraft that I had seen earlier and walked around it and boldly opened the door to peek inside. A man came out of the office and approached me and asked me if I wanted to take an airplane ride. I

STARDUST FALLING

told him that I didn't have the money to take a ride and confessed to him that I had been fired from my job a few minutes before. I also told him that I would be in big trouble with my parents when I got home that evening.

This man introduced himself as Harry Reed, the airport manager and asked me if I would like to wash the little Taylorcraft. He told me that if I did a good job on the plane, he would take me for a ride when I was finished. I was happy to accept the offer and went into the hangar for the bucket and sponge to get busy at the chore. By mid-afternoon, I had the airplane spotless and sat in the shade of the wing waiting for my ride.

I had ridden in an airplane several times before, and had sold ride tickets and strapped the passengers into the cockpit for a barnstormer that occasionally came to our town in his Travel-Air biplane. He would land in a field near some event that was taking place for the purpose of taking as many people as possible for an airplane ride. I think that it was a buck per person for the short ride. The bi-plane carried two passengers on each flight. I always had the honor to ride with him on his first flight of the day when he would make several steep wing-overs to attract attention. This was a definite thrill and he would then fly low over the landing field with both of us waving at the spectators starting to congregate.

These flights were usually on holidays such as the 4th of July, Labor Day, etc. The pilot was a very nice man named Bob Ball from Sterling, Illinois. I would call him at his home in Sterling to advise him when there was to be an event that he might be interested in. It was a thrill for me to see the big maroon and beige biplane with its OX-5 engine roaring overhead, and I knew that it was my friend and that I had a coveted job for the afternoon. If there was time before dark, he would take me for another ride as he was closing out the day. It was usually with another passenger who would be his last paying customer.

This was my total flying experience as I waited that afternoon in the shade for my bartered ride. The date was July 24th, 1939 and it was a beautiful summer day. Harry Reed finally came out to the sparkling Taylorcraft and showed that he was pleased with my effort. I had expected that he would get into the pilot's seat and I would occupy the seat beside him but this was not to be. He told me to get into the left seat and that he was going to give me my first flying lesson. This first lesson lasted for 20 minutes, and it was merely how to keep the airplane on an even keel and to find the place for the nose of the airplane on the horizon to keep it from gaining or losing altitude. The lesson ended all too soon and I was very excited about it. I couldn't wait to tell my parents that I had actually taken a flying lesson.

When Harry Reed and I got out of the airplane, he asked me if I wanted to come back tomorrow to work for him. If I did, he would give me another lesson. I was very happy with this turn of events as I had paid for a full week of rides to Waterman, and hoped that my parents would let me work at the airport for the remainder of the week.

I was in a fine mood until I encountered my father and mother at the dinner table that evening. My father was furious with my cousin Bernard for having fired me. My mother was concerned with the lost income that they had expected that I would earn, but said that they would get by without the money -- somehow. Then I dropped the bomb, telling them about my first flying lesson and that if I could go to work at the airport each day, I would get more flying lessons. My dad said "no" and that I had to go back to work for my uncle on the farm for the rest of the summer. My mother took my side and said, "Art, let the boy have a chance at this if he is set on it." My father said, "How could anyone ever make a living flying an airplane?" My mother stood her ground, and it was agreed that at least for the remaining two or three weeks that I had a ride available, I could work at the airport. Mother packed a lunch for me each day and I happily was on my way. Overjoyed actually!

I intend to start the next chapter under the title of "LEARNING TO FLY" which should more aptly be named "starting to learn to fly." Almost 44 years later I finally graduated, with 29,000 flying hours at age 60 - the FAA mandatory retirement age for any commercial airline pilot. As a military and airline pilot, I soon found out that you never stopped learning your trade. The learning process goes on from your first flight in the cockpit until your very last. I never thought of any other line of work other than flying. I would say that I was a very lucky person indeed.

CHAPTER 2

LEARNING TO FLY

The next morning, even before the hangar doors were open, I was ready for my new job. Harry Reed soon arrived and promptly had me help him move all of the airplanes out of the hanger, after which I was set to sweeping the hangar floor. After lunch I washed Harry's car, then waited in the shade of the wing of the airplane for my next lesson.

As each day progressed, it didn't take me long to learn how to gas up the visiting airplanes and I was always cautioned to use a soft rag to clean the Plexiglas windshield of the plane that I was refueling. When I had time from my other duties, I would help the aircraft mechanic, Clarence "Tink" Towner, with whatever maintenance he was involved in. About every other day I would receive another flying lesson. When my arranged ride to the Waterman airport ended, I hitchhiked to and from work. This was fairly easy, as the same people seemed to pick me up day after day to take me as far as they were going toward the airport. No doubt they had to hear my enthusiastic report of the wonders of being in the air over and over again.

The airport at Waterman, Illinois, was located about a mile east of the small farming town. It was situated on the northwest corner of the intersection of highways US 30 and Illinois 23, and had been one of the emergency airfields on the old airmail route between Chicago and

Omaha. There was a rotating light beacon, a combination weather station and home of the Eakle family and a new hangar had just been built that was about 200 yards west of the beacon.

The old hangar that had burned in 1936 had just been re-built by Dr. Neubauer of nearby Hinkley, Illinois. In the hangar fire of 1936, several fine aircraft were destroyed, including a Stinson Tri-Motor bi-plane. It took a long time for the economy to improve enough for the "Flying Doctor" to decide to construct a new hangar. The old enterprise was named Eagle Airways and that name was proudly bestowed to this new endeavor. Harry Reed rented the entire hangar and airfield and was now the airport manager.

The weather station was operated by Paul and Mary Eakle. The Eakle family was rather large with eight children and each was quite talented. Their father had built a plywood battleship float on a truck chassis. With the float painted silver and an American Legion insignia on both sides, it was in demand for many parades and events in Illinois. The family children participated in a drum and bugle corps to march along with the float and also performed on stage as well. Alice Eakle, the eldest, was an excellent artist as well as an accomplished musician. Next was Mavis and then Johnny, the oldest Eakle boy, who was my age.

In addition to the three older children, there was Nancy, Dea, Joey, and another boy, David Lee "Bucky," and the baby, Angela. Bucky was named after two early-day airmail pilots who, when the Chicago airport was "socked in," would spend some time in Waterman enjoying the Eakle's hospitality. Waterman was one of the last CAA {Civil Aeronautics Association), predecessor to the FAA (Federal Aviation Administration) emergency landing fields before Chicago on the Omaha to Chicago run. The pilots would have coffee and sometimes would enjoy Mary's special fried chicken. The pilots that Bucky was named after were Dave Behncke and E. Ham Lee.

LEARNING TO FLY

I heard many stories about the early days of the airmail history from Paul Eakle. Whenever he was notified by telephone that the weather in Chicago was too bad for the eastbound flight to continue beyond Waterman, Paul would go out onto the airfield and light flares to let the eastbound pilot know that he was to land at Waterman. (There were no radios in the cockpits at that time.)

An incident happened at the airport late in August 1939 that is still indelible in my mind. I was laying flat on the new curved corrugated metal roof of the hangar sawing the protruding bolts that were preventing the final work on the front of the new hangar. At the same time, I was aware that Les Smith was working on the OX 5 engine of his Travelair biplane. He had removed the wooden propeller and was trying to properly "time" the big magnetos on the engine. After much mechanical work, he remounted the propeller but didn't put the big lock nut on the shaft to secure the propeller. It was noon and I saw Les and a friend walk across highway 23 to the truck stop café for their lunch. After my own lunch, I again climbed the ladder to the hangar roof and continued to saw on the bolts.

In the meantime, Johnny Eakle and several of Alice's college friends, including some of the Eakle girls, drifted over to the hangar area to chat and watch the airplane activity. Les Smith turned the big Travelair airplane so that when the engine started it would not blow dirt into the hangar. The airport mechanic, Tink Towner, was in the cockpit and Les Smith was ready to try to start the big engine. At about this same time Alice Eakle, Johnny's older sister, and his younger brother Bucky were approaching the group of friends who were chatting in the area adjacent to the airplane. The little 6-year-old Bucky was following Alice on his tricycle. While continuing my work, I watched from my perch atop the hangar at all of the action going on below.

When Les was ready to swing the big prop to try to start the engine by hand he said, "Contact" and Tink replied, "Contact." Les Smith,

17

with a high leg kick, swung the big prop through its arc. The engine started with a roar and then the unexpected happened. The propeller flew off the airplane, just missing Les as it flew in an arc curving to where it hit Bucky Eakle, who was riding on his trike behind his big sister Alice. Bucky threw his arm up in a reflex action and the tip of the blade cut his right arm off above the elbow. The big wooden propeller completed its arc and clattered to the ground in the midst of the gathered friends. Johnny Eakle was hit in the leg and his friend Mel Elliot was hit in the elbow.

Alice picked up her little brother, and had the presence of mind to put a tight grasp on the bleeding stub and shout for someone to get a car and take him to the hospital in Waterman. Mel Elliot, although his one arm was tingling from the blow on the elbow, ran to Harry Reed's car, and finding the keys in the ignition, raced to the hospital with Alice holding tight to her little brother's stump of an arm.

Prompt action by his sister and the doctor at the hospital stopped the bleeding, and after a few days Bucky was out of the hospital to go through life minus his right arm. Neither Johnny Eakle nor Mel Elliot was seriously injured from the fragments of the propeller that had hit them.

From this accident, I gained a very healthy respect for the tremendous power of a rotating propeller. I was probably overly cautious in not letting anyone go near a revolving propeller after this horrible accident.

A few days after the accident injuring Bucky, I was again sawing at the bolts protruding from the front of the new hangar. I had climbed a long extension ladder to get at the bolts that couldn't be reached from above. I accidentally got a sharp piece of the metal saw debris in my right eye. After climbing down and washing my eye, I continued the task. A day or two later the eye was still dark red and hurting, so my mother took me to an ophthalmologist in the nearby larger town of LaSalle to have the eye examined. He removed a sharp

LEARNING TO FLY

metal splinter from my eye and it healed normally. The eye remained weak, however, and when I went to take my first CAA physical examination, I found that I had to have glasses to read the chart with the right eye. I soon got glasses and passed the physical on my second visit.

The summer vacation of 1939 ended with my having logged 6 hours of dual instruction, mostly in 15 and 20-minute segments in my logbook. I had hoped that I would be flying solo by the time that school started but that wasn't to be. I was now a junior in high school and again participated in all of the sports that the small town afforded, and each weekend I would hitchhike to and from the airport to work.

While continuing to work for Harry, I also helped the local airplane mechanic, Tink, in various chores. He was working at repairing a Kinner Bird biplane owned by Doc Lund of Malta, Illinois. I helped Tink with the fabric work; meanwhile, I enjoyed his many stories of the early days of flying.

It was a very sad day for me when I learned that there had been an accident and that Tink had been killed. He had been steering a tractor that was being towed behind a car driven by Doctor Neubauer (the Flying Doctor). The Doctor was towing it too fast and Tink lost control. The tractor tipped over and trapped Tink beneath. It caught fire and Tink perished. I really missed him and thought of him as one of the old men of aviation, although he was only 35 at the time of his death.

In mid-November of 1939, a Saturday morning with dense fog everywhere, I hitchhiked to Waterman hoping that the fog would lift and that I could fly later that day, or Sunday for sure. The hangar doors were closed, but I was generally kept busy sweeping and cleaning up in the hangar workshop. I heard a police car siren in the distance and went into the office just in time to see "Slim" Sebree, the De Kalb county deputy sheriff, drive onto the airport grounds and up the ramp to the hangar door. Slim Sebree was one of the student pilots at the airfield and was well known to all. He jumped out of the car and asked Harry if any of his airplanes were in the air. Harry said "No" and Slim informed us that he had received a call from a farmer saying that an airplane had crashed and burned in his cornfield. The farm was located near Shabbona Grove, which was southwest of the airport. The farmer had told Slim that two people were dead in the airplane accident.

This farm area was located in the southwest corner of De Kalb County and was unfamiliar to Slim. Knowing that I was from Paw Paw, a bit west of the farm in question, he asked me if I knew where the farm was located. I told him that I thought that I did, and he said, "Jump in the car and guide me." The fog had lifted a bit and Slim made good time, with the siren and lights on all the way to the farm. This ride in the patrol car was a real thrill to me, but I was totally unprepared for what was to unfold ahead of us in that field.

We found the farm without any delay and met Ole Larson and his wife in the yard of their farmhouse, both appearing dazed by the accident. They pointed to a smoking wreckage of an airplane about 300 yards from the farmhouse. It was nose down in a field where the corn had been harvested earlier. Woods bordered the cornfield and it was apparent that the airplane had clipped the top of the trees before nosing into the hard ground. The farmer told us that the pilot of the crashed airplane had survived and that a neighboring farmer had taken the injured man to the hospital in Waterman.

Slim and I made our way across the field to the devastating wreckage of the airplane. It was standing almost straight up with the tail high in the air. The fabric of the airplane had completely burned so that it was just a skeleton framework of metal tubing and charred wood. In the front cockpit where the passengers had been sitting, two bodies were burned beyond recognition. The airplane engine had been pushed back into the front cockpit, crushing their legs. Slim took a long dry cornstalk and pried the two bodies from the cockpit

LEARNING TO FLY

and they fell into the ashes in front of the airplane. The smell of burnt flesh mingled with the smell of burnt aircraft fabric made an indelible impression on me; one that unfortunately I will never forget.

Slim went back to the farmhouse to again interrogate the farm couple, and told them that the coroner would be notified and that the bodies would be removed as soon as possible. Slim drove me back to the airport at Waterman and then went to the Waterman hospital to interview the surviving pilot.

The ill-fated Travelair biplane had taken off from a Chicago airport earlier that morning with an intended destination of Green Bay, Wisconsin. They had gotten lost in the fog and ended up in Ole Larson's cornfield. The weather that particular morning was not flyable, at least not at Waterman.

Just after lunch that same day, a car drove into the airport parking area and a man came into the office. He said that he was from the Chicago Herald American Newspaper and wanted to get directions to the crash site. Someone told him that I had been there and I reluctantly agreed to guide him to the farm.

At first, I refused to go but was finally persuaded with the promise of two dollars for my effort. This *gentleman* of the press was the most "foul mouth" and profane individual that I have ever met. I was shocked and never forgot this character. He had his camera with him and took a picture of me in front of the wreck, with the bodies still in the ashes. The picture was published in the newspaper the next day. He dropped me off at the airport, and I had to ask him for the two dollars that he owed me or he would have driven off without paying. I certainly earned the pay that afternoon.

Finally, on November 24th, 1939, after about 9 hours of dual instruction from Harry Reed, I was able to solo the little cream colored Taylorcraft for a few minutes and was totally in seventh-heaven. The next day I flew dual with Spencer Mack, who was the airport flight instructor, after which he signed me off to fly solo. I was on my way and even *walked* slightly off the ground!

During the weekday, after school, and in the evenings of 1939 and the spring of 1940, I would set pins in my Uncle Harry Town's bowling alley. I was paid 5 cents a line and on a good night I might earn 80 cents. I tried to save enough so that I could buy 45 minutes to an hour of flying time on the weekend. The price for an hour of solo flying time in the little 40 horsepower T-craft was $6.00. By paying for part of my time and working for the rest of it, I was able to build up flight time fairly rapidly.

During my Christmas vacation of that year, Dionne was again visiting her grandparents and we were able to spend time together. On several evenings, we spent pleasant times singing Christmas carols with a group. I don't think that either of us thought that we were dating; we just enjoyed the time together. She would come to my house to visit my sister Audrey, but in truth I think it was to visit with me. I was sixteen and she was fifteen at the time. Although we didn't know it then, this was just the start of a teenage infatuation.

On January 17th, 1940, I flew to Aurora, Illinois and took the first CAA flight test of my career. I had to show inspector Whitter that I could safely fly solo and he issued me my new license number 94655, then named a "Solo License." I still have that number permanently on my flying license. I was now qualified to fly solo anywhere I wished, and was no longer restricted to 25 miles from my home airport. I had 30 hours of total flying time, and on my medical certificate it stated that I was 5' 10" and weighed 140 lbs.

It was at about this time, probably late January 1940, on a foggy Saturday morning that Harry asked me to take his wife's Lincoln coupe into a garage in Waterman to have it lubricated and the oil changed. I told him that I had never driven a car on a hard road (as it was called) as yet. Harry took me out onto the airport grounds in the Lincoln Coupe and we drove along the boundary fence line. He had

LEARNING TO FLY

me back the car up and park next to the fence at a 45-degree angle, as was the way most parking was done in those days. After he was satisfied that I could control the car properly, he told me to take it to the garage and wait for it to be serviced. Harry Reed was to solo me in an airplane and an automobile, both of which showed a great deal of trust. After this, Harry had me drive whenever we were to go anywhere together. He continued to teach me on each outing in the car. Harry was a wonderful confidence-builder for me.

In the spring of 1940, another young fellow from my hometown came to work at the Waterman airport. He was quite mechanically inclined and was employed by Harry to perform some of the duties that the mechanic Tink Towner had been doing. His name was Henry Marks. "Hank" was a couple of years older than me. We were good friends and Harry was busy teaching him to fly as part of his pay. He took a room in Waterman and was now working full time at the airport.

It wasn't too long before spring turned into summer and I had the long school vacation-time ahead of me. I worked full time at the airport that summer, sleeping in the tiny loft over the office. When it was too hot in that small crawl space, I slept on the hangar floor. After a couple of weeks of this, Harry asked me to work for him at night in a pool-hall he now operated in De Kalb, Illinois and he rented a small sleeping room for me in the same building.

Harry Reed was probably 25 or 26 in 1940. Spencer Mack had taught Harry to fly in a little red Taylorcraft that was hangered on the airport at the time. Harry promptly had his wife Edith purchase another Taylorcraft in partnership with another devotee, Ernie Long. Harry was to make money with the airplane that they had bought, and this was the aircraft that I took my first lessons and solo flight in. It was a 1937 model and had a Continental A-40 HP engine. When Harry had settled in De Kalb, Illinois and married Edith, he was the local teamster's union representative. He continued on their payroll while he tried to make the one airplane turn a profit. There were several other airplanes that were normally kept in the hangar, and I suppose the hangar rent for these aircraft helped to pay for his lease on the airport and hangar.

Soon after the cream colored T-craft was his to use, Harry received his private pilot's license. This gave him the opportunity to take passengers with him and soon he turned to charging them. Not long after he started taking passengers for hire, he began instructing. After his instructional period to solo, Harry was completely self-taught, as far as I know. He was a natural pilot and he proved to be very good at his trade. Harry was a promoter and an entrepreneur and was always behind on his bills, a common occurrence during this time. The glamour was there, but "don't quit your night job" was also good advice.

The CAA was very lax in its discipline during this era. There were just too few inspectors to keep up with what was going on in the field. Their Chicago office was located in Northbrook, Illinois. Many pilots throughout the area were disregarding their license restrictions and doing as they wished. The environment then was not at all like it is today.

In the early spring of 1940, I occasionally took one of the other flight students for a ride with me, even though I only had a solo license and I frankly thought nothing of this. About this time, I persuaded my mother to come to Waterman, as I wanted very much to take her on her first airplane ride and to show her all that I had accomplished. It was a sunny Sunday afternoon and I strapped her into the little T-craft. As soon as we took off and got 30 or 40 feet in the air she said, "Wesley that is high enough, don't go any higher." I just laughed and climbed to 500 feet to show her what it was like to ride in an airplane. I was all of 16 at the time. Often, until her death at age 98, someone in the family would remind her of her remarks on

LEARNING TO FLY

her first airplane ride. She would just smile and take the *kidding* with remarkably good humor.

In late April 1940, Harry Reed purchased a new 65 horsepower Taylorcraft; a beautiful airplane of metallic blue with silver trim lines that I was to fly many times.

I have mentioned that Harry was a promoter and always looking for a deal. A fellow from Missouri drove into the parking lot with a truck loaded with cedar fence posts and asked if he could take a flying lesson. Harry took him for a 45-minute lesson in the little T-craft. He came back the next day with a proposition for Harry. He would trade his truck and the load of cedar posts for the little cream-colored 40 horsepower T-craft. He was also to get enough lessons to solo. Harry figured what the posts would bring from the local farmers and what the truck was worth, and decided that it was a bargain.

They agreed to the deal and exchanged titles. Harry gave him lessons for two days and then on the third morning, when Harry and I came to the airport from De Kalb, we found the hangar doors open and the little T-craft gone. There was a note in the office saying that he was on his way back to his home in Missouri. Harry had calculated that he needed a couple more hours of dual before he could solo. A month or so after this, we learned that the man had made it safely home and was now flying the little airplane out of Rolla, Missouri, and was employed patrolling the fuel pipelines in the area for leaks.

The airport family grew as the days went by. In addition to the Eakle family and Hank Marks, there was Slim Sebree, Ivan Coppess, Ray Tucker, and also Ted Coppin, who bought a piper J-4 Cub Coupe from Harry. One of the men that now had a financial interest in the airport enterprise was Selby Proud of Streator, Ill. Selby owned a roller skating rink in Sycamore and a restaurant in his hometown of Streator. He also owned a 65 horsepower Luscombe airplane that I was privileged to fly several times. Selby Proud was apparently

Harry's financial backer in many of the transactions that went on at the airport in 1940.

In May of 1940, Eagle Airways was notified that they had won the contract to commence a CPT (Civilian Pilot Training) program in co-operation with Northern Illinois State Teachers College in De Kalb, Illinois. With Selby Proud's backing, Harry purchased their first J-3 Cub which was to be used in the CPT program that was to begin with the fall semester of 1940. Another J-3 Cub was ordered and on the 22nd of July, I went to Lock Haven, Pennsylvania to pick up the new airplane. This new J-3 Cub was powered by a 60 HP Franklin engine.

This was to be quite an adventure for this 17-year-old pilot. I had never been on a train or outside of the State of Illinois before, when I boarded the afternoon train leaving Chicago for the east. Early the next morning, I transferred to a local (milk run) train that was to take me to Lock Haven and I arrived at my destination around noon. I walked to the Piper Aircraft factory on the edge of town.

After making inquiries, I found that I couldn't take possession of the new J-3 Cub until the *next* day. I was then taken on an escorted tour of the Piper factory and introduced to Kenny Kress, the Piper test pilot. I spent the night in the Fahlin Hotel and prepared to leave the following morning. I flew the new Cub, along with Kenny Kress, on an acceptance test flight and then turned the cashiers check for about $1,400 over to the Piper Company. I wanted to start back later that day but the visibility was just too poor to leave. I spent another night in the hotel hoping to depart the next morning. I began to worry about whether I had enough money left in my wallet to pay for fuel and a night's lodging in Ft. Wayne, Indiana. The extra night in the hotel at Lock-Haven and my meals had cut into the money that Harry had given me for the trip home.

The next morning, although visibility was still poor, I decided to head out. I had only a road map that showed the main highways, the railroad tracks, and most towns, but little else. This was the same map that Harry had used when he had brought the first Cub from Lock Haven, and he had the route and check points noted. When we bought our Cubs, they were picked up at the factory with no expensive options; meaning no compass and no tail wheel were included. Harry felt that he could install the two needed components at our airport, thus saving enough money to pay for the ferry flight home. All went well until I thought that I was nearing my first destination of Du Bois, Pennsylvania. The only way for me to locate my position was to follow a railroad track until I came to a town. Flying very low, I read the name on the railroad depot. I then climbed up to a higher altitude and circled the town until I found it on the map and followed the railroad track to my destination.

The next leg to New Castle, Penn. was nearly a repeat of the first leg of my journey with visibility still quite poor. I was glad to get out of the mountains of Pennsylvania and into Ohio. The flight across Ohio was easy compared to the earlier part of the trip. I knew that I could make it to Ft. Wayne before dark and intended to stay there overnight. I also knew that I would have to call Harry that night to wire more money to complete the journey home. I just didn't have enough money left to pay for the hotel in Ft. Wayne *and* the needed fuel to make it home.

As I was following the long, straight highway across Ohio, I spotted a county fair in progress. I circled the fairground and since I didn't see any barnstormer airplane working the area, I decided to land in an adjacent field to see if I could pick up a little extra cash, hopping passengers. A crowd soon gathered and I started to take them up, for a dollar a ride. I made each hop short and kept adding the dollars to my larder. After I'd taken six or seven passengers for their ride, a group of men came from the fairground. It appeared to me that they were officials from the fair and either wanted to see my license or a cut of the proceeds. I turned the tail of the airplane in their direction and dusted them off as I proceeded on my journey. I now figured that I had barely enough money to make the trip back to Waterman.

It was almost dark and after refueling at Ft. Wayne, Indiana, I spent a dollar renting a bunk in the hangar bunkhouse. The next morning, I departed without breakfast and used the last of my money to buy fuel at Valparasio, Indiana, and arrived back home at Waterman airport in the early afternoon. I hurried across the highway to the truck-stop café for a hamburger and a coke. I had just 40 cents in my pocket, which was enough for the meal and 15 cents to spare.

The summer of 1940 saw a lot of activity at the airport. New airplanes were in abundance. First we bought a Cub Cruiser as a demonstrator. It was soon traded to Doc Lund for his Kinner Bird biplane. Then there was a trade of some sort and we received an Aeronca K. The "K" had a weak, 2- cylinder engine of about 40 HP, but was still fun to fly. A Stinson SM8A then was purchased and was used for passenger hops. This airplane would accommodate "four" passengers and the pilot. A Cub Coupe (J-4), which was owned by Ted Coppin, became available for me to fly as well. Eagle Airways acquired a second Stinson, the next model above the SM8-A. Passenger business was picking up nicely. We were getting ready for the fall semester college term and their students would be flying on a regular schedule in the CPT program. Meanwhile, Harry Reed had opened another airport at Streator, Illinois, so that he could carry on his illegal flying activities without endangering the upcoming CPT contract.

During the spring and summer of 1940, I spent as much time with Dionne as I could. I would hitchhike to her farm home near Shabbona, which was the town just west of Waterman on US 30, and would normally spend the night there. Her father insisted that I get up at 4:30 and help him and her brother with the morning chores, followed by a big farm breakfast. I'd then hitchhike back to the airport for work. Dionne and I were getting quite close by this time

LEARNING TO FLY

and we were definitely dating and "going steady," as it was then known.

I spent the last month of the summer vacation in 1940, primarily at Streator. The airport at Streator was a joint venture of Selby Proud and "Chuck" Melvin, owner of the Melvin Truck Line. Chuck owned the farm immediately east of Streator, about 60 acres of which he devoted to an airport. I often slept in the Melvin home and ate "for free" at Selby Proud's restaurant. I would ferry the J-3's back and forth between Streator and Waterman almost daily.

One Sunday in August, I was working in the office at Waterman when I had a call from Harry. He was in Streator and wanted me to ferry the Stinson SM8-A down to Streator so that he could accommodate the many passengers that had congregated at the airport. I told him that I had never been in the left seat of the Stinson airplane, let alone soloed in it. He said that it was just another airplane and explained how I was to get the big heavy tail up on takeoff by using the stabilizer control lever. I took off in the big airplane and landed it at Streator without any problem - this was my first solo flight in a large, 215 horsepower airplane.

Around the end of August or the first of September, Harry Reed left Waterman just ahead of the CAA, who was threatening to take his flying license away from him. He fled to Canada to join the RCAF.

School started again and I was back to the "old grind." As before, I set pins at the bowling alley for money to fly. Spencer Mack took over as the airport manager, and two instructors were hired to instruct the CPT students. One of these instructors was a colorful woman named Opal Anderson. She came to Waterman with her Laird "Speed-wing" racing biplane. I said "colorful" and that was an understatement. She was the most profane woman that I had ever been around. She was good to me, however, and gave me several hours of dual instruction free when I was getting ready for my private pilot's license. The CPT program was funded by the government and it was a good way for any airport operation to have a steady income. I was still hitchhiking back and forth to the airport on weekends in the final months of 1940, and at the end of that year my logbook showed a respectable 260 hours of flying time.

Just before I started the second semester of my senior year in high school, Spencer Mack asked me if there was any way that I could work full time at the airport. I told him that I had enough credits to graduate now and I would see if anything could be done to be able to accept his offer. I would mainly be the office typist as there was a lot of paper work connected with this contract. I was also to be the driver for the two round-trips a day picking up the students at college. This round-trip was roughly 20 miles and we had a new Ford "Woody" station wagon for that purpose. I talked this job offer over with my parents, and it was agreed that I would go to see the high school principal on the first day of school in January.

I went to the principal's office and talked the situation over with my school principal Mr. Barton. He agreed that I now had enough credits to graduate in June of that year, but he also said that there was one hitch. Illinois history, which was mandatory, was only taught in the last semester of the senior year to keep anyone from leaving school early, just as I had proposed. He went to great length to discuss the world situation with me and was convinced that we would soon be at war and that it would be my generation that would have to do the fighting. He was a naval veteran of WWI and had been in several battles at sea; he knew first-hand the dangers of war. Mr. Barton was also my history teacher so he was the one that taught Illinois history to the seniors. He made a deal with me, saying that I could leave school that very day if I would come back every Friday afternoon and be questioned on the history assignment that he would give me.

I was delighted by this turn of events, as history was the only subject that really interested me. I made it back home every Friday,

LEARNING TO FLY

as promised. I also brought my laundry for my mother to do and always had a good noon meal at home with my family. If the weather was good, I would be given one of the spare airplanes to fly to Paw Paw for my history lesson. There was a farm field directly behind the high school and it became my landing field. If the weather was not flyable, someone would lend me their car for the day. Mr. Barton would discuss everything in the world with me on these Friday sessions, but never asked me one question about my assigned history lesson.

By the spring semester of 1941, Opal Anderson had quit and moved on to a job ferrying airplanes to England. The other instructor had moved on before Opal left, and Duane Cole was hired to take his place. Duane was pursuing his license to instruct in the advanced CPT program while he was instructing in the primary phase at Waterman. Duane Cole was to become one of finest acrobatic pilots in this country. After WWII, the "Cole Brothers Air Show" thrilled crowds with their acrobatics at nearly every major air show in America. Duane was the headliner in his T-Craft. His wife Judy rode standing on the top wing of their Stearman bi-plane in the later years, with their young son Rolly, piloting the biplane. Rolly would fly over the airfield, in front of the crowd, upside down, with his mother's head not more than 20 feet above the ground. A thrilling sight for sure!

Duane was also very good to me and gave me several hours of dual in his own J-3 Cub to ready me for my commercial license. When Opal moved on, Hi (Hiram) Piper was hired to replace her. He was 19 and had just gotten his instructors rating. He came to Waterman with his Aeronca "Chief" airplane and his motorcycle. Hi would lend his "Chief" to me to go home on some Fridays. I was always giving various people rides on these trips home, and during one of the Friday visits, I convinced Grandpa (Alf) Burnett to take his first airplane ride over his and other farm properties. He was quite taken with the

31

smallness of everything on the ground and told everyone of the wonders of flying with his grandson.

Duane Cole had become my good friend, as well as my mentor, in the way that Harry Reed had been before him. I was well coached in the air maneuvers that needed to be demonstrated for a private or a commercial license as soon as I was 18.

I had purchased a 1932 Chevrolet 4 door automobile in April or May and it was my most prized possession. I was able to buy it in practically new condition for the sum of $35. I could now drive my own car to Paw Paw on Fridays, if the weather was not flyable, or an airplane was not available. It also made it possible for me to take Dionne to a movie in De Kalb when I could afford it. I was always able to fill my gas tank from the pump at the airport for free.

Hank Marks was doing most of the mechanical work at the airport while I worked in the office typing. We had to test hop each J-3 in the morning before the students were allowed to go up solo. Hank and I roomed together in a boarding house in Waterman after I came to work full time for Spencer Mack. We took turns driving the college students back and forth five days a week. We both were able to get in a considerable amount of flying time despite our other work. We often flew somewhere for airplane parts, or to Northbrook, Illinois for maintenance on our airplanes. I flew to Chicago Midway airport for parts a couple of times. This was an interesting procedure. I would land at Elmhurst Airport and call the control tower at Midway Airport, on the telephone to ask for permission to land at their field. I would give them the approximate time of my arrival and they would tell me to watch for the signal light from the tower - red was to pull up and go around, green was OK to land.

I had to be 18 to get my private license and so on May 12th, I went to Northbrook, Illinois to take the test. CAA inspector Peacock gave me the flight test and I had no trouble getting the license. I was now

LEARNING TO FLY

finally and *legally* able to take someone for a ride in an airplane whenever I wished.

After Harry Reed had departed and turned the airport over to Spence Mack, we were encouraged to live by the rules. After Spence took over, I didn't take a passenger for a ride while using the Waterman airport; that is until I had received my private pilot's license. I had now logged 290 hours.

I flew my usual Friday leg to Paw Paw to meet with Mr. Barton in late May, and as a *final exam* took my beloved principal and teacher out to the "air strip" (the flat piece of ground behind the high school) and flew him for several circles over the town. I returned home for my high school graduation and my formal education had ended.

During the busy summer of 1941, Dionne and I agreed that we should date other people and so we did. Spencer Mack's niece, Janice Lindus and I began dating. Janice was my age and a wonderful young lady. She would go into nurse training in the fall, and upon graduation from her studies she became an officer in the U.S. Navy. We kept in contact by letter while I was overseas flying combat. Although the romance with Dionne had cooled, we still dated occasionally as neither wanted to break off the friendship. This new arrangement seemed to work well for both of us.

At about this time, I was flying solo in the Kinner Bird bi-plane but didn't have any dual time in it. I was just *expected* to be able to fly it. The hardest part was "take-off's and landings." With no brakes and only a tailskid, it was a *learned art* to be able to handle the Bird on the ground. In the air it flew like any other docile airplane and it was fun flying an open cockpit bi-plane.

I was now busy studying for my commercial pilot's license and felt that I was ready to take the flight test, but I had to pass the written test first. The written exam was longhand written explanations of the questions, rather than the later multiple choice. Your written answer to the question had to satisfy the inspector that you had sufficient knowledge to pass the test. The test wasn't graded, you either passed or not; it was up to the inspector. Dick Fender was the inspector and he flunked me on navigation and motors (engine mechanics) and told me to go back and get one of the instructors to give me some ground-school and come back.

Some time earlier, the CAA had changed a lot of the licensing procedures and the Solo License was now called a Student Permit. The second time I went to Northbrook to take the written, I had the multiple-choice exam and this was a complete surprise to me. I only had to take the two subjects that I had missed on the first exam, and this time I passed engines but failed navigation.

I went back to Waterman very disappointed. Harry Reed had come back to De Kalb on leave from the Royal Canadian Air Force at about this same time. He came to the Waterman airport and I had a chance to talk to him about his experiences. He had become an instant officer upon his graduation from the conversion training school at Picton, Ontario and was now stationed at Trenton. Which was the Canadian equivalent of our "West Point of the Air." He was an acrobatic instructor at Trenton and had been promoted to F/O, (Flight Officer, which was equivalent to our 1st Lieutenant). Harry felt that both Ivan Coppess and I should join the RCAF and that we would be rated pilots in the Canadian military within three months. He warned me that because I was only 18, he felt that I would be graduated as a Sergeant/Pilot. He said that I would probably be assigned to fly at a bombing and gunnery school for a while. I then would most likely be trained to be a combat pilot and sent to England.

This was exactly the right time for me. I had again not passed the commercial written exam and was very discouraged. I thought that this change would be welcome. My good friend Ivan Coppess and I talked it over and decided to go to Canada. War was looming and we thought that this would be a good decision.

I went home to Paw Paw and talked it over with my parents. My dad thought that it was a bad idea and that I should try to go to college. I was pretty sure that I would be drafted before I could achieve much in college. My mother sided with me, as usual. She said that she hated to see me get into the war and that if I would promise her that I would not volunteer for combat, she would sign the paper allowing me to join the Canadian military.

I had a grand total of about $10 saved so I needed to borrow some money to go to Canada. My mother said that she had $35 saved up to buy a new rug for the living room and would give that to me. I told her that I would sign over my 1932 Chevrolet to her and she was pleased with that. This was the first automobile that my parents had ever owned. My father was quite unhappy that she had given me the $35 that she had saved, and she soon sold the car for $50 to keep peace in the family.

I was to leave for Canada with Ivan in a couple of days. The evening before we left, I drove to Shabbona and broke the news to Dionne. We were dating more often again by then. I knew that I would miss her companionship a lot.

Ivan came to pick me up early on the morning of Sept 11, 1941. He told me that we were to go to De Kalb and pick up Harold Long, who was going with us to Canada. This was the first time that I had heard that there were to be three of us going on the trip. Harold had heard of our decision and called Ivan and asked to go along. Harold Long was a young fellow about 19 or 20, and I knew him only casually. He was a pilot at Waterman who had perhaps 50 or 60 solo hours of flight time. When we left for Canada that morning, Ivan had at least 250 hours and I had a total of 425 hours of flight time experience.

With the three of us sharing the driving, it was easy to drive straight through and we crossed into Canada at Niagara Falls on the

12th of September, and spent the night in a hotel near Hamilton, Ontario.

CHAPTER 3

ROYAL CANADIAN AIR FORCE

We passed through Toronto, Ontario, on Saturday Sept 13th, 1941 and stopped to say hello to Harry Reed. He gave each of us a letter attesting to our flying experience and ability, and told us where to go in Ottawa, or more correctly, in Hull, Quebec, to enlist, as it was just across the river from Ottawa. We left Harry and drove on to Ottawa, which took all of that day. We found a hotel room for the night at a cost of $6.00 for the three of us.

We spent Sunday the 14th sightseeing. Out in the countryside, the leaves were starting to turn and drift downward over the very picturesque split rail fences, green fields, and rolling hills. This was a very relaxing day and we enjoyed it thoroughly.

Harry told us that he thought that Ivan would have a problem getting into the Staff Pilot Conversion School without proof of having graduated from high school. He was also fairly sure that Harold Long did not have enough flying experience to be qualified for the conversion school, but Harold was determined to try for it anyway.

After a good breakfast on Monday morning, Ivan went out and found a printer that made him a few pages of stationery with the Waterman High School letterhead on them. In the hotel lobby writing and reading room there was a typewriter available to the guests (as was often the case in those days). Ivan set upon composing a "To Whom It May Concern" letter, stating that the High School in

Waterman, Illinois, had burned in 1938, along with all the records. The letter attested to the fact that Ivan Coppess had graduated from said high school with honors that year. A fictitious High School Principal's name was typed in, and I did the signature honors. Ivan had me practice the signature several times to make it look "authentic."

On Tuesday Sept. 16th, armed with Ivan's letter and our high school diplomas, we proceeded to Hull to enlist. We had our letters from Harry Reed, our personal logbooks and also, in my case, as I was 18, my parental consent to join the RCAF. I had 425 hours of flying time logged in my logbook. It was all actual flight time. Ivan had padded his logbook before he left Waterman and it showed about 350 hours, about one hundred of which were "Parker Pen" time (logged but not actually flown). Both Ivan and I held a Private Pilot's License, and Harold held a Student Permit. Harold had padded his logbook to up over 100 hours, although he had in reality only 50 or 60 hours. None of us knew exactly how much time in the logbook was enough to get into the conversion training school.

We walked into the RCAF enlistment headquarters, and told them that we would like to enlist in the Staff Pilot program and go through the conversion training school. They looked through our paperwork and gave each of us a physical examination, after which we were officially sworn into the RCAF. I had no trouble passing the physical even though I had to wear glasses to read the eye chart. We had to pledge allegiance to the King, but did not have to renounce our U.S. citizenship. Both Ivan and I would be going to the conversion training school, pending a flight check, and Harold was to go to the RCAF aviation cadet school. If either Ivan or I didn't pass the flight check, we would go with Harold to aviation cadet school. We were in the service now and there was no turning back. We were given the rank of AC-2, the lowest rank in the RCAF. Although we didn't have uniforms, we were billeted nearby for the night and scheduled for the check ride at the airbase outside of Ottawa the next day.

Sept. 17th dawned bright and clear. I was scheduled to fly on the first flight check. The airplane was a North American "Yale." It had a 450 HP engine and was definitely an advanced airplane for me. I looked to be about 16 years old at the time and the check pilot, F/O Miscampbell, asked me my age and experience. He then patiently, orally talked me through the cockpit controls, advising me as to the parachute operation, if necessary, and strapped me into the front cockpit of the airplane.

The check pilot started the 450 HP engine and taxied it out for takeoff. We received the green light from the tower and were on our way. He made the takeoff and gave the controls over to me after we were airborne. According to his instructions, I made some climbing turns and then was asked to make a level flight stall and recovery. A stall is when the airplane is allowed to get too slow to fly, and the recovery is to push the nose down and apply the power to pick up speed again. He then had me make a steep turn in each direction, and then by way of the intercom asked if I had ever done a slow roll. When I replied that I hadn't, he demonstrated the maneuver to me and told me to try it. It was a pretty poor performance, and the check pilot had to take over to complete the maneuver. We then entered the pattern and I completed the landing, which was OK but I did have some trouble holding it straight down the runway. He wanted to know why I didn't use the brakes to keep it straight and I realized that I hadn't been aware of the fact that there were wheel brakes on the rudder pedals of this airplane.

Ivan was next, and while F/O Miscampbell was inside the operations room, I gave Ivan all the info that I had on the ride including the fact that wheel brakes were there to be used. Ivan's ride went well, and Miscampbell didn't ask him to make a slow roll or any other type of acrobatic maneuver. The upshot of it all was that

39

Miscampbell passed Ivan and flunked me on the test. I felt that he had included the slow roll demonstration to show me, in no uncertain terms, that at *my age* I probably needed to go through aviation cadet training. I had lost most of my confidence during this check ride and was ready to agree with him that I probably should go all the way through aviation cadets. The old "lack of confidence" bug had bitten again...

That same day, orders were posted for the three of us to go to #1 Manning Depot, Toronto, Ontario. The next day we drove back down the highway through Trenton to Toronto. Harry was flying, so we left him a message that we were to be in Toronto for our initial training. We reported in to #1 Manning Depot late in the day and were assigned bunks high up in the enclosed stands ringing the arena. #1 Manning Depot was situated along the shore of Lake Ontario, in a beautiful setting named Exhibition Park. The RCAF base had completely taken over the park for the duration of the war. New recruits were sent there, as it was the RCAF "boot camp" and our indoctrination into military life.

The next morning, we were to "fall in" and "form up" and were sent to the commissary to get uniforms, top to bottom. We were given directions to the mess hall and to the area where we were to find our daily schedule, and other basic information posted. Next, we again formed up and marched to the barbershop where we each received a GI haircut. On the second day we were to "fall in" at 7AM in the arena. There were 25 or 30 of us in this group, with a half-dozen being American. One of them, Don Lawson was to become a close friend. The majority of this group was Canadian farm and city boys. First thing after we formed up in some sort of formation, the Sgt. in command of our group asked if any of us could type. I sensed an office job and immediately held up my hand. There were half a dozen of us that had volunteered to *type* and we were marched away, handed a broom and told to sweep the arena floor.

I realized then that I hadn't come that far from sweeping the hangar floor at Waterman. After this experience, I decided that this would be the last time I'd volunteer for anything in the military. Later, Ivan told the Sgt. that he had done office work and was assigned to work in the office. This became a big break for me, as we will see later.

The normal workday began at 6AM with breakfast in the chow hall, a large exhibition area under the stands of the arena. Breakfast was scrambled eggs or French toast with greasy bacon or sausage, toast with jam, and coffee, tea, or milk. The large meal was at noon and the evening meal was somewhat smaller. There was always good soup for the two regular meals. I imagine that the food was very comparable to the enlisted men's food in the U.S.

We would march several times each day and learned how to come to attention, salute, and how to stand up straight with our backs arched. We were expected to polish our shoes and tunic buttons each and every evening, which was no small chore. We had some form of entertainment most evenings in the arena consisting of movies, boxing, or sometimes a stage show.

Often when we were marching, it was to the accompaniment of a bagpiper, tunes that have no "beat" as far as I could ascertain. It was very difficult to stay in step with the piper playing. The marching commands were "Old British," like "left wheel/right wheel, etc." We marched with arms held stiff and thrust alternately forward, with the fist clenched and the thumb pointing down and forward with arms pumping. We braced at attention and were inspected daily. We would march outside in the park if the weather allowed, and if not, we marched in the arena. We were directly on the lakefront and marching in the brisk fall weather was quite pleasant, but when you let yourself enjoy the surroundings *too* much, you would miss a command and get a real "chewing out."

On the third or fourth day at #1 Manning Depot, we were scheduled for shots. We marched for an hour or more of practice and then were marched to the dispensary for our shots. We each had to receive 3 or 4 shots, and each one really hurt. It seemed that the needles were dull and in need of sharpening. (In those days the needles were sharpened only when absolutely necessary and used over and over again after being sterilized.) We were given a light schedule for the remainder of the day and I took a nap in the afternoon. There was a boxing match down in the arena that evening and the three of us went to watch. In an area off the arena under the stands we could buy beer. Drinking was not "off limits" for me at age 18, as the Canadians felt that if you were old enough to fight for the country, you were old enough to drink. Ivan went out for paper cups of beer and we settled in to watch the boxing match. When we finished the beer and it was my turn to go for more, I got up from my seat and fainted dead away. When I could walk, Ivan and Harold took me to my bunk. I had consumed only one beer, and I didn't think that was the cause of my "problem."

My arms, where I had gotten the shots, were hot and feverish and hurt something awful. I told them to go back to the fights and that I would join them if I felt better. As it turned out, I spent a feverish night and could not make roll call that next morning. They reported me sick and a medic was sent to my bunk to take my temperature. He felt that I was having a reaction to the shots and I stayed in the bunk all that day. I was able to answer roll call the following morning, but didn't know if I felt a lot better or if I was just inordinately hungry. It was a few more days before my arms felt normal again.

We were restricted to our area through the first weekend. The following Sunday, however, we were given passes allowing us to go into downtown Toronto sightseeing. It was the last Sunday in September 1941, an exceptional day, and Toronto is a truly beautiful old city. All of the stores were closed and people were out enjoying the sunshine. As a way of meeting girls, we would take pictures with our camera of the girls with either Don or me with an arm wrapped around their shoulder. We would promise to send a copy of the snapshot to the address they gave to us. Of course, there wasn't any film in the camera but it was a great way to get acquainted, and try to get an afternoon date. Don was quite a character.

The next week was more of the same at #1 Manning Depot - marching, saluting, polishing buttons and shoes, and lots of PT (Physical Training) each day, with many lectures on military conduct. Ivan was working in the office and was often excused from this everyday routine.

The next weekend, the first in October, we were given passes to go off base, and we traveled in Ivan's car to Trenton to visit Harry Reed. We had talked to him on the telephone, and he had invited us to see him with the idea of giving us some dual flight time in the Cessna Crane. The "Crane" was a twin-engine aircraft that carried two pilots and two passengers. (It was used as a multi-engine trainer and as a personnel transport type airplane.) Although Harry was primarily an acrobatic instructor, he was flight-qualified in all of the aircraft types at Trenton. He procured the twin Cessna Crane for our ride, and took us for a flight down the lakefront, as we approached Toronto he turned inland to Port Perry and Lake Scugog.

I had asked to see the island in Lake Scugog, as this was where my Grandmother Burnett was born and grew up with her grandparents. It was there also that she and my Grandfather, Alf Burnett, courted and were married. He had been a hired man on a nearby farm on the island before moving with his family to Paw Paw, Illinois. He went back to Canada to marry my grandmother, and took her back to Paw Paw to live and raise their family.

We returned to Trenton and were treated to a fine dinner in the Officers' Club. The dining room was of beautiful dark hardwood. The four of us were seated at an individual table, and we ordered from

STARDUST FALLING

a menu. This was a great way to spend our Sunday, but then it was back to #1 Manning Depot before curfew. Harry talked as if he could somehow fix it so I could go to conversion school with Ivan, but I doubted it. Harry had me make the landing on our arrival at Trenton. I made a good landing and didn't forget to use the wheel brakes to keep it straight on the roll out. My old self-assurance was somewhat restored. Harry Reed was always able to renew my confidence, whether it was flying or driving.

We had one more week at #1 Manning Depot to complete. On the Monday of the next week, our orders were posted for our transfer out of Toronto. My name was miraculously on the same orders as Ivan, going to Picton, Ontario, to Staff Pilot Conversion School. We were to report for duty on the 15th of October.

While working in the office, Ivan had gotten hold of the flight-check report pertaining to me by F/O Miscampbell, and destroyed it. He then put my name on the orders to go to Picton with him. I never knew if Harry had a hand in this or not, but he did not seem surprised that I was going to Picton instead of cadet school. Harry may have *suggested* to Ivan to destroy the flight check report and be certain that I was on the roster to Picton.

Harold Long, as predicted, was on orders to go to cadet school. We parted, and Ivan and I were on our way to Picton on the 14th of October. We stopped at Trenton to see Harry, and he gave each of us several takeoffs and landings in the twin-engine Cessna. He said he knew most of the personnel in the school, which was only about 20 air miles from Trenton.

On the same orders sending us to conversion school were Don Lawson and Art Stevens.

The RCAF Conversion Training School was located on the RAF bombing and gunnery base at Picton. The base was close to a small town located near the shore of Lake Ontario. The nearest large town was Bellville, Ontario 20 road miles distant. The base was an RAF

ROYAL CANADIAN AIR FORCE

base and the RCAF unit was a tenant there. The RAF (*British* Royal Air Force) used the Fairey "Battle" and the North American AT-6 "Harvard" for training their gunners. Some of the Canadian "Harvards" were built in Canada by Noorduyn Aircraft in Montreal, under contract with the U.S. North American Aviation Corp. The target for gunnery practice was a sleeve towed behind the Fairey "Battle," and the gunnery students peppered away at the sleeve with a machine gun mounted on a ring in the rear cockpit of the "Harvard." The RCAF Conversion Training School also used the AT-6 "Harvard" and the Fairey "Battle" for the pilot conversion flight training.

We were housed in RAF barracks, ate in an RAF mess hall, and lived under RAF conditions, which were somewhat more austere than we had experienced in Toronto. The most notable difference between the two was in the mess hall. I had a good appetite but the food was so bad that I often left the mess hall hungry. Breakfast usually consisted of stewed (canned) tomatoes and beans, often with some kind of oily fish. The toast was fried on the grill, and if you pressed down on a slice of the "toast" with a fork, the grease would squirt out. Lunch and dinner usually had some kind of soup. The main meal occasionally had some type of greasy, boiled meat, and vegetables and boiled potatoes that were normally cold. We never were treated to mashed potatoes and gravy, the old mid-west standby. Thank God for the soup, that with bread was usually all that was edible. For desert there might be bread pudding or unfrosted cake. At every meal there were large urns of hot tea, which contained about half and half powdered milk and tea, and was always pre-sweetened. There was no whole milk on the table or butter for the bread, only jam.

There was a small canteen adjacent to the mess hall that had coin machines dispensing cans of pork and beans, and Vienna sausages, and soup. These were great, providing you had enough money. After I called home and described the food situation, my mother sent me a little more money so that I could use the canteen. The food machines

STARDUST FALLING

were electrically heated so that the canned food came out somewhat warm. Often we would take the bread from the mess table and go into the canteen and eat, as well as buy a soft drink. Tea was the mainstream, never a cup of coffee in either the mess hall or canteen. I *really* missed steaming, hot coffee.

The RCAF Training was very compressed and intense. We were scheduled 5 days a week from morning until 9 or 10 in the evening. There was ground-school training in navigation, weather, radio code, and many other subjects. We also had some limited drilling and PT. We really didn't have a minute off except on the weekends, which suited me fine. I was eager to learn everything that I could about flying.

It didn't take very long for me to start getting acquainted with the AT-6 Harvard airplane. Two days after we reported to classes, I was to take my first flight with my instructor. The pilot that was assigned to give me my training was Sgt/Pilot Keenan, and he was one of the more experienced in our squadron, or "flight," as it was called. I was in the front seat and he was in the rear of the (AT-6) "Harvard." He had me take over the controls after takeoff, and make gentle turns and other familiarization maneuvers. He then told me to relax and he did two snap rolls, one to the right and one to the left, and then had me take over once again. Apparently he had a penchant for snap rolls, as I went through several on every flight with Sgt/Pilot Keenan. I got used to it; when he said "relax," that meant for me to brace myself because he was about to snap roll the aircraft. (A "snap roll" is one *very fast* barrel roll). In our flight training we included a tailspin maneuver on almost every dual flight instruction period. The AT-6 did a very tight spin, and we would normally hold the airplane in the spin until we had made at least three complete revolutions before we began the recovery procedure. It was great fun!

The "Harvard" was quite a bit advanced for me. It had a 600 HP engine and weighed about 5,000 lbs., fully loaded with fuel and two pilots. The airplane that we were flying that first day, was a Harvard Mark I, one of the early models of the Canadian Harvard. It had rounded wing tips instead of the squared off wingtips of the later Mark II Aircraft. It had a full caster tail wheel, with no tail wheel locking device or detent to make certain that the tail-wheel was straight on takeoff and landing.

At the end of the session, we entered the landing pattern and Sgt. Keenan took over the controls on the landing approach. He had me follow through on the flight controls to give me the general feel of the first landing. He made a good "touch down" but when he eased the tail down, the tail wheel was not straight and we promptly did a "ground loop" to the left. As the airplane spun around on the ground, we dragged both right and left wingtips. Major damage was done to the airplane, and when Sgt. Keenan shut down the engine and we got out, he said, "That is NOT the way to do it," and was embarrassed by the accident. It was said that they were "phasing out" the old model Harvard Mark I airplane and we felt that this airplane would never fly again. That assumption was wrong.

I flew every day that week except the 23rd. On the 24^{th,} Sgt. Keenan had me do takeoffs and landings for 50 minutes and then had me set the parking brake and let him out. I then took off and soloed for the first time in the Harvard. I had memorized the one "checklist commandment" for the Harvard landing: G-U-M-P (gas, undercarriage, mixture, and pitch.) I had, as a kid, followed the cartoons of "Andy Gump," so this was easy to memorize. I had logged a total of 8 hours, 30 minutes in the airplane and about an hour-and-a-half of that flying time had been "under the hood," simulated instrument flying. This amount of flying time for my first solo was right on the curriculum. Both Ivan and I were near the top of our class. My confidence had returned and I could now get on with flying the bird. I soon had about 20 hours of flying time in the

"Harvard," about half of which was dual. I had my first night solo on October 30th, which was about 2 weeks into my training.

Night flying in the Harvard, at Picton was an adventure in itself. We were not allowed to use the landing lights for takeoff and landing. The runway lights were purposely dim and there was only a lighted "Christmas Tree" (a small tower of lights) at the approach end of the runway to give the pilot some appreciation of the height of the airplane above the end of the runway. This was to give us training in the type of night flying that we would encounter in wartime England. I finally had logged about 6 hours of night flying by the time I left Picton; most of it was solo.

At about 30 hours of flight time, I was introduced to my first flight in the Fairey "Battle." This was the airplane that I would be flying when I towed targets at the bombing and gunnery school at Lethbridge, Alberta, Canada. Both of my dual instruction flights in the "Battle" were on the same day and with F/O Lance Call. He was an "old timer," and his method of instructing was to "holler and shout" at the student constantly. I hated him so much that I thought that no matter what I did, I couldn't please him.

I just shut him out in my mind and made the airplane do what I wanted it to do. This was apparently exactly what he wanted and I was completely surprised when he had me stop and set the parking brake. He got out of the rear seat and came forward on the wing, and patted me on the shoulder, and said "Kid, take it around the pattern once and bring it in to the tarmac." He jumped off the wing, turned his back on me, and strode toward the office. This was my introduction to the "Battle," the airplane that I would fly my remaining time in the RCAF.

I again flew the "Battle" solo for a couple of hours of takeoffs and landings on the morning of the 24th of November. On that same afternoon, I flew an instrument flight check and then a 35 minute "Wings" check in the AT-6 "Harvard." This just happened to be the same "Harvard Mark I" that Sgt. Keenan had ground-looped on my first flight. With both of these check flights completed, my conversion flight training ended, and I was now a rated pilot in the RCAF.

The next day, as a reward for being one of the first to finish the course, I was given a "Battle" to fly solo wherever I pleased. I flew along the coastline of Lake Ontario just a short distance offshore for an hour, and I could see Niagara Falls quite clearly in the distance. I returned a bit inland and I could see the beautiful city of Toronto just off my right wing. I flew directly to Lake Scugog to once more circle the island where my grandparents had courted and married. I made two lazy circles around the island, and I am sure that it hadn't changed that much from 50 years ago when they both lived there. I completed the flight back home to Picton. The flight had lasted 2 hours and 20 minutes and had covered about 350 air miles. It was a magnificent day and I reveled in the fact that I had been given this big, powerful airplane to fly purely for my pleasure. It was a reward for finishing the course a day early and I had earned it.

The Fairey "Battle" was a large, single-engine airplane, and was at one time a first-line British light bomber and fighter that had come into service in the RAF in May 1937. However, like the German "Stuka," it was soon to become obsolete. In 1941 it was used only for training bombardier and gunnery students. I was to tow targets and to pilot gunnery students in this airplane for another 365 hours.

The Fairey "Battle" was a "low-wing" monoplane and was almost twice as large as the "Harvard," and twice as heavy. It weighed in at 10,800 lbs and had a wingspan of 53 feet. It was 40 feet long and stood 15 feet high. A Rolls-Royce Merlin engine of 1030 HP originally powered it. The later models had a much more powerful engine, however. It cruised at an air speed of about 160 mph and landed at about 55 or 60 mph. The "Battles" that we used to tow targets at #8 Bombing & Gunnery School at Lethbridge, Alberta, had the big 1350 HP Merlin engine. The British were to build 2,185 of these big, single-engine aircraft before they stopped production.

On November 26th, we had a formal "Wings Parade," where we had the cloth wings of the RCAF pinned on our tunics. Our mentor, F/O Harry Reed, came to Picton to pin the wings on Ivan and me. He had flown over from Trenton in a Cessna "Crane" to participate in our ceremony. We both considered this an honor and were grateful to Harry for his consideration. It was a wonderful surprise when he came striding up to our formation and greeted his friend, our C/O, F/O Jack Ladd. Apparently, he had called Jack to ask when the "wings" ceremony would be held and said that he intended to be there. F/O Ladd later told us that Harry had been checking with him each week to hear about our progress.

Immediately after the "wings" parade, we said goodbye to Harry and saw him off for Trenton, then Ivan and I headed out on our car trip to our new bases in western Canada. Our travel orders would allow us to stop off at home for a couple of days, provided we drove non-stop on each leg of the trip. We took time before we left Picton to have our sergeant stripes and wings sewn onto our tunics. I was to report to my new base at Lethbridge, Alberta, Canada, on December 1st, 1941. Taking turns at the wheel, Ivan and I drove straight through to Illinois.

It was pleasant to be home again and see all of my old friends. Dionne and I were able to spend one day together on this stopover. She was now a senior in high school in Shabbona, Illinois. It was very enjoyable to wear the new RCAF uniform with the Sergeant stripes, and especially the coveted RCAF wings. I was 18 years old and this was "big time" for me. I was even invited to my high school to address the students in the study hall. I described the military duty and the flight training on the way to winning my wings. This was held in the same study hall that I had attended as a student, less than one year before.

This short stopover in my hometown ended all too soon, and Ivan came to pick me up before dawn and we continued our trip to Western Canada. We had figured that with both of us taking turns driving, we could make the 900-mile trip to Winnepeg, Manitoba, in about 20 or 21 hours. I had to be there in time to take the 7AM train the morning after we left home to be at my new base at Lethbridge on schedule.

We arrived at the Canadian border just after midnight and looked forward to being in Winnepeg, Manitoba, in a couple of hours. I planned to sit in the train station until my train left that morning.

This was not to be exactly as we had hoped. We had intended to refuel the car at the Canadian border, but there were no filling stations open on either side of the border at midnight. We doubted that we had enough fuel for the remaining 60 miles that we still had to travel to get to Winnipeg. We felt sure that we would find some place to get fuel along the highway, but there were no stations open for business. Finally, when Ivan thought that we were very nearly empty of fuel, we parked at a filling station in a small village and waited for them to open up in the morning. I was certain that I would miss my 7AM train from Winnipeg to Lethbridge, and that I would be late for my new assignment.

We were cold and shivering in the freezing weather, and ran the car heater periodically with the little remaining fuel that we had. At about 4AM, a Royal Canadian Mounted Police car drove into the filling station parking lot. The officer asked us if we needed help. He saw from our uniforms that we were RCAF Sgt/Pilots. We told him our story of my need to get to the Winnipeg train station to catch my train to Lethbridge and we needed fuel. He said that he would go to the home of the filling station owner, wake him up, and have him fill our tank so that we could be on our way.

The RCMP officer came back with the station owner in his police car, and the man was happy to open his station and fill our fuel tank. There was a real feeling of "anything for the boys" at that time. The

Canadians were happy that we Americans were enlisting in their forces and were pledged to do our duty for Canada. America was not in the war as yet, and the British Commonwealth needed all of the help it could get from America. We paid for the fuel and thanked both the station owner and the RCMP officer and drove off.

We proceeded into Winnipeg and I said goodbye to Ivan at the train station when he dropped me off. Ivan was to drive alone to his new base at Saskatoon, Saskatchewan. I kept in touch with him, both by telephone and letter, but when he dropped me off that morning, it was to be the last time I would ever see him. He was killed in a mid-air collision while towing targets in an AT-6 in the U.S. Army Air Corps about 18 months later in Ajo, Arizona.

The train ride from Winnipeg westbound was pleasant but a bit boring. We made a stop at several small towns and then arrived at Regina, Saskatchewan. We had a bit of time there and I got off the train to stretch my legs. The train ride was an adventure to me, as this was only the second time that I had traveled by train. It had been 18 months since my train trip to Lockhaven, Pennsylvania to pick up the Piper "Cub" for Harry Reed. However, this was the first time that I had traveled in a "sleeper" car and had a comfortable bunk for the overnight trip to Lethbridge.

The route across Canada took us through towns with quite colorful names, like Moose Jaw and Swift Current, and after we entered Alberta, we went through Medicine Hat. After Medicine Hat, I looked forward to our arrival at my destination of Lethbridge. This rail trip across Western Canada had taken almost a day-and-a-half and I had made the most of the allotted travel time from Picton, Ontario to my destination If it hadn't been for the intervention of the RCMP officer, I would have been late getting to my new base.

I arrived in Lethbridge at noon on the 1st of December 1941, and was met by an RCAF bus that was regularly sent to transport anyone wishing to ride from the rail station to the base. There were several

ROYAL CANADIAN AIR FORCE

other Sgt/pilots and Officers that were on the train with me. I suppose that some were returning from a leave of absence, while others may have been reporting to the station for new duty assignment, as I was.

When I entered the base, I was surprised to see the permanent brick buildings and what appeared to be huge hangers and an airport control tower made of brick. The bus driver dropped me, and my luggage off at the headquarters building and I reported for duty to the base adjutant. He welcomed me onboard and referred me to the office next door, telling me to report to the Flight Sergeant at the desk. The Flt. Sergeant informed me that I would be posted to "Drogue Flight," and I was given my quarter's assignment. I then went to the wooden building, found my room and stowed my gear. My quarters were directly across the street from the Sergeants' Club and the Sergeant's mess hall building.

I walked down the road toward the flight line and saw the large letters on one of the hangars, "Drogue Flight," and knew that I had found my new home. In the flight office I met my new O.C. (Officer Commanding), Flt/Lt. Anderson, who introduced himself as "Andy" and made me most welcome. He was an American, hailing from Wenatchee, Washington. He introduced me to several of the other pilots in "Drogue" flight. I was soon to get acquainted with my new colleagues, about two-thirds of which were American. The pilots in "Drogue" Flight were about evenly divided between officers and Sgt/pilots. Sgt. Don Lawson had also been transferred to Lethbridge from the conversion training school with me.

Don Lawson became like an older brother to me, as Ivan Coppess had been earlier. Don Lawson had driven his car to Lethbridge, and while he was en-route had visited his older brother, an RCAF officer pilot, stationed in Moose Jaw, Saskatchewan.

In my new quarters I had a very comfortable room with a table, chair, and a bunk bed. The floor was varnished wood and it was quite clean and neat. A civilian came in to my room to meet me and

53

introduced himself as the "batman" for our floor. Our "batman" was more than just the janitor. If we left our shoes outside of the door to be shined, they would be ready in the morning. He told me that if I had laundry to be sent out, to place it in a bag by my door and he would take care of it. Frankly, as a Sergeant, I hadn't expected all of this. I knew that the officers were treated this way in the RCAF, but I was unaware that the ranking Sergeants also shared "batman" privileges. All of the Sergeants on our floor were expected to pay him a small amount each week. I suppose that he was on the military payroll as well.

On the fifth of December, I rode in the back compartment of a "Drogue" Battle. On this flight, targets were streamed and released. It was a regular gunnery target mission, and I was able to somewhat observe the pilot's procedure and also the work of the man in the back, who was in charge of streaming a new target on the pilot's command. On these gunnery missions, the pilot would follow a path plowed into the flat land for perhaps five or six miles. He would have a gunnery airplane behind him with students firing at the target. I was to quickly learn that it was a "no-no" for the gunnery airplane to fly even with or ahead of the airplane towing the target while the gunnery mission was in progress. The only time that the gunnery airplane could come up even with the tow ship was to signal that the mission was over.

The next day I flew in the front seat of our dual controlled Battle nicknamed the "Camel," so called because of the hump that the rear cockpit made as it protruded behind and somewhat above the front cockpit. One of the veteran pilots in our squadron had me fly out to the target area and go through the whole drill of a tow target mission. He had me come into the drop zone, low and slow, and simulate dropping a target and streaming a new one. We would approach the drop zone into the wind and slow the airplane to just above the stall speed, and then fly low over the drop ground. On the pilot's command, the winch operator would release a new target. The new target would automatically release the old target at the end of the toe line and it would flutter to the ground to be scored by the ground crewmen below.

I was scheduled to fly the early flight the very next day, which was to be my first solo tow target mission. I was awakened by our "batman" before dawn, and went across the street to the Sergeant's mess hall for breakfast. Then it was off to the hangar to get ready for the day. There I met Sgt. Emsland, who was to be my winch operator. We both dressed in warm flight clothes and remarked at how cold and windy it was. The big "Drogue" Battle was out in front of the hanger and the crew chief had it all warmed up for me when I was ready to board. Both Emsland and I climbed aboard and started our preflight check. After the crew chief had fastened my seat and shoulder harness, he closed the canopy and jumped off the back of the wing. He then took up a position to pull the chocks from under the wheels at my command. When the chocks were released, he moved out into a position to salute us off. I saluted back and taxied to the edge of the ramp to get further instruction from the control tower for departure.

The control tower directed us to the takeoff runway, and with the "before takeoff" checklist completed, I asked for permission to takeoff. There was a considerable crosswind, on the runway but the effect of the engine torque partially made up for the crosswind and I had no trouble keeping the airplane centered on the runway. It was quite turbulent on our way to the target however. We settled in at our assigned gunnery target altitude and waited for the first gunnery aircraft to arrive. With our target streamed out behind, we started our first flight down the line that was clearly marked on the ground. We "waggled" our wings to indicate to the gunnery ship that it was OK to start firing. At the end of the line we made a turn around with the gunnery ship changing to the other side of the target, and the firing on the towed target continued.

When the second student in the gunnery aircraft ran out of ammunition, the pilot of the gunnery airplane came up along side of us and waggled his wings, indicating that the firing exercise was over and that he was departing for home. We then started to descend to our drop altitude and prepared to head into the wind to drop the first target sleeve. The first drop was successful, although the air was very rough and I couldn't slow down as much as I would have liked had the air been smoother. We streamed another target as we released the used one and waited for the next gunnery airplane to arrive. It soon made its appearance and we again started down the firing line. The air was getting rougher, and I wondered how the poor gunnery students could possibly hit the target with any consistency. When we finished that run, I had a call on the radio from the airport control tower telling us that the gunnery period had been cancelled and that we were to return to base.

We again approached the drop zone and sent out a "dummy bell" to release our target. On the way back to the base, the winch operator, Sgt. Emsland, reeled the long tow wire in. The crosswind was even worse than it had been earlier. With the large vertical fin and rudder, the "Battle" was not all that difficult to handle in a crosswind. I made a good landing and turned off the runway to go directly across the grass to my flight, as was the normal procedure. I was soon to learn a lesson on how to taxi a "Battle" in a downwind and crosswind situation.

The wheel brakes on the airplane were operated by compressed air. The pilot had to move the rudder bar to the left or right, and squeeze a handle on the joystick to apply the proper wheel brake pressure. The compressed air was supplied by an air pump driven by the engine. It took more than idle engine RPM to keep enough air pressure in the air tank to handle the wheel brakes. Taxiing downwind with the throttle in idle soon meant that we ran out of brake pressure, and the airplane completed a wide turn around into the wind. I was now headed straight into the wind again and with a little more than idle engine speed, I was just barely moving forward. I soon had a full tank of air pressure, and proceeded to turn around and again taxi toward our flight. The air pressure went lower, and lower and I again made and uncontrolled turn around into the wind. When I had enough air pressure, I set the parking brake and called the control tower and asked them to telephone our flight and tell them to send a tug out to get us.

After a 15-minute wait, a tug came out and we were towed back to the hanger. This ended my first tow target mission. This just *happened* to be on Sunday, December 7th, 1941. I will remember that first mission and the date forever.

I hung around the flight operations office for a while and finally word came down that gunnery practice was over for the day, due to the rough air. I took off my flight suit, but put my fur-lined jacket and boots back on and made my way to my quarters. It was probably about noon, and I washed up and got ready to go across the street to the Sgt's. Club and mess hall for a late noon meal. Just as I was leaving my room, our "batman" met me at the door and breathlessly said, "The Japanese have bombed Pearl Harbor." I thought that he was kidding me, but I hurried across the street and into the Club lounge to find everyone huddled around the radio absorbing the news. It was then that I came to the realization that this was no joke.

After listening to the radio for a while, I went into the mess hall part of the Club for lunch. After eating, I went back into the Club lounge area to again listen to the radio reports. It was overwhelming news. I thought that the U.S. would have no trouble in making short work of this war in the Pacific, and it was difficult to understand how the Japanese could think that they could attack one of our possessions and get away with it.

I went to bed that night thinking that this new war would be over before I had a chance to be in it. I had no doubt that the Canadians

57

would back the U.S., and I felt that being a pilot in the RCAF would put me in a good position to see some action in the Pacific war.

The next couple of weeks went by quickly as I was flying almost every day and loving every minute of it. Among both the Americans and the Canadians, there were rumors of what was to come next. We heard almost every rumor possible, although I do not recall anyone suggesting that the Americans serving in Canada would be allowed to transfer back to the forces of the United States.

Our base was to go on half-schedule for the holidays. Half of the personnel would be given five or six days off over Christmas, and the other half would be given time off over the New Year.

Sgt. Don Lawson and I were given the Christmas period. The time off was too short to attempt to go home, so we decided to take a leisurely car trip into British Columbia. We threw our duffel bags into the back of his little Willys coupe and headed west.

Our route took us through a very scenic and picturesque part of Canada, and as night approached, we found ourselves in Fernie, B.C.

Fernie was a pleasant, medium-sized town, which was festively decorated for Christmas. We found a nice hotel and were happy that they had room for us. We were advised at the hotel desk that their dining room was the "finest in town" and that they would soon be open for the evening meal.

Don and I went up to our room and washed up after our daylong drive. We were both wondering about what we could do for entertainment that night, it being Christmas Eve. Soon the proprietor of the hotel knocked at our door, and welcomed us to his hotel and told us that we were the first *American* RCAF men to visit Fernie. (All of the Americans in Canadian service wore a little arm patch on the left shoulder of the uniform saying USA.) He also told us that there was a traditional Christmas Eve dance at the community hall that evening and that he thought that we would enjoy attending. He said that all of the cafes, including his dining room, would be closed on Christmas Day, however, we were invited to have Christmas dinner with his family and friends. We thanked him and told him that we would talk it over and give him an answer soon.

During dinner, we decided that we would indeed stay over another day and night and advised the manager that we would be very happy to share Christmas dinner with him and his family. We thought that it would be nice to spend Christmas Day in Fernie and then head back to Lethbridge the following day. This was such a beautiful and friendly environment to spend our first Christmas away from home.

After receiving directions to the hall where the Christmas Ball was to be held we again went to our room to prepare for the dance.

When we arrived at the hall, we were greeted cordially and many came over to us and introduced themselves. Most wanted to know where in the U.S. we were from. We had no problem getting partners for each dance (girls outnumbered the men two-to-one) and spent an enjoyable evening dancing and talking to the young people at the ball. We were sort of the center of attention, as we were the first RCAF pilots from the United States to enjoy their hospitality. We danced all evening and met some very pretty girls. Both Don and I had made a date for the following evening. We were told that the local theater would be open on Christmas night, and suggested to our new friends that we would like to take them to the movie. We both thought that it had been a Christmas Eve to remember. There was so much going on around me that I really didn't give much thought to the fact that it was to be spent without my family. Every day and night was a new adventure.

Christmas morning dawned bright and clear. The icicles were hanging from the eves and the snow was dazzling. We enjoyed the morning strolling about the town, watching the kids trying out their new toys. It was very reminiscent of Christmas mornings back home.

Promptly at 1:30PM on Christmas Day, we went to the hotel owner's quarters and were cordially ushered in. We were taken up a

STARDUST FALLING

flight of stairs and into a large festive room that may have been a ballroom at one time. It was probably now used for private parties or large dinners. It had an entrance and stairs to the street three stories below. The long table was set for at least 25 guests. The whole room was decorated, and at one end there was a large lighted Christmas tree. The other guests started arriving and we were introduced to them as they came. There were name markers at each place setting with the name on both sides so those who left them in place were easily identifiable by first names. This made it very comfortable for me to carry on a conversation at the table.

Our first course of the dinner was oysters on the half shell. I had never eaten oysters raw and watched Don Lawson dip his in the cocktail sauce and swallow each one whole. I thought that I would try it, and the first oyster got as far as the back of my throat and I couldn't get it to go down. I finally was able to bring it back out on my napkin, the same way that it had gone in. I was embarrassed but the host and hostess just smiled and gave me a new napkin. I was to leave what was left of the half dozen oysters on the plate uneaten.

We were served a beautiful salad and then the entrée, which was beef and wild venison, after which we had plum pudding for desert. It was an absolutely wonderful Christmas dinner and when finished, the host passed Cognac around to all who wished. Don took a small glass of the Cognac but I passed. I was still embarrassed about the oyster and since I had never tried liqueur, I thought it prudent to decline. As the guests started to leave, we thanked our host and hostess for a beautiful Christmas and left to go to our room and have a little nap before the evening entertainment. (It was to be about a year later before I learned to eat and love oysters on the half shell as well as cognac.)

That evening we went to pick up our lady friends. Fortunately my date lived within easy walking distance of the theater and Don dropped me off at her home and said that he would meet us at the

ROYAL CANADIAN AIR FORCE

movies. It was a good thing that we could walk to the theater, as four in that little "Willys" coupe would have been something to see.

After the show, I took my date home and saw her to her door and then made the long walk back to the hotel. It was a cold and crisp evening and I was well bundled up in my fur boots, heavy uniform jacket, and scarf around my neck, and was feeling on "top of the world." Don returned a bit later and said that his date had invited him in where the parents were waiting to meet him with a cup of hot cider.

After breakfast the next day, we thanked our hosts for a most wonderful Christmas and said goodbye to picturesque Fernie. We were on the road back to our barracks in Lethbridge, arriving late in the afternoon; both still having three full days left on our vacation. I had relatives on my grandmother's side of the family in Edmonton, Alberta, who had invited me to come to visit. This being an excellent opportunity, I bought a round trip ticket on Western Airlines for the flight to Edmonton.

I boarded a Western Airlines 247D airliner in the forenoon and enjoyed the flight through Calgary to Edmonton. It was to be my first flight on a commercial airliner.

I enjoyed the cordiality of my relatives that I had never known before, and they enjoyed showing me the city of Edmonton. In the evening they took me to the local ice rink for a curling match. It was educational, as I had never before heard of the sport. Curling is somewhat like bowling, but takes place on the ice with bowls that look like large marble teakettles with a handle. It is a slow-moving sport but it was fascinating to me. After the second day in Edmonton, I again boarded the airliner for my flight back to Lethbridge; ending my marvelous Christmas vacation of 1941.

I was scheduled to take the early morning flight of January 1st, 1942. I was a good pick for the dawn patrol as I didn't drink much and had no intention of partying on New Year's Eve.

I went to the Sgts. mess hall for the evening meal on New Year's Eve and had liver and onions for supper, one of my favorites. I opted for a second helping and then dessert. I went to my room after reading the local newspaper in the Sgts. Club, I then re-read some of my recent mail, and prepared for an "early to bed." Before I had a chance to retire, I started to get a fierce bellyache. It was quite intense and seemed to be on my right side about belt level. It soon hurt so bad that I made my way to the nearby base hospital and checked in. They put me in a bed and a doctor came in and examined me and said that he thought that it was appendicitis. I had them call my flight duty officer and tell him that I wouldn't be answering the bell for the dawn patrol the next morning. The doctor had said that they would watch my temperature, and if it started to rise they would have to do an emergency appendectomy.

Meanwhile, there seemed to be a New Year's Eve party going on in the nearby ward. The nurses came in to check on me periodically, and I soon realized that I didn't want anyone doing any emergency surgery on me *that* night. They gave me something for the pain and something to put me to sleep. After a while the pain seemed to ease and my temperature stayed near normal and I drifted off to sleep. I awoke in the morning groggy, but had somehow passed the overload of gas that the greasy fried onions had built up. They kept me in the hospital until noon that New Year's Day, and I welcomed 1942 into my life.

I was fit to fly the next day but wasn't scheduled until the 4th of January. A couple of weeks later they had liver and onions on the menu again. I hadn't suspected the fried onions in my New Year's Eve meal, so I went ahead and had the favored dish. Again, I had the severe bellyache but this time I just "toughed it out in my quarters." I was not scheduled to fly the following day, so I took it easy and stayed in my room. It was to be many years before I tried liver and onions again, and forever have gone easy on the onions.

ROYAL CANADIAN AIR FORCE

Time seemed to move along swiftly in January as I was flying most days and logged nearly 60 hours of flight time that month. There were many rumors floating about; we were to go into combat training, we were to be transferred to Alaska; all sorts of rumors. But I still never heard anyone mention that we might be transferred to the U.S. forces.

In one of his "fireside chats" in late January or early February, President Roosevelt announced that he was requesting the return of the U.S. servicemen that were presently in the RAF and the RCAF. I believe there were about 6,000 Americans that were serving in these two services. This was a "bomb shell" to us Americans in Lethbridge. I made an instant decision to transfer as soon as possible. The information about the transfer, however, was slow in coming, and again there were rumors by the dozens.

Sometime early in March, I talked to my friend F/O Harry Reed on the telephone and he told me what he knew about the actual transfer. Harry said that we would be able to pick the branch of service that we wanted to transfer to, and that he intended to choose the Air Corps. He urged me to do the same and to try to get into multi-engine training.

At about this time, Don Lawson received a telephone call informing him that his brother had been killed in an accident in Moose Jaw, Saskatchewan. He left immediately on emergency leave to be with his family.

Very soon after talking to Harry on the telephone, the information on the transfer was posted on the bulletin board in our flight operations room. All of us for which it applied took it down and read it. It gave the date that the transfer would take place in our area as the last part of May 1942. The information papers also stated that we could choose the branch of service that we desired. It further stated that anyone who had completed 400 hours of flying time in any foreign service would be promoted one grade in rank.

It was now the first week of March, and I knew that I had a 14-day vacation coming the last two weeks of the month. My heart sank when I realized that I would have less than 220 hours of flying time in the RCAF at the time of my scheduled vacation. I appealed to my O.C. Flt/Lt Anderson to let me pass on the vacation and stay in the flight to try to fly enough to have the 400 hours before the transfer. He said that he understood, but that I would have to take the vacation. I was to leave Lethbridge on the 13th and return from my vacation on the 29th of March.

I went by bus to Cut Bank, Montana, and boarded the "Empire Builder" train bound for Chicago. I spent a carefree time at home, spending as much time with Dionne as was possible. She was a senior in high school and spent her weekends at my home in Paw Paw. The leave was over all too soon and I again boarded the "Empire Builder" for the trip back to my base.

When I returned to Lethbridge, I was resolved to fly as much as was possible to try to get the coveted 400 hours of flight time in before my transfer date. I talked to my O/C "Andy" Anderson about getting in as much flying as possible. He agreed that he would speak to the scheduler and have me fly as much as was possible, but cautioned me about not getting my "hopes up." He said that he was afraid that I would be too young, at age 18, to be a commissioned officer in the U.S. forces. I reminded him that I would have a birthday on May 1st and that I would be 19 before the chance to transfer came. He suggested that I go to the Gunnery Flight in my "off time" and volunteer for some extra flights there.

The Gunnery Flight agreed to let me fly their aircraft and students when I was available. On many days in April, I would fly a drogue flight in the morning and three or four gunnery flights in the afternoon. By the end of April, I had logged 108 hours for the month, not including the six hours that I flew on the 30th and 31st of March. I

ROYAL CANADIAN AIR FORCE

now had 330 hours and I knew that, weather permitting, I should have the required 400 hours by the last week of May.

I flew both morning and afternoon drogue flight schedules on many days, and did have enough spare time to get in 8 or 9 gunnery flights in the month of May.

I topped the 400-hour mark on the 21st of May and it was a good thing that I did. I was able to fly another tow target mission on the 22nd and then the weather was non-operational for the next three or four days. I went to the Gunnery squadron and begged two flights on the 26th of May; this was my farewell to the Fairey "Battle." It had been a "fine old horse" and in many ways I was going to miss it.

On the 27th of May, I went to Flight operations to have my flight logbook certified and signed by the O/C. I collected all of the RCAF papers that I would need the next day when I was to meet the transfer train in Calgary. Quite early on the morning of the 28th, we left our base by RCAF bus, and arrived at the railroad station in Calgary before noon.

The method used to transfer the Americans from the Canadian forces to the U.S. forces was somewhat unique. The transfer train was brought into the Calgary station and was put on a siding. The American transfer personnel had the first three or four of the rail coaches and the RCAF occupied the last two. We entered the first railroad car and were greeted by a U.S. Army Air Corps (USAAC) officer who explained the transfer process. He told us that if at any time before we were sworn into the U.S. forces we had a change of mind and wished to stay in the RCAF, that we were to inform them and the procedure of transfer would go no further. By no means did all of the nearly 6,000 or so U.S. airmen in the RCAF and RAF wish to transfer, but I would estimate that perhaps seventy-five percent did so. The lure of flying new and different airplanes and for many, a promotion to one grade higher in rank, was a powerful incentive.

There were many papers for me to complete; one of them asked for the branch of the U.S. service that I preferred. Another asked the amount of airplane experience that I had in the RCAF. My logbook was checked and the numbers that I wrote on the paper were certified. The USAAC Sergeant that was helping me with the paperwork commented on the fact that I had just barely made it over the promotion edge.

Next we were given a complete physical and again, I had to wear my glasses to pass the eye exam. I was then taken to the next railroad car where we were all awaiting orders officially establishing us in the U.S. forces. When the new orders came, I now knew that I was to be a 2nd Lieutenant. In a small compartment at the rear of this coach, there was a small room that served as the place that each person was individually sworn in to the U.S. service.

We then proceeded to the first of the two cars at the rear of the train. In the first rail car we were officially discharged from the RCAF. Our remaining pay was calculated and we were paid in cash. We then went to the last car of the train and received orders for our travel to our reporting station in the United States. A paper was handed to each of us thanking us for our support of the Commonwealth war effort.

I was to report to Mather Field, Sacramento, California, on the 8th of June. My orders routed me through my hometown in northern Illinois, and it appeared that I would have less than a week of home leave.

We again boarded the RCAF bus back to our base at #8 B&G and arrived early in the evening. I went over to the Sergeants' Club to see if any of my compatriots were there, but only a few of the Canadians were in the lounge and bar area. I saw my Sgt. Major, Flt/Sgt Plant, and told him that I had transferred and would be leaving the next day. He said some kind things to me. He told me how much they

ROYAL CANADIAN AIR FORCE

appreciated my enthusiasm in the flight (squadron) and how happy he was that I had earned enough hours to receive a promotion.

I went back to my room and reflected on the events of the day. I had left my bunk early that morning as a RCAF Sgt/Pilot and returned to it this evening as a 2nd Lt. in the United States Army Air Force. This was quite a day for me. The next morning, I went to the Sgts. Club to pay my club bill, and then paid the quarters "batman" his wages for May. I made my way to the flight line to say goodbye to my Canadian pilot friends and the winch operators that had served with me on my tour of duty.

Don Lawson and I went into the town of Lethbridge at noon and said goodbye to our civilian friends. We exchanged mailing addresses, with the promise to write and let them know how we were doing. We returned to the base, stripped off our uniforms, and bundled up everything that we had been issued in the RCAF. We then took the bundle of clothing, shoes, belt, hat, and all of our issued gear to the supply building to be turned in and accounted for. We requested to keep our RCAF wings and that was granted. Our wings were separated from our tunics with a razor blade, and I stuffed mine in my pocket and departed the base in civilian clothes.

I originally had planned to ride to St. Joseph, Missouri with Don Lawson and go from there by train to my home in Illinois. Don elected to drive to Moose Jaw, Sask. to retrieve his brother's belongings, so I decided that I would take the "Empire Builder" straight through to Chicago and not lose a day going with him.

I know that Don Lawson felt bad that he didn't have enough hours in the RCAF to qualify for a promotion. I was the only Sergeant that had come to Lethbridge in early December 1941 that was promoted in the transfer. Don had lost precious flying days when he had accompanied his brother's body back to St. Joseph earlier in the year. Certain duties always come first.

I had been in contact by telephone with Ivan Coppess and he had been transferred as a USAAC Sgt/Pilot about two weeks earlier than me. We missed each other in Illinois, as he had already left his home near Waterman, for his new assignment when I arrived at my home on the last day of May.

CHAPTER 4

U.S. ARMY AIR CORPS
ROSWELL & B-17 COMBAT TRAINING

I left Lethbridge on the afternoon of the 29th, with 10 days travel time to report to my new base at Mather Field. My travel orders were routed through my hometown in Illinois, so I could spend some time there before reporting to Sacramento. Again, I boarded the "Empire Builder" at Cut Bank, Montana, and went straight through to Chicago for a visit with my parents and family.

The weather was great, as it was early June of 1942. I again was able to spend considerable time with Dionne. She had just graduated from high school and was soon to take a job in nearby De Kalb, Illinois. I arrived in civilian clothes, as I couldn't buy my new uniform until I reached my new base. Most of my old "civies" were quite tight, having gained weight on the good food at my RCAF base in Canada. We enjoyed being together although the time was all too short.

I went by train to California, arriving at Mather Field on June 8th. We former RCAF pilots from western Canada were assembled for indoctrination into the U.S. Army Air Corps. Most of the people in the classes that I attended had been officers in Canada, but for a few former RCAF Sgts/Pilots like me, it was a "whole new ballgame."

I needed to get an appropriate new uniform immediately. Rather than being issued a uniform as in Canada, I had to go into downtown

STARDUST FALLING

Sacramento and buy my apparel. We were directed to a clothing store that specialized in military clothing, and it was suggested that since it was summer, we only buy what was immediately necessary. I went to the store with my orders in hand and purchased the uniform I needed for the time being. This included gold 2nd. Lt. Bars for the shirts and Air Corps (prop and wings) insignia for the collars, as well as the silver pilot's wings that I was so proud of. The wings were metal and pinned on instead of the cloth wings that were sewn on the Canadian uniform. The uniform shoes were brown rather than the familiar black of the RCAF uniform. As I previously stated, I had gained some weight in Canada and it was a relief to get some properly fitting clothes. I still had most of the "mustering out pay" from the RCAF, so I was able to pay cash for my new purchases.

We had classes in military conduct, and endless marching. We learned how to march all over again, the commands being quite different from the RCAF. I was taught to return salutes from the enlisted men and to salute all officers of a higher rank than mine. On the 18th and 19th of June, I was given a familiarization and check-ride in a BT-13A Vultee airplane. This was a U.S. basic training single engine airplane that was somewhat similar to the AT-6 that I had flown in Canada. The check-ride on the 19th went well. At this time, we were asked if we preferred a single-engine or multi-engine assignment. I selected multi-engine, as that was what I had hoped for. I received orders to report to my new station on June 28th, 1942, at Roswell Army Flying School (RAFS), Roswell, New Mexico. This school was dedicated to the training of multi-engine pilot and bombardier cadets. I was to pilot the Beechcraft AT-11, flying the bombardier cadets on their practice bombing missions.

There were several officers in training with me at Mather that I had known at Lethbridge. I elected to share an auto ride with them as far as Los Angeles, where they all went to different bases, except Capt. Ernie Bickell, who was assigned to Roswell along with me. As we drove down the coast of California, this was my first view of the Pacific Ocean - any ocean for that matter. It was a very beautiful drive but it took all day. I stayed in a hotel in Hollywood that night, and the next morning I was picked up by Capt. Bickell to continue the trip to Roswell.

We proceeded east out of Los Angeles and stopped for lunch in Palm Springs. I took a picture of Ernie in front of his coupe while we were stopped. It was extremely hot there and very hot driving all of the way to Roswell. (Unfortunately, there was no automobile air conditioning in those days.)

We stayed overnight in Phoenix and the next day made it to El Paso. That night, we stayed in the Del Norte Hotel in downtown El Paso and left early the next morning for Roswell. Our route took us east out of El Paso and then, after passing Guadalupe Peak, we turned northeast, leaving Texas and re-entering the State of New Mexico. We passed through the towns of Carlsbad and Artesia and arrived in the late afternoon at our new assignment.

I was happy that I had chosen to make the trip from Sacramento to Roswell by car because I was able to see such diverse scenery and culture for the first time. On this trip, I experienced the coastline of California, the mountains and deserts of Arizona and New Mexico, and became aware of the different nationalities of the people of these regions - the Navahos and Mexican cultures that were all so new to me.

I had never heard of Roswell before being sent there. It was a medium-sized town surrounded by ranches, and was also the home of the New Mexico Military Institute. I can't think of anything remarkable about the City of Roswell at that time and it was years before the famous incident that put Roswell on the map. Roswell was at an elevation of about 3,500 ft. with the ground sloping gradually up west of the city, until encountering the Capitan Mountains which have peaks over 10,000 ft. The temperature in the summer was hot with an occasional thundershower in the late afternoon. The winter was mild, with some dusting of snow; making the weather good for flying all-year-around, which made this area a good selection for the creation of a flying school that could be quite productive.

The airfield at Roswell was new and had recently been built from the ground-up. It was located just south of the town proper on what had been open rangeland. Construction was started in the late fall of 1941, and had proceeded at a leisurely pace until after Dec 7th, when work on the airbase quickly accelerated. The new airfield was designated RAFS or Roswell Army Flying School. (The Air Corps was still a part of the U.S. Army throughout all of World War II.)

The airfield consisted of a large landing pad, which was constructed using a huge amount of soil-cement mixture. This large landing pad allowed the student pilot cadets to practice takeoffs and landings simultaneously, side-by-side, accommodating a very heavy flow of air traffic. Primarily the bombardier school, for their takeoffs and landings, used a separate traditional east-west runway on the northeast side of the mat, as they went back and forth to their practice targets. This runway was also used for the visiting aircraft, leaving the mat almost exclusively for the twin-engine pilot school. Work on another runway had just begun when I arrived.

Upon our arrival on June 28th, 1942, there were only 3 or 4 officers' barracks or bachelor officers' quarters (BOQ's) completed and I was assigned a room on the second floor of the latest completed building. It mainly housed officers who were the instructor pilots from the twin-engine pilot school, and the pilots and bombardier instructors from the bombardier school. Being built quickly and poorly, the BOQ's were hot in the summer and cold in the winter. All of the buildings and hangers were constructed of wood and were serviceable but quite unattractive. Across the street from this barracks area was the Officers' Club. This was both comfortable and roomy, with a large dining room where we were seated six or eight to a table and served family style. There was a large bar and a lounge facility for reading or relaxing and a card room and a billiard room with several pool tables, which made for a comfortable setting. The dining room was used as a dance floor on Saturday night and the drinks at the bar-lounge were inexpensive.

As officers, we did not have a "batman" as the officers and sergeants did in Canada but each BOQ did have 2 janitors; one for the upstairs and one for downstairs. We had to make our own beds, but the janitors swept the rooms and of course kept the bathrooms clean and the windows washed as required.

The largest difference between this airbase and the one in Canada was that many of the jobs on the base were held by women who were almost everywhere except on the flight line. Women could come and go at will, a distinct contrast to the RCAF where all civilians, especially women, had to be escorted when on the base. At RAFS, the officers would bring their wives and girlfriends to the Officers' Club for drinks in the evenings, and on every Saturday night there was a dance-band, consisting of talented GI musicians playing dance music at the club. About once a month there would be a formal dance and this was a gala affair where full-dress uniform was required.

The base airfield was not quite completed when we arrived, so we did our first flying out of the Roswell Municipal Airport that was on the northwest side of the town. The twin-engine pilot school was in operation and they trained out of an auxiliary field nearby. The bombardier students in training were flown out of Roswell Municipal Airport until the 4th of July, when the airbase runways were officially opened. Then, *all* military flying was conducted at the new airbase thereafter.

My checkout in the twin-engine Beechcraft AT-11 was started at the Roswell Municipal Airport on July 1[st.] My first two flights were with 1st Lt. C.E. "Gene" Hersche (pronounced as Hershey), who would become one of my two best friends at Roswell. The first two flights with "Gene" were mainly familiarization with the twin-engine aircraft. Starting on the 4th of July (which was open house at the new airbase, attracting about 6,000 locals). I continued my twin-engine training with 1st Lt. Ed Gholson. About a total of 15 hrs of flying time was consumed in this stage of my training. The instruction was to get me ready to pilot the aircraft that was the platform to train future bombardiers. Although some of the training was simply takeoff and landing practice, much of it had to do with emergency procedures, target location, and practice with the Honeywell autopilot installed in the airplane.

Some instrument flying practice was included and about three hours of night flying was accomplished. I was checked out on the airplane by Lt. Gholson on July 17th and went along with Lt. Hersche on a medium-low altitude training-bombing mission on the 23rd. I had one more training flight with Gene Hersche on the 24th of July that was a high altitude (17,000 ft.) bombing training flight. This completed my training. I remember that Gene asked me if I had to shave yet. I told him that I did; however, "not every day." The evening before my last training flight, Gene suggested to the squadron commander that he thought that since I had so little night flying time, I should make some night takeoffs and landings solo before I took my first night flight with bombardier students on board.

That night I made two flights of 1 hour and 45 minutes each making takeoffs and landings. On each flight there was a sergeant from the maintenance department riding along. I have often thought that if they really knew how inexperienced I was at night flying, they would have thought twice before they begged to tag along. It was nice to have company and I felt competent doing this night flying. Starting on the 24th, after the high altitude checkout by Gene Hersche, I took my first solo flight with two bombardier aviation cadets aboard.

US ARMY AIR CORPS ROSWELLL & B-17 COMBAT TRAINING

I had a total of about nine hours of night flying (including my Canadian time) when I checked out to fly night solo at Roswell. Night flying in the RCAF and the USAAC were somewhat different. In Canada all night flying was done *without* the use of the landing lights. In the USAAC we could and did use the landing lights for the purposes that they were intended, for all ground operations and also for takeoff and landing. This made night flying a lot easier.

The second officer that I became acquainted with was John Fannin. He and Gene were buddies and both were 1st Lieutenants and lived in the same BOQ as I did. Gene was from Kansas and John was from Floresville, Texas, a short distance southeast of San Antonio.

An amusing incident happened when we three first went into town for dinner. I had never had a Mexican meal and John, being from Texas, wanted to show me what *good* Mexican food was like. The Mexican meal was very spicy and the pinto beans were especially "hot." I really wanted water to accommodate the burning in my throat from the beans so John told the waiter that I wanted "mas frijoles." I thought that John was asking for water when he was, in reality, ordering more beans for me. I continued to chow down the beans until I thankfully got the water, and both John and Gene had a good laugh at my expense.

The weather in New Mexico was good and we often flew over 100 hours a month, which suited me fine. All I wanted to do was fly, although I was not quite the "eager beaver" that I had been in Canada.

The AT-11 airplane was one of the twin-engine versions that were produced by Beechcraft in Wichita, Kansas; this same type of airplane was used as a navigation trainer and courier aircraft. It was an all-metal airplane with two Pratt and Whitney 450 HP engines. The airplane was about 35 ft. long, 10 ft. high, had a wingspan of almost 50 ft., and weighed about 9,300 lbs. empty. The airplane cruised at 150 mph and had a top ceiling of 20,000 ft. It could fly for 750 miles without refueling, it was designed to be flown solo, and had room for a bombardier instructor and two cadet students. The bombardier instructor sat in the right front seat beside the pilot, and the two students sat on jump seats behind the practice bombs near the rear of the aircraft during takeoff and landing.

    The forward section of the aircraft was glass, and the student knelt over the Norden bombsight and made course corrections as the instructor sat on the step beside him. The student, as he made the course corrections, sent a signal to the pilot through an instrument on the pilot's panel indicating whether to alter the course to the right or left, and the pilot responded by changing the course accordingly. The bombsight could also be connected into the airplane autopilot so that the course corrections to the target could be automatically made through the autopilot. Often, if the student made a large correction, the airplane would be in a bank as the bomb was released and the bomb would hit outside of the marked target area.

    The target areas were in the wide-open range and any miss was not a danger to habitation. Occasionally cows or sheep might wander into these training areas; however this was unlikely as there were fences enclosing each target. The target was marked in circles, much as a vertical gunnery target, with a wooden pyramid (called a shack) at the center. As the 50 lb practice bomb hit, it would emit a white puff of smoke and the instructor or the other student not at the bombsight would record the hit on a chart. At night the target was lighted, with the shack at the center lighted as an "X" and the rings extending out having a light at each ring intersecting the four cardinal compass points. When the practice bombs hit at night, they emitted a flash of light and thus could be scored by the observer.

    Fortunately, the service was quite lenient in allowing us to have an airplane for a weekend jaunt. We could leave first thing Saturday morning as long as we had the aircraft back by six on Sunday evening. I took several such trips during my stay at Roswell. Most of the flights were to Texas with John Fannin and Gene Hersche aboard.

US ARMY AIR CORPS ROSWELLL & B-17 COMBAT TRAINING

On the first weekend of October 1942, I checked out an AT-11 and with John and Gene aboard, flew to San Antonio. This was a flight of about 2 hrs. and 30 minutes. I had chosen to go to San Antonio, as there were several men from my hometown who intended to get together there for the weekend. We were all invited to the small home of Bill and Roberta Wetzel for the gathering. Ray Rogers, Chet Gaines, and several others from my hometown were there for the weekend. We had a very good time talking about our hometown and the challenges we faced in the service. It was quite late that night when I went back to the visiting officers' quarters at Kelly Field.

The next morning when it came time to leave, there was a low ceiling and rain was falling. Since I had very little instrument flight experience, John and Gene thought that it would be prudent for them to pilot the airplane on takeoff and climb out through the clouds, while I was to sit in the back in one of the student jump seats. I didn't object and we proceeded to depart San Antonio in this fashion. I forget whether it was John or Gene that was in the pilot's seat on takeoff and climb out; however, I noticed that they were concerned at the aircraft's poor rate of climb and the escalating cylinder head temperatures encountered on the climb. I thought that the wings were getting iced up but when I crawled forward to the cockpit, I saw that the landing gear green lights were still on, indicating that they had forgotten to retract the landing gear. This was the cause of the poor climb rate and the high cylinder head temperatures. I suggested that they retract the gear, and immediately the climb improved and the temperatures returned to normal. We soon popped out on top of the clouds and they decided it was time to let me fly my airplane back to Roswell.

I went home for a short leave in mid-October. Dionne and I had a chance to be together and I was able to take her to the Palmer House in Chicago for an evening of dinner and dancing. It was very nice to be back in Paw Paw in the fall of the year. My grandfather, Lee Coss, died while I was home on this vacation; however, I could not stay for his funeral as I was due back in Roswell by the 17th.

I used one of our airplanes for a weekend jaunt in late January for a flight to Victory Field, Vernon, Texas. I was to spend an evening visiting two of my friends from my flying days at the Waterman Airport. The following morning, as I was preparing my flight-plan for the trip back to Roswell, the commanding officer of Victory Field came out to say goodbye. While this may seem unusual, remember that this was a primary flying facility that had only Stearman biplanes trainers based there. A visitor in a twin-engine airplane was a rarity. The commanding officer suggested that I *buzz* the field on departure *if I so desired*. There was no local traffic, being a Sunday, so I climbed out east of the field and put the AT-11 in a shallow dive and picked up speed to around 200+ mph and gave the field a good old-fashioned low-level legal buzz job. I pulled up in a steep climb and continued westbound on my course to Roswell.

Several times, on a military sponsored bus trip, I visited Carlsbad Caverns for a tour of these famous caves. For recreation at Roswell, there was a picnic area on the Pecos River about 5 or 6 miles southeast of Roswell known as the "Bottomless Lakes." As an outing, we would take beer and dunk it deep in the lake so that after an hour or so, it was sufficiently cooled to be drinkable.

My experience in trying to find someone to date in Roswell was totally unsuccessful. I was at an awkward stage, being too old for the high school seniors and too young for the more mature ladies that circulated on the airbase. I attended a couple of events in town that the USO put on but met no one new or interesting. In Roswell society, the matrons wanted to see that their daughters were interested in New Mexico Military Academy cadets only, as these cadets generally came from the wealthier families. The mothers of the daughters of Roswell made a definite effort to keep their young ladies from being courted by *mere* RAFS officers.

Getting back to business, one base incident that I recall, sadly, was the time I ground looped the airplane on takeoff. By this time, I had several hundred hours in the AT-11 and was quite confident in my ability to fly the airplane. I was in front of half a dozen other airplanes from our squadron and I made a much too hurried engine run-up and control check and called the control tower for takeoff clearance. (It was normal for us to give the aircraft serial number and the pilot's name to the control tower when we requested takeoff clearance.) I was given clearance, and in my haste I forgot to lock the tail wheel before I brought the power up for takeoff. The power from the two engines did not come in evenly and *without* the tail wheel locked straight ahead, (as it should have been), the airplane headed off the runway in a large ground loop. I closed the throttles and traveled in a large 360-degree turn that put me back at the tail end of the line waiting for takeoff. The people in the control tower asked if everything was OK and I assured them that everything was fine. The only damage was to my pride, which was badly bent. I took a lot of ribbing from the pilots in my squadron about this incident. Cockiness and over-confidence just doesn't pay!

On the AT-11, there was a left and right main fuel tank, and also a reserve fuel tank that we normally used en-route to the target before switching to the main tanks. Once, on an early morning flight, I forgot to switch to the main tanks and flew the entire training mission using the fuel from the reserve tank. We were using one of the targets nearer to our base just east of the Pecos River. Returning to the field, I throttled back and started descending at a fairly rapid air speed and just as I crossed the river east of the airfield, both engines ran out of fuel. I was advancing the throttles to level off at about 2,000 feet above the ground with the early morning sun shining over my left shoulder on the instrument panel and I had failed to see the two fuel low pressure lights illuminating to tell me of an imminent engine failure. I again throttled back to keep the engines from over-speeding as I attempted to get fuel flowing from the main tanks to the engines. I switched the fuel valves and, using the hand wobble pump between the pilots' seats, pumped furiously and finally got both engines running again. I was able to level off at about 1,000 ft. above the ground. It was fortunate that I was going fast enough that I didn't lose more altitude while I was getting the engines restarted. Needless to say, this was a heart-stopping incident in my young life. One more lesson learned! *Keep your head out of you know where and use the lessons you've been taught.* The Beechcraft AT-11 was a responsive, nimble aircraft and was a dream for me to fly.

As my first winter in the USAAC approached, I had purchased a complete officer's uniform. I also purchased an elegant, fingertip-length greatcoat. I didn't have the money necessary to buy all of this new uniform clothing, so I bought on credit, which the stores were more than ready to extend to the military men. In late fall, I had gone shopping for a used car that I felt that I could afford. I zeroed in on an old La Salle that was on sale for $125.00. I soon found out that it burned about as much oil as it did gas. It was transportation to and from town and to the "Bottomless Lakes," and that was about all I used it for.

On one occasion, Gene Hersche and I and several other officers from our squadron went to a saloon just north of Artesia, New Mexico to drink and dance with the local girls. Artesia was about 40 miles south of Roswell. We soon had a confrontation with the local cowboys who objected to our dancing with *their* girlfriends. This escalated quickly into a near-fight situation, and we were happy to see that a small group of tough oil field workers came to our rescue and afforded us the opportunity to make a hasty exit.

In the 9 months I was stationed at Roswell (which included two vacations), I added 750 hours of flight time in the AT-11. Once I rode as co-pilot with Gene on a search mission trying to find one of our downed aircraft. This flight totaled 3 hours 50 minutes, so the AT-11 had at least 4 hours of fuel on board. We would be scheduled to fly a week of morning missions, a week of afternoon missions, and then a week of night missions, in that order. The weekends were pretty much off as most of the equipment and targets were down for maintenance and inspections.

I had a chance to drive with friends into the mountains west of Roswell to Ruidoso, New Mexico. This was all new to me and I enjoyed it a lot. One weekend I took a bus trip from Roswell to Albuquerque. The bus driver made a rest stop adjacent to a cowboy open range round-up camp. They were cooking fresh young beef over an open fire, and the passengers were invited to partake of this meal of beef and pinto beans with the cowboys. It was indeed a delicious meal and fun experience.

I was promoted to 1st. Lt. on February 2nd, 1943, while I was still 19 years old. I think that at about this time, both Gene Hersche and John Fannin were promoted to Captain. I had been a 2nd Lt. for 8 months. Because of the date that I had received my wings in the RCAF (11-25-41), I was promoted to 1st Lt. along with the USAAC class of 41-H, which had the nearest graduation date to my receiving my Canadian wings.

I went on a 15-day leave on Feb. 6th, 1943 and returned to Paw Paw. Again, Dionne and I had a good time being together as much as possible. My folks had a car by now and I was able to borrow it, as fuel and tires would permit. I was still in touch with Janice Lindus but she and a girl from my high school class named Betty Krueger were in training to be nurses at Swedish American Hospital in Rockford. It was nice to be home, even though it was quite cold compared to Roswell. Both my sister Audrey and my mother were working at the munitions plant in Amboy, Illinois at this time, as Audrey was waiting to go into nurses training as soon as she turned 18. My youngest sister Norma was employed as a telephone switchboard operator in Paw Paw when she wasn't attending school.

81

When I returned from my February vacation, I learned that Gene Hersche had gone to Hobbs, New Mexico for B-17 training and combat duty. John Fannin had signed up to be on the next list for transfer to the same school and also would leave soon. I hadn't seen a lot of either of them for several months as they were often assigned to fly the RAFS brass and the West Coast Training Center Commanding Officer on frequent official flights.

On March 6th and 7th, I took Capt. Ernie Bickell, our maintenance officer, to Wichita, Kansas, on a cross-country flight. He had requested that I fly the airplane on the trip. This was the same Ernie Bickell that I had known in Canada and had ridden with from Los Angeles to Roswell.

On the night or early morning before John Fannin was to leave for Hobbs, he knocked on my door and came into my room, and asked me if I would be best man at his wedding the next morning. Of course I said yes and in the morning, as soon as the stores were open, I went with him to purchase the wedding ring. I had never met Jane, the lady that he was to marry, but he had told me recently that he was dating someone quite special in Roswell. She was the daughter of a minister. We assembled at Jane's home at noon and her father married the couple. Her mother and I were the witnesses. There was no time to celebrate, as John had to report to Hobbs that very day. I kissed the bride and shook John's hand as they dropped me off at the airbase, and he and Jane headed for his new assignment in Hobbs.

I was determined to go to B-17 school also and when the next list of volunteers was posted, I was the first name on the list. I received orders to report to the B-17 school at Hobbs, New Mexico on April 19th, 1943. I was to be at the B-17 transition flying school just one month before going on to combat phase school and assembling my combat crew.

My old La Salle automobile was doing OK but I wasn't comfortable driving it as far as Hobbs. It had never let me down but I certainly didn't trust it for a long trip. I decided to sell it back to the used car dealer that had sold it to me. The salesman was named "Toad" Breneman and he had said that when I was transferred he would give me 75 bucks for it. I took him at his word and pealed off the seventy-five dollars from a roll of bills in his pocket and the *gem* was ready to be sold to the next eager GI.

There were several pilots that I knew or flew with at Roswell that I would later be re-united with at Continental Airlines after the war. This group included Gene Hersche, John Fannin and Harold Spores, all of whom were in my squadron. I also knew Danny Gray and Bob Wampler at Roswell and later at Continental. It was almost like Roswell all over again when I went to work as a co-pilot for Continental Airlines in the spring of 1946.

It was time to move on, I had logged over 750 hours in the AT-11 by this time. I had been in Roswell about 9 months, which was a longer time than at any other place in my short military career. I had virtually no contact with any civilians in Roswell. I don't recall dating one girl in Roswell, even though I had met a few interesting ladies on the frequent cross-country flights that I made. I still wrote and heard from Dionne regularly and corresponded with Janice. Some of the girls from my high school class also wrote from time to time, as it was the thing to do then. Harry Reed and I kept in touch by phone and letters while he was a Marine Captain at Cherry Point, North Carolina, and was training to be a marine fighter pilot. I also kept in touch with Ivan Coppess by phone when he was stationed at Ajo, Arizona. Harry Reed was to go on to serve two full tours of combat duty in the South Pacific.

I was to report to Hobbs on April 19th, so on the 16th, I checked out of the BOQ, paid my bills, and got one of my friends in the squadron to fly me in an AT-11 to my new base at Hobbs, New Mexico.

When I checked in on the afternoon of the 16th, I got settled in at the student pilot quarters and found my way to the Officers' Club.

STARDUST FALLING

The first person that I ran into was Capt. Gene Hersche. He had been made an instructor and was near graduating his first or second class of students. Gene told me that John and Jane Fannin had rented a small house off the base and had set up housekeeping there. John was also a B-17 instructor like Gene. I was invited to go along with Gene and his two students on a flight the next morning, April 17th. This was to be my first flight in the B-17, and to me it was very impressive. Gene was giving his students emergency procedures, such as engine failures on takeoff, landing, and so forth. About midway into the flight, when he wanted to give the students a breather, he put me in the left pilot seat and had me make a couple of touch-and-go landings. This was a terrific way to start out my B-17 training. I had made my first flight in the AT-11 with Gene Hersche, and was now doing the same in the B-17.

When I checked in at Hobbs, I was again a student; this meant limited drilling and ground school training, and of course flight training. The schedule was quite compressed, as we were to complete a 6-week course in one month flat. We were scheduled almost every day, attending both ground school and flight training. Included in this course was about 15 hours of simulator (Link) instrument training, and we were scheduled at all times of the day and night to complete the assignment. The ground school covered everything about flying the B-17, for we were to become totally familiar with the airplane and its characteristics.

I saw Gene often and visited the Fannin home several times. John and Jane had a small cottage in the town of Hobbs. The "main drag" of Hobbs was paved, but all the side streets were covered with tar or oil to keep the dust down - the street in front of the Fannin home was no different. It was very comfortable for me to spend an evening with them in their home and I had lunch or dinner with Gene Hersche at the Officers' Club quite often.

US ARMY AIR CORPS ROSWELLL & B-17 COMBAT TRAINING

While I had hoped to have either Gene or John as my flight instructor at Hobbs, I was assigned to Capt. Arnold. The flight instruction started with basic air work including stalls and steep turns, etc. Then we practiced takeoffs and landings, cross-country flights, and some under-the-hood instrument practice. I had one flight to 30,000 ft. with Capt. Arnold, and then on the 5th of May, I took a flight with Capt. Grover (as his co-pilot) to Randolph Field, Texas. We landed the B-17 on the grass runway at Randolph Field, which was quite a thrill.

There were three models of the B-17 in use and they were the B-17E, the B-17F, and the G model. The most common at this time was the B-17F, which was used in my training at Hobbs. It had an empty weight of 34,000 lbs. (This was a considerably larger and heavier airplane than the AT-11.) The B-17F could weigh as much as 56,500 fully loaded with fuel, oil, crew and armament, and a full load of bombs. The B-17 had a cruising speed of about 180 mph (more like 170 mph in combat formation), with power supplied by four Wright nine cylinder engines of 1,200 horsepower each. The propeller was 11' 7" in diameter and each engine was equipped with a turbo-fan supercharger that allowed the engine to perform very well at the higher altitudes. The airplane was 74' long, 19' high and had a wingspan of 104'. The fuel capacity was 2,520 gallons, which was contained in the wings.

There was very little time for socializing at Hobbs. The airbase itself was almost a carbon copy of Roswell, where all the buildings were temporary and the student quarters similar in layout. The student officers were welcome at the Officers' Club and we would occasionally have a free evening off and visit the "State Line Café" for drinks, dinner, and dancing. Gene Hersche introduced me to this watering spot. It was 5 or 6 miles east of Hobbs, and was on the Texas state-line; the "State Line Café" straddled that state line. New Mexico being a "wet" state and Texas a "dry" state made for an interesting situation at this cafe. One could drink and dance in the New Mexico part and then step through an open archway into the Texas side and have a great steak dinner. You could order a drink at a "hand through" between the bar on the New Mexico side and the dining room on the Texas side, but you had to hand carry your drink to your table. The waiters couldn't serve you a drink directly from the New Mexico bar as long as you were seated in the Texas part. This was a very popular place, not only with the citizens of Hobbs and the Air Corps personnel, but the ranchers, cowboys, and oil field workers in the area.

I was qualified for my first solo flight in the B-17 on May 6th, and then with a few more flights I was certified as a crew pilot in the airplane. Most of the last few days at Hobbs were taken up in instrument practice. One cross-country flight was from Hobbs to Omaha to Texarkana and return to Hobbs with no en-route landing. This was a 6-hour flight.

We had some formation practice almost daily, which I thoroughly enjoyed. On May 15th, I received my final checkout at Hobbs. I had logged a little over 100 hours in the B-17 in just one month. In the final few days at Hobbs, we had worked the airways radio range (for instrument practice and beam bracketing) at Wink, Texas. Just south of the Wink radio range was an airbase at Pyote, Texas. I would occasionally see it on my training flights and hoped that I wouldn't be sent there for combat phase school training. It was in a god-forsaken area of west Texas, a bit south of the New Mexico border and about 80 air miles south of Hobbs.

My training over, I received my orders to go to combat school as an aircraft commander on the 17th of May 1943. I was to go to 1st phase combat training at (where else) "Rattlesnake Army Air Base" in Pyote. This wasn't a surprise but I had hoped for better. Before starting the combat phase of training, I was given a leave to go home. I left Hobbs on May 18th on this special leave and was to report to

US ARMY AIR CORPS ROSWELLL & B-17 COMBAT TRAINING

Pyote on June 1st, 1943. As before, I saw Dionne on the weekend; however, she had a job at Interstate Aircraft Co. in De Kalb, IL, so we weren't able to spend much more than the weekends together. My friend Janice was busy in her nurses training at this time and although I didn't see her, I did talk to her on the phone. My brother Jerry was 9 and my sister Norma was 16; both were in school and about to start summer holiday. My sister Audrey was now 18 and was waiting for the next class of nurses training to commence. Both she and our mother continued working at the Green River Munitions Plant in an area not too distant from our home. It was soon after Audrey left for nurses training that our mother also quit her job at the munitions plant and became the U.S. rural mail carrier for the post office in the Paw Paw area. All of the men who had previously carried the rural mail were in service and it was now a woman's turn. (After the war, when the men returned, she was to work in the post office as a substitute postal clerk until she was 75 years of age.)

With the month of May and my leave coming to a close, I said goodbye to my friends and was driven to Mendota, Illinois to board a train to my new base at Pyote. I remember showing my travel orders to the railroad station agent in Mendota and to his surprise he found a routing from Mendota to Pyote, Texas. I was issued a ticket and boarded the train for the two-day trip. I think that I changed trains twice; once at Kansas City or St. Joseph, Missouri, and once again at Ft. Worth, Texas, for the final leg west to my destination.

I remember arriving at the little train station at Pyote, with its cattle pens next to the railroad siding. The town of Pyote, a couple hundred yards north of the railroad tracks, was little more than a widening in the road connecting Pecos, Texas, to Monahans, Odessa and Midland, Texas. It had a grocery store, a filling station, and a couple of beer joints and that was all. I was to be stationed in the middle of "nowhere" for the first stage phase training for combat in

87

the B-17. I quickly decided I was going to be saving a lot of my take-home pay.

We were taken by military bus to the airbase located about a mile south of the train station. At the front gate was a sign saying, "Welcome to Rattle Snake Army Air Base, Pyote, Texas." This was the official name of the facility, and a carbon copy of the temporary type wooden buildings that we had at both Roswell and Hobbs. The streets were dusty and the atmosphere was very hot and parched. There were the usual two-story wooden buildings for the officers and enlisted men. The picture was completed with an Officers' Club/mess hall, a gym, a theater, a PX, and a chapel at the end of the street. Wooden hangars lined the flight ramp where dozens of B-17's were parked, all of which was very typical for an Army Air Corps Base of its day.

I signed in and was directed to my quarters. It was nice to relax in a bed after the last two days on the train. I unpacked my B-4 hang-up bag and duffel bag and relaxed (to the best of my ability). I had brought an old electric fan from home that my father had procured for me. It had needed the motor re-wound and a general overhaul but now worked as good as new. It was an oscillating fan and was a big help in keeping me comfortable. (I still have the fan as a relic of the past and astonishly it *still* works.) We were told to report for a mid-afternoon briefing and given our training schedule for the remainder of the week. We would be assigned a crew the next day and all of our future training would be as a crew.

After a good night's sleep, I reported to the large briefing room where the crew assignments were posted. I wrote down the names and went searching for my new team. When I had gotten them all together, we shook hands and got somewhat acquainted. There were now two officers and six enlisted men assigned to me, all of us being quite young. As a matter of fact, I was the youngest member of the entire final 10-man crew. The two officers assigned to me were

Robert Johnson, my co-pilot, and Ernest Jenkins, my bombardier. I was to get a navigator at the next phase of combat training to round out the team.

We went to another briefing together as a crew and got our training assignment. We were told that we weren't to be surprised if we found that most of the ground school was in the middle of the night, as it was just too hot to study in the classrooms in the daytime. Of course there was no air conditioning and fans were too few to be of much use. We got used to going to class at midnight or 0200 to 0400 (AM that is). In the day we might be scheduled to fly in the AM and then we were supposed to sleep from noon until our next ground school assignment. If I hadn't had the fan, I am sure that sleep would have been nearly impossible in the hot Texas afternoon. The only relief that we had from the searing heat was in the early morning or when we were flying and were at a cooler altitude.

Rattlesnake Air Base was aptly named. There were rattlesnakes, often on the flight ramp or roadway seeking a bit of early heat in the cool morning air. We were all aware of the danger of being bitten and did not venture off the paved roads and walkways where the snakes could be easily seen.

The ground school consisted of basically cross-training each crew member. We had to learn to use the Norden bombsight, which was easy for me, having practiced on it several times when I was flying bombardiers in training at Roswell. We learned all about the 50-caliber machine gun and all were required to shoot each of the guns on the airplane. This was an interesting exercise for me. I turned the airplane over to Bob Johnson, my co-pilot, and we cruised up and down the gunnery range while the gunners assigned to each position instructed me in firing their guns. All of this went well until Sgt. Harold Rice tucked me into the ball turret in the belly of the airplane and explained how I was to maneuver it and fire the two guns. He shut the hatch and I tried to maneuver it around up and down. It was very hard to stay orientated unless I could see the underside of the wings or belly of the aircraft. I fired off a few rounds and called on the intercom that I was ready to come out. I now had a very healthy respect for the fellow down there in the ball turret and *definitely* did not wish to trade jobs with him.

Our training in the airplane consisted of a lot of formation flying, which I enjoyed very much and prided myself on how well I could hold my position, no matter what maneuver the leader made. The B-17 was an airplane that was heavy on the controls and you had to work at flying it. After a half-hour or so of close formation, I would give it to my co-pilot for him to get some work in and for me to have a few minutes to relax a bit. This was the normal routine; we alternated flying the airplane regularly. My co-pilot practiced making landings from the right seat, as it was always possible that with an injured pilot he would have to land the plane from that position. Bob was a good pilot and I was always comfortable when he was at the controls.

The days and nights went by at Pyote, while we continued our phase-one combat training. We were given a pass to go to town about every eight to ten days. This meant boarding a bus to Monahans or Pecos, and once we went into Midland, Texas for the day. Monahans was one of our favorite places as there was a restaurant there that served cold beer and the biggest steaks that I had ever seen. They were even larger and better than the steaks at the State Line Bar & Café east of Hobbs. One evening, the café at Monahan's served fresh shrimp and oysters on the half-shell, and what a feast this was in the most unlikely place that I would have expected shellfish to be served. They must have had it shipped in, on ice of course, by train from New Orleans or Houston. We devoured as much as we could possibly handle.

We were based in Pyote for five weeks where we flew as a crew. Our bombing practice was from low and high altitude. We practiced firing on the gunnery range, high altitude formation flying, flying on instruments, and participated in endless ground school.

Most of the "bull" sessions with the other pilots in my class, and also my crewmembers, were held in my room, as I was the only one with a fan. I got well acquainted with the other crew leaders having been together at both Hobbs and Pyote, and would stay together until we were assigned to our combat unit. Some of the other pilots that I particularly liked and hung out with were Claude Scott (Scotty), George Perry, and Jesse Wheeler.

Time went by fairly fast in Pyote, flying many multi-task missions. It might be bombing practice and then instrument practice. We would have gunnery practice and then high altitude bombing practice, etc. Formation practice was almost a daily routine as were simple takeoffs and landings. As a crew, we flew a total of 67 hours in the B-17 at Pyote.

We spent a week at Alexandria, Louisiana, before they decided that they weren't ready for us. We were then transferred as a group to Dyersburg, Tennessee, arriving on July 16th to continue our combat training. I had received my navigator, 2nd Lt. Walt Amundsen, just before we arrived at Dyersburg, now completing my ten-man crew. I was advised that I would likely lose my co-pilot, as he would be promoted to pilot and have a crew of his own. He was certainly qualified, but this didn't materialize and he remained with me the entire time.

At Dyersburg, we were in our final phase of combat training, that consisted of more formation, high altitude bombing, and long-range navigation, with both day and night formation. Night formation was interesting, as we flew without navigation (wing tip) lights. As a matter of fact, with the exception of a faint blue light under and above the mid fuselage, there were no lights on the aircraft at all. It wasn't all that difficult, however, as we could clearly see the glow of the turbo-superchargers of the airplane we were to fly in formation with. By that orientation, it was possible to keep quite good formation.

The flying was more interesting in Dyersburg, having been designed to be as near to combat flying as possible. We went on a 1,000-mile over water navigation mission and did both high and low altitude navigation, as well as bombing from both altitudes.

I remember one long-range, low-altitude navigation mission in mid August. I chose a cross-country flight path at low altitude the length of the State of Illinois, to a point northeast of my hometown of Paw Paw. I had called my parents the night before the flight and alerted them that I would pass over town at a low altitude the next day. My mother, in her typical fashion said, "Wesley, don't fly too low." I assured her *I wouldn't*.

We were to simulate bombing a bridge or dam at low level and then to return to Dyersburg. The flight plan had us fly at low level and then near our IP (initial point) we were to climb to 3,000 feet above sea level and cross the IP at that altitude. This procedure was to enable us to see our target better and get our bomb run in. Over the IP, we were to concentrate on finding the target and start a descent to be at about 500 feet above the ground and level flight at "bombs away." We were then to execute a steep climbing turn after releasing the bombs to avoid the effect of the bomb blast. Thereafter, we were to go back to low level and return to our base. This was primarily an exercise in low-level navigation and bombing. This type of navigation is not easy and I knew that it would be a good test for both our navigator and bombardier.

I also knew that we couldn't use the Norden bombsight on the bomb run, as we were changing altitude and airspeed constantly, so the bombardier would have to "eyeball" the target and drop on *instinct*.

The next day, everything went well and we flew to Aurora, Illinois, our IP, crossing it at the prescribed 3,000 feet, and then started a left turn and a powered descent to pass over Paw Paw at 500 feet above the ground. I was able to sight Paw Paw on our descent and aimed at the water tower. I pointed the airplane at the target and hoped to be at the assigned altitude in level flight in time to give Ernie a good bomb run.

We came in over the town from the northeast and the bombardier simulated his bomb drop. We then did a sharp left turn pull-up and were supposed to go back to our base. *I changed the plans a bit*, when I decided to swing back around to the right and come down the main street from west to east at a low level, so I could have a look at my home. I missed seeing my parents out in the yard so I decided to come in from the north at a slower speed and lower altitude so the guys could have a good look. I could see Dad and Mother and my siblings clearly on this pass. I was satisfied with this and having fulfilled the initial mission, we proceeded back to Dyersburg.

That evening I had a call from my Dad, saying that some of the people in my hometown were upset that I *rattled* the little town and he was afraid that they would report me. (I later heard that we had broken some dishes that fell from the shelves, and that my Dad went around and paid each person for the damages if they asked.) My Dad said they might report me and I could be in trouble. I told him to not worry about it and I thought, "What could they do to me, send me to combat?" That was the last I heard of this. It was one fun training mission in spite of my parent's displeasure and the flack from my hometown folks.

During the time that I was in Dyersburg, my sister Audrey and my girlfriend Dionne came to visit me and I took them to Memphis for an evening of dinner and dancing at the famous Peabody Hotel. It was very nice seeing Dionne again and I came very close to proposing marriage to her there in Memphis. I realize now that we were both much too young to marry, as I was barely 20 and she was 18. My bombardier Ernie Jenkins had his wife, Sarah, come to Dyersburg to be with him and also our tail gunner, Jim Hoskins, and his new wife were together in Dyersburg during this time.

Our time at Dyersburg ended on Sept 6th and we were given a 10-day leave before going to combat. We had flown 123 hours in this phase of training at Dyersburg and had now completed our combat training. We left Dyersburg and I spent my leave again in Paw Paw, much of the time with Dionne. Although Dionne and I were close, I decided to tell her that I expected her to date while I was away. She said, "Date who? They have all gone into service." It was left at that.

I made one auto trip to the now closed Waterman Airport and visited with the Eakle family and caught up on all of the local news. I knew that Hank Marks was now in Pilot Cadet training. We were all just a bit careless and free in our confidence level and attitude in those days. "Nothing could touch *US*," we thought!

When I was leaving the Eakle home, Alice Eakle Marks gave me a beautiful pin-up drawing that she had made of a seductive young lady with a candle in her hand on the way to her bedroom. It was done with crayon and was drawn on a window shade that, when rolled up, would fit nicely in a footlocker. I told Alice that I would name the new B-17 (that I fully expected to take to combat) the "Shady Lady." While Hank Marks had been given her first drawing, (Alice and Hank were married by this time), I carried her second into combat and Harry Reed received the third or fourth drawing created by her. Alice was to complete more than 40 different renditions of the "Shady Lady" that she gave to the men going into combat. The lucky servicemen receiving these prized window shade pin-ups treasured them, just as I did, during my combat tour.

We were to report to Dyersburg by midnight the 17th of September for overseas assignment. I boarded a train in Chicago about noon of the 17th for the direct rail trip to Dyersburg, and my co-pilot, Bob Johnson, and navigator, Walt Amundsen, were on the same train. When we arrived in Dyersburg, we were met by officers from the base, with orders that we were to board another train immediately for Grand Island, Nebraska. We were concerned about our belongings at the base but were assured that they had been gathered up and were already on the train with us. We boarded the train and met Ernie Jenkins, our bombardier, who told us that he had cleaned out our rooms and had packed our footlockers for us. We were now on a two-day trip to Grand Island, Nebraska.

When we arrived at our new temporary base, we took the regular physicals and had our insurance papers and will updated, and were briefed on our upcoming overseas assignment. We were all sure that we were to go to England to join the 8th Air Force. I had one short check-flight in Grand Island and the crew picture was taken in front of a B-17 parked on the ramp. Unfortunately, my waist gunner, Joe Kinanne, was not available for the picture "shoot" as he had a dental appointment. I lost my radio operator, Sgt. Parks, at the last moment in Grand Island as he was hospitalized with spinal meningitis.
I was assigned another radio operator/gunner, Sgt Najarian. He fit in well with the crew and was well liked by all. The crew was now declared fit and ready for combat duty.

I still had the lingering hope that we would be assigned a new airplane to fly overseas and that I could name it "The Shady Lady." Harry Reed named two of his planes "Shady Lady" (both were shot out from under him) in his two Pacific combat tours as a Marine pilot. To be able to name your airplane "The Shady Lady" was indeed a tribute to Alice Eakle Marks and her artistry and generosity; this, however, was not to be. We were bussed to the railroad station and shipped out to the east coast by rail.

Mom & Dad

My Sisters & Brother
Norma, Audrey & Jerry

My friend, Tommy Boyle pretending to shoot an apple off my head.
Next time, I get to shoot the arrow!

Wes and the "T" craft

My sister Audrey

Cousins Marvel Coss and Bill Town with Wes

Dionne Firkins

Hank Marks, Harry Reed & Wes

Myself in 1940, wearing glasses that were necessary to pass the CAA physical. I usually wore corrective sunglasses when flying.

left to right: Wes Coss, Spence Mack, Henry Marks, & Ivan Coppess

At right is one of the big Stinson airplanes that I flew in 1940 at the age of 17.

Some of the "Old Gang Around Waterman Airport"

When the fuel tanks were empty at the hangar, it was just "push her across the highway to the truck-stop and fill 'er up!"

The J-3 Cub at Progress Corner Gas Station

Sunday afternoon's with people sitting in their cars watching the airplanes takeoff and land. Maybe some are waiting for a bad landing.

School Principal - 1940
Mr. Henry Barton

My girlfriend Dionne pictured with the "T" craft that I often used to commute to school on Fridays for my history lesson.

Paw Paw High School

This was our simulated target on Aug 7, 1943, which shook the sleepy town and broke a few dishes!

Two important people. One helped me to leave Paw Paw early and one helped me return to Paw Paw sooner!

S/Sgt. Ambrose Moore

Photo provided by Mark Clark Courtesy Aircraft, Rockford, IL

Above is a Canadian Harvard AT-6 that I flew during my RCAF Days.

RCAF Days

Sgt/Pilot - Ivan Coppess RCAF

Sgt/Pilot RCAF Wes Coss at age 18

F/O (1st Lt.) Harry Reed RCAF

Fairey "Battle" Gunnery Aircraft

Captain Gene Hersche

Captain John Fannin

These men were my closest friends at Roswell and Hobbs.
We were reunited while flying for Continental Airlines after the war.

Photo courtesy of Paul Bowen Photography

One of the models of the Beechcraft AT-11 aircraft used to train bombardier students at Roswell

A picture of me taken while I was stationed at Roswell, New Mexico

This beautiful pin-up was created by Alice Marks. It was drawn with crayons on window shades and could be rolled up and put in a footlocker. She created these wonderful drawings for servicemen as something to lift their spirits while away from home fighting the war. I was fortunate to receive drawing #2, which I took overseas with me. (Her husband, Lt. Henry Marks, received #1) Our friend and mentor, Major Harry Reed, received the next window-shade drawing. He named two of his Marine fighter planes "Shady Lady." This is one of the few photographs that remain today of the 40 or more that Alice created for servicemen of WW II, each one different from the others.

Photos courtesy of Mrs. Alice (Eakle) Marks and her sister Nancy (Eakle) Coss and her daughter Melissa (Marks) Van Drew

"Shady Lady" by Alice Marks vintage: early 1940s

CHAPTER 5

NORTH AFRICA AND ITALY

We had endured a long and gritty two-day train trip from Grand Island, Nebraska, finally debarking near Newport News, Virginia on September 25th. Camp Patrick Henry was located in a sandy, piney woods and the accommodations were quite temporary, but sufficient. This became our home until we shipped out. There were eight officers in each hut with four double bunks. Since this was a staging area for personnel being sent to Europe, everything had to be checked again.

Before we had left Grand Island, the officers had been issued a 45-caliber automatic pistol, a steel helmet, and a shelter half for a 2-man tent. We also received all of our flight gear (overall flight suit, fur-lined jacket, fur-lined flight boots, etc). We had been provided with a footlocker and a duffle bag in Dyersburg. We packed all of this new stuff away in them, except for our lighter weight leather jacket, our good uniforms, our everyday uniforms, and all of the things that we wanted to travel with us in our cabin on the ship. We kept all of this in a hang-up bag known as a B-4 bag.

We were convinced that we were to go to England to fly with the 8th AF, so we packed away all of our light-weight clothing in our foot locker, and were now wearing our gabardines in anticipation of the cool weather we expected on our arrival in England.

STARDUST FALLING

We had been advised to stock up on heavy long underwear, as this would help us keep warm at the low temperature of flying at high altitude. The long underwear that we bought was light gray and of the two-piece type. We also were told to stock up on heavy wool socks. Whether we smoked or not, it was suggested that we also take along cigarettes, as they could be used as barter. We couldn't buy bottled liquor at Patrick Henry, but a few of the fellows had brought liquor from home to be consumed upon finishing their combat tour.

We were allowed one chance to shoot the new gun on the pistol range. This was fun and I enjoyed shooting it and was amazed at the "kick" that it had. I had never before shot an automatic handgun, let alone a 45.

I checked with our enlisted men every day to see if they had any problems. In a letter home, I told my folks that I was eager to get overseas and to fly again. I had established a bank account in my hometown bank and I deposited some of the pay that I received on October 1st. I intended to continue to send money home while I was overseas, and I did so. We were tightly restricted to the camp and no one could go off base for any reason, so there was nothing else to do but play cards most of the day. Jesse "Wheeler-the-dealer" always had a game going. Our pilots and their crews were virtually the same as we had trained with at Hobbs, Pyote, and Dyersburg. The crews were known by the name of the pilot, like Lt. Wheeler's crew, Scott's crew, Perry's crew, Coss's crew, etc. Our group of 10 replacement crews was known as the Chambers Group. Someone said that a Major Chambers was in charge and responsible for our transfer overseas. I do not remember ever meeting the gentleman. (Chambers Group may have been a code name for our transit.)

We finally received our orders to ship out on October 7th, 1943. We had been in Patrick Henry almost 2 weeks; more of the Army's "hurry up and wait routine." We were sent by army bus to the nearby port of Newport News, Virginia. Our baggage was sent on ahead by truck, and we carried what we needed for the voyage, which we stored in our cabin.

We found that the ship that we were to embark on was the newly renamed "Empress of Scotland." The former "Empress of Japan" was a large vessel that had originally been in the service of the Canadian Pacific Steamship Lines, and had been in passenger service between our west coast and ports in Japan and Asia. After Pearl Harbor, it was pressed into military maritime service and was renamed. The ship was a fast vessel and the ship's crew was confident that she was too fast to be a target for German submarines. Now that the vessel had been converted to wartime troopship duty, she carried about 5,000 GI's.

The sendoff was quite traditional. There were Red Cross ladies with cookies, coffee, and fruit, as well as a small military band to see us off while we made our way on board. We all went to the rail as we cast off and were tugged out into the harbor. People on shore were waving, and we all did our best to not think of the serene peace and security that we were leaving.

We left Newport News at noon on October 8th, 1943. As the shoreline receded, I remember standing at the rail on the fantail of the ship wondering if I would ever see the soil of the USA again. This was sort of a "sinking" feeling, which soon passed with all the activity aboard the ship.

We officers were soon assembled in a large lounge area, and the 1st Lts. and Captains were given their emergency station location. We were to be in charge of the passengers (GI's) that were also assigned to that lifeboat area. We took all this emergency drill seriously, being fully aware of the German "U" boat threat. We were afraid that we were quite vulnerable to a sub attack, even though the "Empress" was said to be too fast to be intercepted by a submarine in the open ocean. There were 2 double bunks for the four of us in our small compartment, but at least we did have a window (porthole) for light in

STARDUST FALLING

the daylight. The ship had very subdued interior lighting at night and, as a consequence, we didn't stray far from our quarters, except perhaps to see the movie.

Most of us had packed our light-weight clothing with the "hold" baggage because we were so sure that we were going to England, but we were soon to learn that winter clothing definitely would not be needed in North Africa. My enlisted men were berthed in a fairly large area below the waterline. The bunks were stacked 5 or 6 high. My entire crew was comfortable, but still engaged in the normal amount of "bitching" that is a staple in the military.

We were accompanied out of the harbor by two destroyers and a blimp. The blimp stayed with us until dark the first day. The second day at sea the destroyers left us at noon and we were now on our own. On the third day of our voyage the Captain of the vessel came on the loudspeaker and told the ship's crew that shorts were now in order. He then told us that our destination was Casablanca. I knew only that Casablanca was in Morocco, and was on the west coast of North Africa.

Most of the ship's crew was British and it was apparent that the ship had been taken over by the British Maritime Service. The food aboard ship was good and I was sure that the food supply, along with the U.S. Army cooks, were boarded at our departure port.

The steward assigned to our cabin was a "Brit" named Chester. He was about 5'6", a happy fellow who wouldn't hesitate to do anything in his power to make us comfortable. At the end of the voyage, we four officers generously gave him much of our U.S. currency as his gratuity. It was a smooth crossing and all went well. We now knew that we were to be stationed in North Africa but we were not certain where. We thought that we would eventually be flying out of Italy and perhaps already might be headed there.

What we didn't know was that this had already been resolved and that the 12th AF was to be split up, and the 15th Air Force would be

NORTH AFRICA AND ITALY

created on November 1st, 1943. The newly formed 15th had the heavy bomber units of the 12th, including its bomber protection fighter planes. Its headquarters was to be in Tunis with Major General Jimmy Doolittle as its first commanding officer. Subsequently, the 15th headquarters was moved to Bari, Italy on December 1st. The heavy bomber groups started to move from their bases in the Tunis area to the Foggia, Italy area commencing in early December. General Doolittle remained the commanding officer until January 3rd, 1944, when he was transferred to England to command the 8th. General Twining then took over as commanding officer of the 15th.

When the 15th was officially activated on November 1st, 1943, it had 6 heavy bomber groups, four B-17 groups, and two B-24 groups. It also had three P-38 fighter groups and one P-47 fighter group. These fighters were to provide escort for the heavy bombers. In January 1944, three additional B-24 groups were added to the bomber force.

We sighted the African shore on October 15th, 1943. Our steward, "Chet," had said that he expected a fast turnaround and would be back in the U.S. in less than 10 days. I dashed off a letter to my folks for him to hand-carry back with him with instructions to mail it to my parents as soon as he arrived on U.S. soil. I knew that this was the fastest way to let my folks know that I had arrived safely, and I asked my parents to call Dionne and tell her the news. I also asked my parents to not acknowledge receipt of the letter, as it was uncensored. (My mother kept that letter and all of the letters that I sent home while I was overseas. She kept them in a little cardboard stationery box and I now have all of the original 38 letters.)

I remember my first sight of Casablanca – how aptly named. All of the homes and buildings were stark white, as the name implies. There was really very little other color except the green tops of the palm trees peeking through. Most of the homes and commercial

109

STARDUST FALLING

buildings had flat roofs, so you saw no roofs, tile, or other coverings to break the monotony of white on white.

I said goodbye to my "limey" friend Chet, gave him my letter to mail, and lined up with the others to debark. It was around noon on Friday the 15th of October. We were put on trucks along with our hand baggage for the short trip to camp Don Passage, on the outskirts of Casablanca. The camp was a staging area, and was quite near the airport from which we thought that we would be airlifted to our new assignment.

The camp was another tent city, full to bursting with replacements like us. The weather in Casablanca was ideal fall weather. It is situated at about 33 degrees north latitude, about the same latitude as San Diego, California. Our leather jackets were welcome at night but a bit too warm for daytime wear. We had decided that we would post one of the replacement crew pilots at the airport to await the arrival of air transport for the crews to go to our station, which we now knew was to be Tunis.

In the meantime, I had a fine time exploring Casablanca. The city was relatively clean but did have a rather strong odor, which we finally deduced was the smell of camel manure. We were told that the manure was used in the leather tanning process, and that the leather products sold there retained their *distinctive aroma* for quite a long time after tanning, if not forever. The smell of camel manure is truly unforgettable.

We were getting acquainted with using the French franc as our currency in Casablanca. While on a USO sightseeing tour of the city, we were invited to visit one of the Sultan's palaces. We were told that the Sultan had 7 palaces in Morocco, one of which was in Casablanca. It was a very beautiful place. The Sultan was said to be quite young, only 27, I believe. He had eight wives and 290 ladies "in waiting" who worked in his various households. They were of all nationalities, including ten Americans. He apparently was a tennis fan, for he had an elaborate tennis court with a little building next to the courts. His principle residence was in Rabat, Morocco, the capitol, which is near the seashore, north of Casablanca. His residence at Fez was said to be his favorite palace and was reported to be the most elaborate and beautiful.

As the days dragged by with no transportation orders, we were again reminded that the army is always in a "hurry up and wait" mode. When it was my turn to spend the day at the airport looking for transportation, I was about to conclude that my day's mission was fruitless, when I saw a sight that I have never forgotten. On the approach for a landing at this airport (which was both commercial and military), was a very old commercial airliner that had three wings and four engines. The engines were contained in two nacelles (cowlings), however. Two of the engines were in each nacelle; one propeller at the front and the other at the back, making it a pusher and a puller. I don't remember the make of this particular airplane; it may have been a Farnham. It had a very slow landing speed and a short landing roll.

After it had parked at the ramp and the passengers and pilots had deplaned, I climbed into it and beheld the 10 or 12 wicker passenger seats. I then wanted to see what the cockpit was like. I climbed up the short bamboo ladder and stepped over a high sill (the wood center wing spar) and into the cockpit. It had a most simple rudder bar instead of rudder pedals, and wooden steering wheels on a metal control column. The wood steering wheels reminded me of the one on the old Stinson SM8-A that I had flown earlier at Waterman. All-in-all, this was a terrific experience for me. I hitched a ride back to camp Don Passage, excited to relay what news I had and of what I had seen to my companions.

On Sunday, the 18th of October, my co-pilot Bob Johnson and I were enjoying the sights and sounds of downtown Casablanca. The downtown area was very French and it had numerous restaurants with tables in front of the cafés, usually under an awning or an umbrella.

STARDUST FALLING

We were enjoying sipping our cognac (I had learned to enjoy this drink by this time), when I saw something that has remained in my memory for all of these years. "Picture this if you will," across from where we were sitting having our libation was a small park. There was a man sleeping on a park bench, covered with a dark pea coat. He appeared to be British or French, probably a merchant marine seaman. An Arab man came along the street and took a good look at him. I called Bob's attention to the man, as we watched. The Arab quickly and carefully removed the man's shoes without waking him. The Arab put the shoes up under his robe and promptly strode off up the street without missing a beat. What a surprise the victim must have had when he awoke "shoeless." This one incident perhaps contributed to my early opinion that Arabs were untrustworthy and shiftless, for certainly that is the way that they appeared to me at the time.

Finally, orders came through for us to proceed to Tunis by rail. This was to be on the narrow-gauge French railroad that spans the northern coast of Africa and was quite an experience in itself. This would have been a long, tiresome trip in peacetime, but in wartime it was especially difficult.

There was a railroad siding next to Camp Don Passage, and we packed up our belongings and prepared to board the train. There was a couple of Pullman-type coach cars, and perhaps a dozen or more small wooden freight type cars (known as 40 and 8 boxcars) to carry us to our destination. At least seven or eight of the 40 and 8 boxcars were loaded with our enlisted men and others in transit. The other boxcars carried our supplies and baggage and other freight. The wooden freight cars were placarded in French to be for 40 men or 8 mules.

I think that there were approximately 20 men assigned to each boxcar. They were expected to sleep on the floor of the boxcar on their shelter halves. A Lister bag provided water for each boxcar, and

112

had several spigots near the bottom of the canvas bag that contained 30 or 40 gallons of water. The bottom of the Lister bag reminded one of a cow's udder. The area under the Lister bag seemed to always be wet. The enlisted men eventually put all of the Lister bags in one boxcar in the middle of the train, where they would go and fill their canteens as needed at the frequent stops along the way.

An officer was responsible for each one of the boxcars. My co-pilot, Bob Johnson, was one of the officers that made this entire trip on the floor of one of these miserable cars. Another officer who made the trip on the floor of a boxcar was J.O. (James) Grizzell, who was Jesse Wheeler's co-pilot. The officers had all of our hand baggage with them wherever they were to ride. This arrangement was the same for the men in the boxcars, and since the enlisted men weren't issued a B-4 bag, they used their duffel bags as pillows when they tried to sleep on the floor.

The Captains and 1st Lts. and other officers not assigned to ride in the boxcars rode in the coaches. In addition to our replacement flight group, there were other personnel on board the train. There was one "Lister" bag in each Pullman car across from the toilet and it leaked, keeping the floor in that area constantly wet. The rations for the day were stacked at the other end of each railroad car. There was no lavatory provided for the men in the boxcars. The only way for the enlisted men to relieve themselves was out of the boxcar door, or to wait until the train stopped and go into the desert.

There was no running water in the lavatory in the coach. The toilet was permanently opened to the roadbed. After filling our canteens from our Lister bag, we would sometimes put some water in our steel helmets and use it as a washbasin to try to keep clean. We had been on a cruise-type ship to Casablanca, plus our time in Casablanca was almost like a vacation. Now, reality was setting in, and we were getting a taste of the discomfort that war provides. It was not pleasant.

Several times along the train route, we saw white crosses indicating the place where war casualties had been hastily buried, apparently where they fell. There was also evidence of the battles that had taken place along the route, with many burned out trucks and tanks. Reality was really setting in.

The meals were all canned rations and when eaten cold, were very unpalatable, (if you can imagine eating greasy, canned corned beef hash cold, you have an idea of what it was like). If there was some way to warm the food it wasn't too bad, but there was just no easy way to accomplish this. I can only imagine how uncomfortable this ride must have been for the enlisted men and officers that were in charge of each car, and had to ride in the boxcars all of the way to our destination. Bob Johnson said that the men in his boxcar put some flat rocks on the floor of the car and lit a fire on the rocks to heat their rations to make them more palatable. J.O. Grizzell said that the men in his charge would try to light a fire alongside the roadbed with anything that would burn to try to heat the canned food. Many times they would have to abandon the half-heated food to climb hurriedly back aboard the train. We tried getting our steel helmets filled with hot water from the train engine boiler on the frequent stops, but it wasn't very successful in heating the canned food. I guess "we officers" weren't smart enough to think of building a fire in the desert or in the middle of our coach.

Nearly every time the train stopped, Arabs trying to sell any manner of goods surrounded it. Most of us bought fruit to supplement the rations. The oranges that they were selling weren't very sweet but it was still better than nothing. The Arabs were good at bargaining, so we soon learned not to buy until the train started to move and then the price went down dramatically. Our navigator, Walt Amundsen, was especially shrewd at this maneuver.

We had departed Casablanca around noon of October 24th, 1943. Our route was north along the coast to Rabat and then into the mountains to Fez, where we then proceeded on to Oran and Algiers, and finally to Tunis.

It was an uncomfortable trip for all, and early in our train trip we found that the cars were infested with lice and bedbugs and other creatures that feed on flesh and blood. I had been bitten by lice (bed bugs or whatever) especially around the wrists and ankles as I wore the long two-piece underwear all of the time. I was also bitten around the neckline and they were in my hair. (It was reported that the Arabs brought the lice aboard when they hitched a ride on the empty trains returning to Casablanca.) Although they preferred the Pullman cars and made those the primary carriers, they rode wherever available, including the wooden boxcars.

The enlisted men and officers in the 40 and 8 cars were not as badly infested with the creatures, according to Lt. Grizzell. He reported that the men in the boxcars took some delight in the fact that the officers were especially lousy and uncomfortable up front. The train crews said that they fumigated the cars before they were boarded for the trip eastward, but that the lice would just hide. As soon as the train was boarded in Casablanca, it was lunchtime again for the bugs.

On the first part of the trip we had French railroad crewmen, and east of Algiers they were all American. I made my way to the engine several times at the stops and visited with the engineer and fireman. Once I was invited by an American crew to ride up in the engine cab for a while. The engineer of our train on that section of track was from Pennsylvania and had been a railroad fireman before the war. He told me that the only sport that they had on their daily grind was to outsmart the Arabs when they were bargaining with them at the frequent stops.

He had a GI-issue mattress cover that he had cut in half across the width to make two out of one. At the next stop, there were Arabs bargaining for the mattress cover, when in reality it was only half of a cover. He did all of his bargaining from the height of the engine cab

115

side window. He kept arguing about the price until he got the green light to proceed, then he sold the cloth to the highest bidder. As soon as we started to move, I looked back and saw that the new owner had just shaken out the cloth and saw that what he had paid for was only half the size of what he thought that he had bought. The engineer laughed and said that he felt that this was only fair, as he argued that the Arabs would cheat you every chance they got.

When we would stop out in the open countryside, the men and officers would jump down and wander a short distance into the desert for body relief needs and then return with the sound of the whistle as the train began to move again. At times, the train moved forward so slowly that the men would just walk or jog along side for exercise.

Keeping clean was a bit of a chore and we took advantage of every stop to improve our sanitary situation. When the American train crews were in charge, many of us would go forward to the engine and have the engineer or fireman hose some hot water from the engine boiler into our steel helmets. The officers and enlisted men could then be seen sitting or kneeling in the soft dirt or sand beside the idling train, trying to wash or shave as best that they could. It was a luxury that we had access to the steaming hot water from the engine boiler.

On the occasional stop where the enlisted men had a fire started beside the track, we would try to heat our cans of food when they had finished with the fire. When we opened the ration can we would leave the top partially intact as a handle. In heating the rations, it was very easy to burn what was in the bottom of the can and barely heat what was at the top, and often you would burn your fingers retrieving the can from the fire. When you thought that you finally might have a warm meal, the whistle would sound and the half-heated can was retrieved and eaten "as is."

We stopped once at some town east of Algiers for a couple of hours to change to another engine, and a new crew and some of the men and officers wandered into the town. Most came back with an armload of wine, and we all sat in the shade of the railway cars passing the bottle and drinking the poor wine. This was the real, glamorous war. We were hot and dirty and lousy, and on top of that, we had miserably bad wine for comfort.

We found early in the trip that it was nearly impossible to clean our mess kits, so we abandoned the kit routine and ate the rations out of the container. After the third or fourth day, we realized that we would be on the train a bit longer than we had originally anticipated. We had hopes that eventually we would tie into what we thought must be the main line and then we would be at our destination quickly. What we didn't know was that we were on the main line, and that this slow pace was to be our lot all the way to Tunis.

On the morning of the day before we were to arrive in Tunis, I went forward to the engine at one of the frequent stops with my steel helmet to get hot water to wash and shave. I had left my leather jacket in my compartment, as I hoped that we would be stopped long enough to be able to shave and wash before the train started to move again. I held the steel helmet out at arm's length for the fireman to fill with hot water. He held the big hose close to my steel helmet, and when he turned on the hot water, it went in one side of the helmet and out the other, burning my left arm and wrist.

I was wearing a long-sleeve shirt and long underwear top, so it took some time for me to get the hot cloth off the area of the burning flesh. It was a pretty severe burn, and all the treatment that was available was some salve in the medicine kit aboard the train. It hurt like crazy and I realized that if it had happened before we had passed through Algiers, I would have had to get off the train there and seek medical help. As it was, I could just tough it out to our destination in Tunis. A Captain who was traveling with us was a medical doctor, and he applied some of the salve and a loose bandage. He did what he could but I wasn't able to sleep much that night because of the pain.

It was some comfort to learn that evening that we were to arrive in Tunis early the next morning.

The entire trip took a total of 8 days and we arrived at our destination on the morning of November 1st. This, coincidently, was the first day of the assignment of the heavy bomber groups of the 12th AF to the newly created 15th. Our ten aircrews went to the 99th Bomb Group airfield at Oudna #1.

When we arrived in Tunis, we were transported to an area for de-lousing. The medics stationed there treated my burned arm with something that seemed to take some of the pain out of the burn. The de-lousing process was something else. They had us strip bare and tag all of our clothes and put them into a large revolving cylinder, where the contents were heated and exposed to a fumigating powder. As for our bare buffs, we were told to get a hot shower in the area provided for us. The time in the hot shower would have been great if it hadn't been for my burn. I had to hold my left arm high over my head to keep the hot water off my forearm, but it still felt great to be clean again. After drying, we were generously de-loused in all the areas of hair on our body with a white powder sprayed from a "flit" gun. We hastily dressed and boarded trucks along with our baggage, and were transported to our assigned bomber group.

There were four squadrons in each heavy bomber group and our group had the 346th, the 347th, the 348th, and the 416th. My crew was assigned to the 347th along with several of our companion crews. The pilots of these crews were the same men that I had gone through B-17 pilot transition training with at Hobbs, New Mexico. Most of these pilots were 1st Lts. We had all become well acquainted with each other in training, on the boat, or in our adventure riding on the "roach coach" train.

The arrival of 100 new crewmen at the 99th BG put a strain on billeting everyone. Many of the new officers were "sandwiched in" with older crews, and some of the enlisted men had to sleep on the ground out in the open. It was a couple of days before more pyramid tents were erected so that all the enlisted men had shelter.

I was bunked with the officers of an older crew that was nearing the end of their 50-mission tour. They showed me around the camp and also gave me many tips that would be useful in my future combat tour. On the 3rd day that we were in our new airbase at Oudna #1, the commanding Generals of the new 15th Air Force and 5th Wing, to which we were now attached, came to visit our group. The 99th Bomb Group had just completed their first 100 combat missions, all of which were from bases in North Africa. Among the visiting officers were General Spaatz and General Doolittle. We had a big celebration with a barbequed roast goat with all the trimmings. The goat was as "tough as old shoe leather," but the beer flowed freely so it really didn't matter. It rained but nothing dampened the spirits or the speeches.

I was able to visit the city of Tunis soon after we arrived and I found it to be French and Arab. Here again, we used the franc for spending money. Tunis was quite a modern city and did not have as much damage as one would have expected in a war zone. The railroad yards were somewhat torn up but had been restored enough to be functional. Tunis was not as clean as Casablanca, but there was a lot to do. There were sidewalk cafes and bars that we could visit and get wine or cognac or most any other mixed drinks except a martini. There were olives galore but not a martini in sight.

The French were cordial but the Arabs were somewhat subdued. You sensed that the Arabs did not like the Americans as they viewed us as occupiers and probably felt the same way about the British. The "old hands" told us that it was advisable to wear our sidearm holstered when we went into town or anywhere else off the base. The holstered gun tucked under our leather jackets, where the bulge could be seen, was enough to discourage problems.

Our airbase, Oudna #1, was in a flat area about 15 miles southwest of the city of Tunis, and was surrounded by olive groves wherein each squadron had their tents pitched. The tents were floored with white rock and usually covered by a mat beside each cot. Most of the tents had a couple of clothes racks and many had an improvised wooden door for the tent. It appeared that many of the doors had come from homes or the railroad coaches that had been destroyed in the bombing of the Tunis railroad yard. Some of the tent doors sported a window, which was a really nice touch. Each crew had somehow left its mark on their abode with creature comfort improvements. Each tent was heated by an oil stove, and electricity was provided for a few hours each night. It was quite comfortable, even though our cot had only a mattress cover stuffed with straw. We had plenty of blankets so it was warm enough at night. It was some walking distance to the latrine and also to the Officers' Club mess hall for our meals.

After I had been at Oudna for just a couple of days, while I was still bunking with the veteran crew, we were out in front of our tent playing volleyball when someone nearby yelled "FIRE." When I looked around, I saw that *our* tent was the one on fire. The oil heater had become overheated and had caught the wooden center pole on fire. My cot and belongings were near the back wall of the tent, and I was able to pull up the canvas wall of the tent and get all of my stuff out except the new trench coat that I had purchased in Rockford, Illinois. It was hanging on a clothes rack and was lost in the fire. All of my other belongings were in my B-4 bag under my cot and I was able to snatch it out before the flames chased me away. The veteran crew that I was bunking with lost everything, however. That afternoon, I checked out new blankets and a cot and filled a new mattress cover with clean, lice-free, straw. I was assigned to move in with another group of guys while awaiting a permanent tent for myself and the officers of my crew.

The group had over 100 missions by this time, and that meant that all of the original crews had completed their tour and had gone home. Some of the first group of replacement crewmembers were now getting close to their 50th mission and were looking forward to rotating home. We were the start of the second set of crewmember replacements to be infused into the 99th Bomb Group.

On November 15th, one of the old crews rotated out and left for the states, and we received their tent for our own. It was nice to be rooming with my own officer crewmembers again. My enlisted crewmembers had gotten their own tent a few days earlier and were settling in. The group had an abundance of new crewmembers at this time, so we had to wait our turn to be assigned to fly our orientation combat missions.

In the meantime, when the squadron was not flying a combat mission, we "new hires" were scheduled to practice formation flying with an experienced combat pilot in the right seat. My first practice mission was with Lt. Pixler as my co-pilot. He was a veteran combat pilot and he gave me a lot of tips about squadron and group formation, and formation flying in general. We flew in an old B-17F named "The Warrior" and it was a good 3-hour workout. I was learning to fly very tight formation.

The theory was that if you were in a tight formation, the enemy aircraft would not try to tackle you as you had too many guns concentrated on fighting off the attack. One tactic of the enemy was to fly through a formation, breaking it up and cutting out a cripple to finish off (possibly learned from the animal world). If a very tight formation was maintained it was impossible to fly through it. The enemy would go to another group that offered a better chance for success. We were constantly cautioned to keep it in tight. This very tight formation was quite a departure from what we had been taught at Hobbs and in combat phase school training.

The 99th had a reputation for flying the tightest diamond, which probably was reflected in the groups' low loss rate. I found that flying tight formation, was easier than a loose formation but it kept you very busy concentrating on the flying of the aircraft. I soon felt quite

121

comfortable with this type of flying, and it was a pleasure to tuck the airplane in tight and to continually keep it there. My burned arm was healing well, and although it was loosely bandaged, it didn't seem to interfere with my duties.

On the 12th of November, I was assigned to fly a test hop with one of the pilots of our squadron as my co-pilot. He was one of our replacement group airplane commanders and I sensed that he did not like being assigned as my co-pilot; I thought that it was his problem, not mine. This pilot was junior to me in date of rank, as were most of the other nine replacement pilots that had gone through training with me at Hobbs. On this flight, I was able to do some low-level flying and went down along the ancient Roman aquaduct that stretches for miles near Tunis. Some of the local Arabs were walking and sunning themselves on the top of the aqueduct and I made them duck for cover as I skimmed along the top. I thought it was great fun but my companion didn't appreciate it, and said as much. I had one more squadron practice mission on November 19th with Lt. Calkins, a combat veteran, as my co-pilot in a B-17 named "The Reluctant Dragon." This was a 2-hour practice mission and it was to be my last chance for practice flying in North Africa.

On my first few missions, I was to be scheduled to fly with an experienced combat veteran pilot in command of the airplane and I was to be his co-pilot. Bob Johnson had been assigned to fly in the right seat with a veteran crew and he had completed his first combat mission before I did. He was on the bombing mission to Turin, Italy, ball bearing factory on November 8th.

On all of my practice missions in the B-17, I had been occupying the left seat as pilot. On November 22nd, 1943, I was in the right cockpit seat of airplane #25746 named "Stardust," with 1st Lt. Thomas "Red" Craig as the pilot. Our group was recalled by radio when we were only part of the way to the target. Clouds were obscuring the target and we didn't get credit for a mission, as it was a "turn-back."

After arriving back at the base that afternoon, I went to "mail call" and received seventeen letters. This was my first mail from home and it was very welcome. I lined them up according to date and read them in that order. I had some from my parents and, of course, there were several from Dionne.

In our tent, we had racks for our clothes to hang on and we even had a small table. There was an oil heater near the center of the tent and we made certain that it was as far as possible from the center pole. We were careful to be sure that someone was in attendance when the oil heater was used. We had electricity for a few hours each night so we could read or write or play cards if we wished. I had brought my cribbage board and we played occasionally. None of my tent mates were overly excited about playing cribbage with me but they did sometimes just to please me. If the outdoor movie looked good, we would sit on the wooden plank benches under the night sky and enjoy it. On one of these nights, "Arsenic and Old Lace" was playing but it was stopped in the middle because it started to rain hard.. A few days later it was shown again and the projector broke down, canceling the movie at about the same place it had stopped before. I still hoped to see the conclusion of the movie but unfortunately this was never to be. It seemed that every time this movie was shown (and it occurred numerous times during this tour), either the projector broke down or a raid would occur and the movie ceased, causing us to once again miss the ending. Guess I was never meant to find out what happened to these characters and I've been content to just leave it at that.

Cigarettes were rationed at the PX and we were often short of them; it didn't pay to be too generous with your pack of smokes. I wrote to my parents that I had visited Tunis and that it was a nice city, but that everything was quite expensive; for example, it cost 15 cents for one egg and over $2.00 for a pound of poor meat. In almost every letter home, I asked for something to eat. The food at the officers' mess hall wasn't bad, but it was nice to have something to munch on in our tent. The Arabs came to our tent to try to sell us figs and almonds but they too were expensive. We all wrote in letters home that fruitcake or candy or cheese was very welcome, and that we always shared what we received.

On November 24th, I was credited with my first combat mission. It was ironic that it was November 24th, for that is the date of my first solo flight in the 40 HP T-craft in 1939, and also the date of my "wings" check in the RCAF in 1941. The "24th of November," seemed to be a memorable and magic day for me.

The mission was to the submarine pens at Toulon, France. As the co-pilot for Lt. "Red" Craig, I was to learn a lot. The first thing he taught me was to use a wad of tissue paper to clean the outside of the windshield just before we were the number one airplane for takeoff. The Wright engines on the B-17 were famous for leaking oil, and if you were in line behind a squadron of B-17's taxiing out for takeoff, you were sure to have numerous specks of oil on the windshield – they were a distraction when looking for enemy aircraft on the mission. After this first lesson, I always had a small wad of toilet tissue in my flight suite pocket. I would set the parking brake, slide the side window open, and hurriedly clean the windshield just before being the next airplane to move onto the runway.

I remember being more excited than scared on this mission. The time from the IP (initial point) to the target seemed extremely long. This was the time when the group and squadron had to fly straight and level to make a good bomb run. This mission was my first chance to see flak. (Flak was the exploding enemy anti-aircraft shells.) It looked oily and black and there was a lot of it exploding near to us. We felt one jolt of the exploding flak and Lt. Craig had the waist (mid-ship) gunners and ball turret gunner report any damage to the aircraft that they could see. They reported that they saw no damage and everyone reported on the intercom that they weren't injured.

NORTH AFRICA AND ITALY

Lt. Craig felt that the flak had burst under the left wing, and I suppose that he had some concern about whether a fuel tank had been ruptured. I was more concerned that we were still flying and that all of the engine instruments looked normal. Everything was apparently OK and we made our turn in formation off the target after the bombs were dropped. Nearly 400 bombs had been dropped on the sub pens. There was a great amount of damage reported in the target area and this was considered a good mission.

I was interested in our P-38 escort. The twin tailed, twin-engine airplanes were very easy to distinguish. They patrolled the area above us and were a great comfort. They seemed to depart when the flak came up. If the enemy fighters wouldn't try to penetrate the flak, why should our escort? Perhaps they were busy driving off the enemy aircraft. The flak was only considered moderate on this first mission and I wondered what it would be like if it was heavy and intense. One of the airplanes in our group went down into the sea and six parachutes were seen drifting downward. A plane from the 346th squadron flew low over the area and looked for survivors. They were prepared to drop a life raft if they could spot any of the downed airmen. I didn't learn if any of the crewmen who bailed out of the stricken aircraft survived; I certainly hoped so. We prayed for them that night in our tent.

On November 25th, Thanksgiving Day, we were scheduled to fly another mission and did takeoff and form up, but the mission was soon scrubbed and we looked forward to a big thanksgiving dinner. I wrote in my letter home that we had roast turkey and dressing, cranberry sauce, mashed potatoes with gravy, and sweet potatoes. We also had raisin bread with real butter rather than the synthetic stuff that was substituted for butter and was aptly named "axle grease." Our dessert was chocolate cake, candy, and tangerines. We also enjoyed a green salad for the first time since arriving in North Africa. I wrote in my letter that we went to church in the early evening and

125

that it was quite crowded. Comfortably stuffed, it had been a great day.

I received a package of hard candy from Dionne on the 28th of November, and it really hit the spot. We often brought slices of bread home to the tent from the mess area. On this particular night, I wrote home and complained that all there was to go with the bread was peanut butter. I don't like peanut butter, so I was content with the candy.

On November 29th, I flew on my second combat mission and again it was with Lt. Craig in "Stardust." This mission was to Fiano Romano Airdrome in Italy. We arrived at the target area and found that it was completely covered by clouds. The alternate target was also covered with clouds, and we returned with our bombs still in the bomb bays. It was a long mission, 7 hours, and we were a bit short of fuel as we approached our airbase at Oudna #1.

Our gunners were in a much better position to see the enemy aircraft than the pilots as all of the pilot's concentration was on keeping the airplane in a tight position in formation. The gunners were on constant watch for enemy fighter planes. They would call out on the interphone the position of any enemy fighters with their position relative to the formation, and also whether they were below, level, or above us. Thus a call of "twelve o'clock high" meant that the enemy was straight ahead and above our formation altitude.

The name "Stardust" was painted on the nose of 25746 just ahead of the cockpit. There was a bar of music above the name on the left side. The musical bar may have been painted after the original name was completed. I believe that Lt. Tom Craig had about 30 combat missions at this time and was considered one of the veterans. He was a very good man to fly with and tried to give me the benefit of his experience. I really appreciated his comments and instructions.

On the next day, November 30th, we again took off in "Stardust" intending to bomb the submarine pens at Marseilles, France. I was co-pilot for Lt. Craig with most of my regular crew again on board. About two hours after takeoff, we were recalled because of clouds reported over the target area. When we returned to our airfield at about 1100 hours and prepared for a normal landing, we had our bomb load on board (twelve 500 pound bombs), as well as about half of the fuel that we had started with.

Everything on the return flight went as planned and Lt. Craig was flying as we prepared to land. We peeled off from the formation when it was our turn and started our landing pattern. We extended the landing gear and the three green lights illuminated, indicating that the two main wheels and the tail-wheel were "down and locked" for the landing. We were "cleared to land" by the control tower. The wing flaps were extended and our speed was reduced to the approach speed, and then to the touchdown speed. The touchdown was normal, and as the plane slowed the left wing went down, and down and down, until the left wing contacted the ground and we made a ground loop to the left off into the dirt on the shoulder of the runway. Lt. Craig tried to keep the airplane straight with full right brake but the brake had no effect and it wasn't possible to keep the airplane from making the ground loop off the runway. As we came to a stop, there was a big cloud of dust and as soon as we could get the two right engines shut down and the electrical system turned off, Lt. Craig said, "Let's get out of here."

The crew in the forward part of the airplane used the exit below the cockpit. It was a bit closer to the ground than normal but there was room to easily squeeze out. The whole crew ran from the wreck because we all thought that it might catch fire and that the bombs still on board might explode. Ernie Jenkins, my bombardier, later told me that the twelve 500 pound bombs in the bomb bay banged and clanked around during the accident and he thought for sure that they would explode. The whole crew ran a pretty good distance from the airplane before stopping. The dust finally settled over "Stardust" and we

STARDUST FALLING

thought that the chance of fire was now fairly remote. The fire and crash trucks approached the wreck and determined that the entire crew had exited safely, and then they checked with us to find that no one, thankfully, was injured. This wasn't the case with poor old "Stardust," as the propellers on the two engines on the left side were badly bent and the left aileron and left wing flap were badly damaged.

Both Lt. Craig and I were sure that we had seen the three green landing gear warning lights illuminated. We were also sure that the warning horn located in the cockpit did not sound, which would have indicated that the landing gear was not down and locked as we throttled back for our landing.

I am not sure, but the Air Corps brass that soon surrounded the damaged airplane thought that we had made a mistake and had landed without being certain that the gear was extended (i.e., pilot error, as usual). Later that same day, we were told that the micro-switch that stops the gear extension hydraulic motor had slipped out of position and had shut off the "gear down" motor before the gear was fully extended. This same micro-switch turns on the green "gear down" lights in the cockpit, and disarms the landing gear "unsafe" condition warning horn. Lt. Craig and I felt that we were, as they say, "off the hook." We didn't get credit for a mission this day and we were still pretty excited that evening about the accident. We knew that it could have been very serious if the airplane had caught fire. The twelve 500 pound bombs would have made a terrific explosion, and I doubt that any of us were far enough away from the airplane to have survived. All of my crew, except for my co-pilot Bob Johnson, was on board when the accident occurred.

We knew that the group was due to leave for the new permanent base in Italy soon, and we had assumed that we would fly "Stardust" to the new base. Now that it was a wreck, we didn't know if we would be able to fly to Italy or would have to go by boat. We felt that they probably would not repair "Stardust" and that we would be flying another airplane in Italy. The very next day, we were notified that we should pack up and would be trucked to the port of Bizerte, near Tunis, for transport to Italy, by boat.

The damaged "Stardust" was technically a B-17 "F," but the Air Corps contract that was originally written was for an earlier "E" model. Stardust was a mix of the old and the newer B-17 "F." It had the old high-pressure oxygen system and the older type turbocharger controls, as well as the old B-17 "E" - type wheel brakes. Most importantly, it was reported to have the fuel tank capacity of the "E" rather than the additional 30 gallons in the newer "F" model. It did have an excellent cockpit heater, which was much better than the standard "F." It was perhaps the oldest airplane in our squadron and may have been one of the oldest in the group. I think that the old bird had probably been involved in more than 60 missions by the time I first flew in it. We all thought that it would not be repaired and it was all washed up forever in the ground loop accident. The next day we were to leave for Italy along with our squadron ground crewmen. We weren't happy about this, as we were sure that we would miss the chance to fly on some combat missions while we were being transported.

When we arrived at the port of Bizerte, we expected to go straight to a boat and be on our way to Italy. As usual, the army "hurry up and wait" mode prevailed and we had to wait several days for orders to board a ship. I went to the dock each day to see what I could find out about our impending transport. During this waiting period, on my daily visit to the dock, I met a naval officer. My new acquaintance was in command of an LST (Landing Ship Tank) naval vessel. He was awaiting orders to ship out in convoy with his vessel, and he casually asked me if I played the card game "cribbage." I told him yes, that I enjoyed cribbage, and he invited me aboard for a game or two. He said that the officers on his ship didn't play cribbage and he was delighted to find someone with whom he could share the game.

STARDUST FALLING

The morning was spent pleasantly playing cards and at noon he invited me to have lunch with him. I too was pleased, and it was a great lunch with apple pie and ice cream for dessert. He then invited me back the next day for another card session and I was happy to oblige. The cards and good food went on for a couple of days and was a very nice and welcome diversion. He asked me which group and squadron I was attached to and he said that he would try to get our squadron assigned to his ship for the crossing. Our squadron and equipment boarded his ship for transport to Italy the very next day.

As soon as we cleared the harbor at Bizerte, he told me that we were heading for Tarranto, Italy. I tagged along with him all over the boat as he went about his duties. We played cribbage whenever he had the time and it turned into a smooth and fun voyage for me.

The Tarranto, Italy harbor is located at the "in-step" of the boot of Italy. Tarranto harbor was picturesque but quite small. On the voyage, there were several other LSTs and other types of vessels in our convoy. We were escorted first by British naval vessels and later by U.S. Navy ships on our crossing. The trip took three and a half days for the six or seven hundred sea miles. The ship was not fast and, with the zigzagging, it was a fairly slow voyage. I was fascinated by the flexing of the thin metal deck of the vessel even in the light swells that we encountered. I remarked on this and the Skipper said, "You should see it when we are in rough seas." We had some of our squadron flight crews, those who had not flown to Italy, aboard with us, as well as many of our ground crew and equipment.

Upon docking at Tarranto harbor, I said "goodbye" to my Navy friend and thanked him for his hospitality. He wished me well on my combat tour and I told him that I had enjoyed a most pleasant trip across the Mediterranean. Having no duties except to play cribbage with the Skipper could hardly be called a "duty."

After leaving the ship, we boarded trucks for transport to our new base, which we knew only as "Foggia #2." I didn't have the slightest idea where this base was located. Someone had pointed out Foggia on the navigator's map but that is all that I knew about it. Trucks picked us up at about 0900. The trucks that were sent were from our Bomb Group and our driver told us that we were located at Tortorella, about 8 or 9 miles northeast of Foggia. Our driver said that without a German air raid on our convoy, it would be nearly midnight before we would arrive at our new base.

It was a long and uncomfortable ride in the back of our canvas covered truck, and we weren't able to see much of the countryside. The officers of my crew, along with the officers of two other crews, were assigned to the first truck in the convoy. This turned out to be a "bad break" because we would have liked to have taken turns riding up front with the driver. The convoy commanding officer was riding in our truck and was "up front" for the entire trip. We did see a little bit of the local scenery out of the back of our truck as we slowed to pass through villages and towns. We made a rest stop at Bari, Italy, and were told that this was the headquarters of the 15th Air Force. We had been given a box of "K" rations when we left the ship, and we ate them as we progressed along. Another carton of "K" rations was boarded at Bari as we had picked over the first box and had already eaten all of the *good* stuff. The Red Cross in Bari greeted each truck of the convoy with two cartons of "Old Gold" cigarettes.

It was a lot more appreciated than a cookie and coffee, which was the normal greeting whenever the Red Cross met a convoy. Some of us were running short of smokes and were worried that the PX would not be up and running when we arrived at our squadron. Cigarettes, writing material, wool gloves, socks, and underwear were the normal staples of the PX. We could sometimes purchase a carton of cigarettes a week, and this usually was enough, especially if we were operational as it was impossible to smoke at high altitude. Everyone on our crew bought cigarettes, even if they didn't smoke, being great barter and trade items.

We passed through the city of Foggia on our way to our new base that night and were at our individual squadron headquarters at Tortorella about one hour later. The aircraft commanders went to check on the billeting of our crews. When we entered the squadron headquarters building, we were informed that we weren't expected until the next day, and therefore there were no tents or cots available for us. We were told to use our shelter halves and find a place to sleep, either on the ground or on the hard concrete of the headquarters building.

Bob Johnson peered into a small room that was not much larger than a large closet. He saw that the floor was filled with mailbags, hopefully incoming mail. He motioned to us to come with him and we spread our shelter halves on top of the mailbags and finished the night on a very lumpy, uncomfortable bed. I couldn't help but wonder if I might be sleeping on a letter from Dionne. I missed her – she seemed too far away, especially now.

The next morning, we went to the new squadron mess area, located in a pigpen, where a breakfast of French toast and so-called sausages was the fare. Later, I will explain the pigpen or pigsty in which our squadron mess area was located.

After we had finished our coffee, we went out to survey our new base. The squadron headquarters of the 347th was in the main building of a cluster of small farmhouse buildings. One part of the main farmhouse was the living quarters for the squadron commander and the headquarters office. There were three or four other stone houses surrounding the main farmhouse. These were not large but they afforded office space. It appeared that the smaller stone houses were once occupied by the farm workers and their families.

Eventually, one of the buildings was made into the Officers' Club. The interior walls were removed and a kitchen was a new addition. Some windows had to be added to let in more light. This building was to afford a little more comfort to our living conditions at Tortorella.

On the morning of our arrival, the only renovation that was completed was the enclosing of the lower part of the main farmhouse. This was the area where the farm animals had been kept and it now contained the squadron supplies. None of the other enclosed areas had as yet been renovated, so they were lined with cots of the permanent party that had preceded us to this new location. We were pleased to hear that the vessel that had brought us, and the bulk of the ground personnel had also contained enough tents to alleviate the housing problem and we were assured that we would have a tent of our own by nightfall of that day.

After we had gotten acquainted with our squadron arrangement, our next act was to hop in a passing truck to go to the airfield to see how we were situated for "business." This area was known as Foggia #2, but was often referred to as Tortorella landing grounds. The 99th BG, flying from North Africa, had been involved in several bombing missions in this target area. There were many enemy aircraft that were obviously caught on the ground during these raids. There were wreckages of both Italian and German aircraft scattered all around, which was a grim reminder of what our "business" had done to the enemy here.

The area east of the city of Foggia is a flat plain wrapping around the city from the northeast to the south. Originally it had been wet but had been drained and ditched to where it was now very fertile and heavily agricultural. Each section had a hub where there was a headquarters area with grain sheds and substantial buildings. Surrounding this central site, like spokes of a wheel, were the tenant farmhouses. The tenant houses were made of stone and mortar and all were two stories high and exactly alike. The tenant farmers lived on the upper floor of the house, and the livestock, cattle, or sheep occupied the ground floor area. One of these farmhouses served as our squadron headquarters. Our group headquarters was located two miles away where there was a crossroad village. This crossroad area contained a cluster of buildings, including several small buildings used as the radio shack and the photo recon building. There were three or four larger buildings along with a large shed that was used for our group mission briefing room and the movie theater. All had been confiscated by our military with the exception of the church.

The main road from Foggia, northeast to Manfredonia, ran north of our base. There was a perimeter road that connected all of the squadrons to the headquarters and it ran completely around the entire complex. The runway and control tower were at the center of the perimeter. Our squadron was the farthest from headquarters on the north side of the airfield. I don't recall that I saw any old bombed out hangers on this Italian airfield, although it was officially known as Foggia #2.

When we first arrived, there was an Australian RAAF unit just south of the runway and they were inside of our perimeter road. This Australian unit was flying the A-20 type aircraft and they shared use of the one runway on the airfield.

The Army Corps of Engineers had covered the landing area with the heavy clay that was found everywhere. They then laid down a mat of heavy perforated and interlocking metal planking to make a very serviceable runway for the heavy bombers. At the far northwest end of the runway, there was a railroad embankment and small station named Tortorella. This embankment was the only obstacle that could be seen on the approach and takeoff path of the runway. The single runway was oriented northwest and southeast. There were revetments, or hardstands, for each squadron, connected by a taxi strip to the main taxiways. These hardstands were made of the same perforated steel planking as the taxi-strips and the runway. All of the 99th BG hardstands were located on the northeast side of the runway, and the Aussies occupied the area on the southwest side of the runway.

This type of metal runway and work areas were fine when it was dry. When it was wet, however, because of dew or rain or drizzle, the water and clay would ooze up through the perforation holes in the metal planks and would make everything as slippery as ice. When we were cleared to taxi out for takeoff, we had to be very careful not to veer off the narrow taxiway, and when making the final 90 degree turn from the taxiway on to the take-off runway, it was especially hazardous when slippery.

Of course, we knew little of this on our first day at Tortorella. We did find out that our control tower call sign was "sandflea," and this was the code word for our airfield. We caught a ride back to the squadron headquarters and found that nearly everyone was busy putting up the tents. I went to the area where the officer's tents were to be erected and found that Walt Amundsen, had already claimed a tent for the four officers of our crew. Jesse Wheeler and his crew were in a tent close to us.

The officers and crew of Claude "Scotty" Scott and George Perry were in the 416th squadron, and were on the same perimeter road but some distance from us. We set up our cots on the bare ground inside the newly erected tent, and Walt procured transportation and soon returned with a load of dry straw, which we stuffed into our sleeping mattresses. We then put our mattress sheet cover and blankets on the bed and figured that we could finally bed down in our new permanent home.

Before dark we made our way to squadron headquarters for chow. Our headquarters and mess area was about 300 yards from our tent area. We could go to our squadron headquarters on a "round-about" pathway, or could cut directly across to the area, but had to avoid many tents en-route. To cut across was a shorter way but it was a bit hazardous, especially at night. There were tent stakes and pee pipes to be avoided, along with the three foot deep "foxholes" or slit trenches that the Italian workers had been employed to dig near each tent in our area for enemy bombing raid protection.

The Italian workers were always available for a small price. We had a slit trench dug beside our tent the same day that we moved in, and it was a good thing that we did. That very night, at about midnight, the air raid sirens sounded and we all grabbed our pants, shoes, and jackets and dived into the new slit trench. We crouched there for about 15 or 20 minutes until the "all clear" was sounded. The next day, we learned that "Axis Sally" had sent a message congratulating the four B-17 groups on their move to Foggia. She said that they (the Germans) would be over to visit us soon. This may have been one of the attempted visits; I will never know. We heard no bomb explosions but it made for an interrupted night's sleep.

We soon were trying to figure out how we could get our new abode more livable. The first priority was heat, and Walt and Ernie set off to see what they could do about this. They saw several other tents, occupied by the flight crews that had flown in ahead of us, that were heated by homemade stoves using aviation gas, which was stored outside of the tent in a barrel. They thought that they could have a stove like this fabricated and up and running in a couple of days. I told them to "go for it, we needed heat." The regular GI oil stoves that were then on hand were for the squadron headquarters and for the staff use, but none were available for the ground and aircrews at this time. Everyone seemed to prefer the homemade av-gas stoves to the regular oil stoves by the time that the oil stoves finally did arrive, anyway.

It was chow time, and we went up to the pigpen for supper with mess kit and cup in hand, we went through the mess line. Officers and enlisted men were in the line together as there was only one communal squadron mess area as yet. When I refer to the "pigsty" or "pigpen," it really had formerly been a pigpen. There was a lean-to,

NORTH AFRICA AND ITALY

three-sided, long building with a sloping tin roof that formerly housed the pigs on this farm. The pig area had a stone fence around it that probably enclosed an acre. This stone fence was about 4 feet high in some places and perhaps three in other places. The pen had been scraped free of manure and I suppose fumigated before being filled with dirt and clay and then compacted. Voila, it was designated a "mess hall." The tin lean-to building had been whitewashed, presumably to give it some semblance of being a place sanitary enough in which to cook and serve food. Who really knew!

We were on "C" rations and Vienna sausages swimming in catsup for most evening meals. Powdered eggs and undercooked bacon or sausages, or French toast made from the same powdered-eggs, were the normal fare for breakfast. Anything that they could scrape together served as the noon meal, like toasted cheese sandwiches, pork and beans, etc. Hot coffee was welcome on the mornings that we were not scheduled to fly. If we did drink coffee when flying, we had to limit our intake, or get rid of the coffee before takeoff. We did get fried Spam a couple of times for supper and this was the best meal that we could have imagined under these circumstances. Believe it or not, I still like fried Spam.

The port at Bari, Italy, had been nearly destroyed by a German air raid just before we arrived, and all of our food supplies were, unfortunately, now at the bottom of the harbor. There was no local source of food available. We were on combat rations and whatever the mess sergeant could scrape together until new supplies arrived. With our mess kit filled with whatever we thought that we could eat, there was always dessert. It was "usually" a peach half and it was plopped on top of everything else. Then there was the strong coffee for the tin cup, and it was off to find a place to sit on the stone fence or a place on the higher portion of the stone wall to perch the mess kit while we ate standing up. If it rained, as it often did, we had to eat in

STARDUST FALLING

the rain with the rainwater filling the mess kit. This was miserable and was often a very short mealtime.

After we had finished what we could eat, there was a short path that led to 55-gallon trash barrels. All along this line of GI's waiting to dump their leftovers into the barrels were little Italian boys with empty gallon cans, hoping that you would scrape your uneaten food in their can rather than put it in the trash barrel. This was discouraged, of course, but no one enforced the rule and most of the leftover food went into these waiting containers. We were sure that the older siblings or parents were in the dark nearby with a larger pot to collect enough for their family's evening meal. If you chose to remain in the area for another cup of coffee or a cigarette, you would see the same kid back with his can empty, begging again. After we had dumped our leftovers, we would then proceed to another 55-gallon barrel of boiling hot water (the Army's early version of an automatic dishwasher) and dip our mess kit in it to clean off all the greasy stuff and shake off anything that was still clinging to it. There were no rags to finish cleaning or to dry the kit; just shake off the hot water, and put your eating utensils inside your kit and close it up.

By now it was the 13th or 14th of December and I really missed flying. I was hoping for a mission or test hop or some type of flying soon. After "chow" that evening, it was back to a cold and dark tent. We didn't have a stove or electricity as yet, and the only way for us to be comfortable was to get into our cot and cover up to stay warm. We continued our talks from our bed positions about how we could improve our living situation. We expected to get electricity the next day, but this would not happen. We would try to get a stove made tomorrow. If we could have electricity, we could then have a single electric light bulb from dark to about 2100 hours each night. This would be great, and we decided to work on wiring for the electricity. We also needed to build or appropriate a small desk and chair, if possible. We talked about building a doorframe and getting a door for

NORTH AFRICA AND ITALY

the entrance. We planned to brick-in the floor completely. We thought that, in time, we could find a door and brick in the rubble of Foggia. On and on we talked about how we could acquire this and that. The big problem was that transportation was in short supply to fetch these items, but Walt said that he would work on the situation. Walt, our super scrounger, said to leave the commandeering problem to him, and we did.

First things first – Walt and Ernie went to the squadron motor pool where they were fabricating the aviation gas stoves for those waiting for them. One of our sergeants, I think it was Hoskins, was a friend of one of the truck mechanics, and after the man had made a stove for my enlisted men's tent, Hoskins pleaded with the fellow to make one for his lieutenants.

With Ernie and Walt standing by, the motor pool GI took an empty barrel, perhaps 16 to 18 inches in diameter and about 24 inches tall, and cut a rectangular hole in the side near the bottom. He then punched a small hole in the back near the bottom for the fuel line to enter. He asked what size hole we wanted cut for a chimney. Walt and Ernie had no idea, but Hoskins said that he had spotted a long length of six-inch iron water main pipe that had been discarded, and it would do as a chimney for both stoves. The man cut a hole in the top of the barrel that would be a little smaller than the water main.

When the barrel cooled, it was brought to our tent and the two officers, along with Sergeant Hoskins, went out hunting for the section of water main that was to be used as a chimney. They found it, but Hoskins had to go and recruit two other sergeants to help lug it all the way to the motor pool to have it cut to length for the two chimneys. It took five of them to carry the forty feet of iron pipe to the motor pool. Bob and I heard all about the "heavy duty" that we had missed. The guys were then able to find the tubing and other hardware and the empty 35-gallon drums for the av-gas to be positioned outside of the two tents. The truck maintenance area and motor pool was a good place to make friends.

The outside drums were elevated on bricks so that gravity would feed the burners. With the help of most of our sergeant crewmembers, we had both stoves up and running by that evening. This was the "wonder of all wonders" as we had heat in our tent at last! We still had only flashlights at night, so now if we could just get electric lights, we would finally have some of the common and basic comforts of home.

After we had stove heat in our tent, we would occasionally skip the meal and get a couple of slices of bread and bring them to our tent. Walt had scrounged a gallon-can of cheese and we would make, (often burn), toasted cheese sandwiches on the top of our stove.

CHAPTER 6

COMBAT IN ITALY

When we went to the pigpen for breakfast the next morning, I met Lt. Thomas "Red" Craig. He said that #42-5746 (Stardust #746) had been repaired and would be coming in soon. This was good news for us as we felt that we might have an airplane at last. Sure enough, on the afternoon of the 15th, "Stardust" arrived at Tortorella in combat flying condition. The two, 30-caliber machine guns that had been in the nose section of the airplane had been replaced by two new 50-caliber guns. I went to the revetment assigned to #746 to talk to the crew chief after it arrived and asked to see the logbook. I wanted to review what they had done to fix the old broken bird, but the new logbook, a continuation of the old one, had nothing written about the repairs that had been accomplished. The damage was repaired, it was fit for combat, and that was all that obviously mattered.

One thing that did irritate me upon touring the interior of the airplane was the fact that all of the extra armor plating that had been put on the airplane by the previous crews had been removed. This meant that if we did get the airplane, we would have to replace any armor plating that was now missing. It was a "given" that the new crew of any aircraft would go to a junkyard and salvage metal for armor plating that they thought necessary. Of course, the pilot had the final say as to the extra weight that he would permit.

STARDUST FALLING

Right after chow (supper) at the pigsty, I went to operations to see if we were scheduled to fly the next day. Sure enough, we were and I was to be co-pilot in Stardust #746 with Lt. Craig again. It was warm in our tent but we still didn't have electricity; it was a restless night's sleep for me. I was thinking about the mission of the next day. It was similar to the feeling that I had when I was scheduled for my first mission.

The next morning, we went up for chow, then to the latrine, and finally back to our tent to get our flight gear. It was then back to squadron headquarters to board the trucks to be transported the distance to the group headquarters for our mission briefing. The mission was to Padua, Italy, where we were to bomb the railroad yards. The mission went quite well. There was little flak, no enemy fighters, and it was considered a "milk run" (slang for an easy mission). This was Dec. 16th 1943 and mission #3 for me. I felt a lot better after getting into the air again.

Many of the older crews were now completing their 50th mission and would soon rotate home. This gave the replacements an airplane and a regular place on the schedule.

From this point in my narrative, I will indicate where I have quoted directly from letters that I sent home, exactly as they were written. My letters were always intended to my whole family even when I usually wrote "Dear Mom," this was taken for granted by me. Previously, I have used information from my letters home to enhance the story. There were nearly 40 letters in all that I had written home while I was overseas. My mother, bless her heart, saved all of them and they came into my possession after her death, at age 98. I have quoted from a few of them only where they contained some information of interest to the story. They served to be a daily diary of the living conditions and activities of our time spent in combat in North Africa and Italy. Where I quote from the letters, the wording will be in italics, exactly as they were written, poor grammar and all. After we moved up to Italy, I wrote almost daily. I knew that this was necessary so that I could keep a steady stream of

COMBAT IN ITALY

letters coming in from home. I had finally found out that the more letters that I sent, the more I received in return. I often wrote to Dionne. Some of the young ladies in my high school class also wrote newsy letters that were quite welcome. As is the case now, they were encouraged to write to servicemen and some were thankfully quite faithful in this endeavor. The mail of the day was about the only thing, except flying and completing our missions that we had to look forward to. I would read and re-read some of the letters when I was lonesome. The letters that I will be quoting from are still in the little stationery box just as my mother saved them.

In my letter home on Dec. 17th, I wrote: *"I like it here in Italy. There are an awful lot of wrecked German and Italian planes on this and the other airfields around it. We got heat and light now. We found some telephone wire and Walt wired up the tent and now we made a stove out of a 30 gallon drum and a stovepipe out of an old heavy water main, it is getting more comfortable by the day."*

In a letter to my sister Audrey on the 19th, I wrote: *"We have quite a cozy tent with a homemade stove and mats on the floor and a light, although it isn't very bright. They have almonds and oranges here and they are quite cheap. Bob and I are writing at S-2 office (intelligence) and he is finished so I better hurry up and finish so I can walk home with him, he has the flashlight and there are a lot of foxholes between here and the tent to stumble into."*

On Dec. 19th the group was operational, and on this day we were not scheduled to fly. However, our friends, Claude (Scotty) Scott and his crew of the 416th, were among the 32 pilots and crews that were fielded that day. Our crew had a close relationship with the crews of both Scott and Perry that were assigned to the 416th squadron where we often visited, even though we were quite a distance apart. Lt. Kyrouac, co-pilot on Perry's crew, often came to our tent to visit Bob Johnson. Lt. Conners, Scotty's navigator, was an almost daily visitor of Walt Amundsen, my navigator. He and Walt went scrounging together. Lt.

143

Hinson, co-pilot of Scott's crew, often came to visit when Lt. Conners did, and I got to know all of them well. Conners and Kyrouac were big jolly guys and fun to be around. I visited with "Scotty" and George Perry often and they reciprocated, along with Lt. Jessie Wheeler's crew and his co-pilot, Lt. J.O. Grizzell.

We often went to the 416th area for a return visit when we were not flying. When we pilots and co-pilots would get in a "bull session," better known in aviation circles as "hanger flying," it was most enjoyable. Most pilots are good at "hanger flying," then as now. The talk would center around airplanes and girls and girls and airplanes, nothing changes.

On the mission of Dec 19th, the group was led by Major MacDonald of the 416th squadron. Both Perry and Scott and their crew were in the lead squadron. The mission was to attack the Messerschmitt factory at Augsburg, Germany. The main target at Augsburg was covered by clouds, so the secondary target of Innsbruck, Austria was bombed. The group scored good hits on the mouth of the railroad tunnel leading to the railroad yards at Innsbruck. The flak was moderate to heavy over the target and the group was attacked by 30 to 40 enemy ME 109's and FW 190's. Several of the 416th were hit in the enemy fighter attack, including Lt. Scott's airplane.

Several 20 mm cannon shells came into the nose and cockpit of Scotty's airplane. Lt. Conners, the navigator, was killed instantly and the bombardier was severely injured. In the cockpit, "Scotty" was not hit but his co-pilot Hinson was severely injured, along with the flight engineer. This left Lt. Scott the only uninjured crewman in the forward part of the airplane. All four engines were still operating normally and "Scotty" flew the airplane home alone in the cockpit. The injured were carried to the back section of the airplane by the rear crewmembers. "Scotty" told them to take care of the injured men, as he could fly the airplane by himself. He made a straight in approach and landing on our runway. Ambulances were sent to the area to remove the injured as soon

COMBAT IN ITALY

as the airplane could be stopped clear of the runway.

It was a sad day for us when the word came that afternoon that Conners had been killed, and Hinson and the bombardier were quite severely injured. Walt, Bob, Ernie, and I went over to Scotty's tent that night to console him. We all felt like crying at losing our good friend. The other three, even though injured, were expected to survive. Scotty asked us if we would go with him to the funeral for Conners. We said of course we would, if we were not scheduled to fly.

On December 20th, I flew my 4th combat mission as co-pilot for Lt. Lafoon. It was a six and a half hour mission to Athens, Greece, to bomb the Eleusis airdrome. Our group didn't have any enemy fighter opposition but we did encounter heavy flak.

Our airplane received several holes in the fuselage from the flak but no one was injured. This was an exciting mission, but I was still numb from losing our friend Conners the day before.

I was now beginning to worry about my own mortality more than ever. It is absurd to say that I wasn't scared. We were all scared, but we flew anyway. Each night, when we checked the schedule board and saw that we were to fly the next day, it was a restless night. On the one hand I wanted to get my missions in, and on the other hand I didn't want to lose my life over here. It was to fly the allotted missions and get it over with, or be shot down and be a POW, or to be injured or not survive. We had no other viable options. Make no mistake; we all felt this way most of the time. To get the missions in and get it over with was the only really decent option available. Reality had totally set in.

On this same mission of the 20th of December, my bombardier and navigator flew in the squadron lead aircraft piloted by Capt. Shaefer and Lt. Craig, the veteran, as his co-pilot. Ernie Jenkins was the lead bombardier of our squadron that day, and Capt. Shaefer commented afterwards that he would like to have Ernie as his regular bombardier soon. On this mission, just after bombs "away," there was a loud explosion underneath the airplane and two of the engines were badly damaged and were rendered inoperative. Capt. Shaefer feathered the propellers and shut down the two damaged engines, and had his ball turret gunner check underneath for visible damage.

There was extensive damage near the disabled engines and the ball turret gunner reported that they were losing fuel from the tanks on that side. Capt. Shaefer ordered a fuel transfer from the leaking tanks to the ones still able to accept the fuel. The Captain had the crew "check-in" and there was no one injured. Capt. Shaefer had to give the squadron lead to the deputy leader, and they limped home on two engines. They were not attacked by enemy fighters on their long and lonely trip back home, where they landed safely. The entire crew was badly shaken by this incident.

Ernie told me later that evening that Capt. Shaefer told him that it was as close to being downed by anti-aircraft fire as he could ever imagine. (This incident was written up in at least one U.S. East Coast newspaper and the picture of the crew and the damaged airplane was featured. My navigator's name was misspelled but the picture was clear. Either Walt or Ernie received the article in their mail from home a couple of weeks later.) Whoever led the prayer that night, whether it was Ernie or Walt, the prayer of "thanksgiving" for their safe return home was totally fervent and sincere.

On either the 22nd or 23rd of December, we went with Scotty to accompany the body of Lt. Conners to Bari for a military funeral. Walt, Ernie, and I rode in a two-ambulance convoy with Scotty. One of Scotty's enlisted crewmembers rode up front in the lead ambulance with the casket; another of Scott's men rode in the front with our driver. We four sat in almost total silence on the two and a half hour trip to the cemetery at Bari. The funeral was simple. A hole dug in the ground, a GI casket, a chaplain, a man to play taps; and the firing squad, and it was all over. Good-bye friend! It definitely was "real."

On the trip back to our base we all loosened up a bit and told the funny stories that we could remember about our departed friend. We had

COMBAT IN ITALY

the driver stop on the way home to allow us to buy a couple of bottles of wine, and we found a low stone fence behind which to relieve ourselves before traveling on. We lit up cigarettes, and then proceeded on home, drinking from the bottles of wine and laughing and joking to relieve some of the tension of the events of the day and what was now our life.

On December 24th we flew a three and a half hour practice mission with my regular crew of "Stardust." This was to complete my training and I would fly as pilot with my crew on most of my remaining missions. I did have a couple of missions where I flew as co-pilot with the squadron leader or the deputy squadron leader. This was to give me a little experience up front rather than in my usual spot near the back of the squadron. I was also informed on the 24th that #746, "Stardust," was to be our airplane and my crew and I would be scheduled in it normally.

I would like to describe the airplane briefly. As stated earlier, the full number of "Stardust" was 42-5746 and it was a B-17 F. It was the 42nd B-17 produced by Lockheed-Vega Aircraft Company located in Burbank, California. The number 42 on its official identification means that the contract to build it was signed in 1942. It is just co-incidental that it was the 42nd B-17 that Vega built. When Vega received the contract to build B-17s, Boeing was ordered to ship parts and plant equipment to Burbank to allow Vega to build the B17s. The original contract to Vega was for them to build the B17-E model. Before the first airplane came into production, the "F" model was being produced by Boeing and the order to Vega was changed to the "F." Much of the parts and equipment that had been shipped to Vega before the contract change were for the "E," so the first few airplanes were a combination of the two airplane models.

Our "much used" airplane had the molded Plexi-glass nose section of the newer "F" model. Also it had many other important refinements of the "F" but was still in some ways an "E." We thought of it as an "E," and I have it in my logbook as a B17 E. Among our ground crew members it was simply known as a "Vega-built E." It may have had the

147

fuel tankage of the "E," which was 30 gallons less fuel than the "F." It had the "paddle blade" propellers like the standard "F," necessitating shortening the engine cowling a bit to allow the paddle bladed propeller to be fully feathered. The new propeller gave it better performance at high altitude. "Stardust" still had the turbo-supercharger controls of the "E," which were inferior to the newer type on the "F." It did not have the electrical "plug-ins" for heated flight suits.

Finally, the one difference that was most noticeable to us was the fact that it had a high-pressure oxygen system rather than the diluter-demand type on the newer model. This meant that we had to use the type of oxygen mask that had the bag hanging below it and the two sponges protruding from the facemask. These sponges froze at high altitude and we had to squeeze them to break up the ice to make breathing easier. The fact that the airplane may have carried 30 gallons less fuel than the "F" was sometimes a worry on the long-range missions. One pleasant thing for Bob and me was that it had a much better cockpit heater than the newer "F" model.

As in all B17s, there was just one urine relief tube and it was located in the rear of the airplane. It was unusable at high altitude after its first usage as it always froze up solid. We finally devised a creative solution to this problem, however. About the time that we moved up from Tunis to Italy, someone in the squadron or group suggested that if need be, that we use a condom as a urine bag instead of the old method of using our steel helmets as a bucket. Most of the crewmen tried to go the seven hours without emptying their bladder. This was quite uncomfortable sometimes. Whatever you used, condom or steel helmet, it froze almost immediately so it was somewhat easier to get rid of in the frozen state. In the cockpit, we would stand up and remove our oxygen mask for a moment and inflate the condom like a balloon. After replacing the oxygen mask, we would proceed to use the condom for something that it was never intended to be used for. We would then tie a knot in the top and gingerly set it on the floor. In a short while it would be frozen into

COMBAT IN ITALY

an ice ball and it could be tossed into the bomb bay to be dropped along with the bombs.

We were normally issued a couple of condoms along with our pay each payday of the month. Most of us threw them into our footlocker and forgot about them. Suddenly they were now in demand. Our Flight Surgeon kept up with the squadron's demand, although this may have raised some eyebrows higher up in the chain of command. That is until they found out that this tremendous increase in usage amounted to better crew health and comfort for the flight crewmen. (Someone up there may have thought that the 99th had hit a "bonanza location" until they learned the truth.) Some of our guys still stood by the old method of holding it and suffering or using the steel helmet. The disposal problem of using the condom was much simpler, and if we put the frozen ice balls in the bomb bay before "bombs away," it was perhaps more satisfying to allow our imaginations to conger up the idea of our presents raining down on the heads of the German defenders, perhaps on one of their anti-aircraft batteries

Dec. 24^{th,} I wrote a long letter home: *"Dear Mom: It is Christmas Eve here and none of us have any Christmas packages to open. I did get a long letter from you today and it was like getting a Christmas gift in itself. I would like to be home tonight, I guess that Christmas was the brightest time of the year for me. When I get home I hope to have a real old-fashioned Christmas with you. Thanks for the letter. You would be surprised at how a letter helps ones morale. Tell Jerry* (my kid brother) *that our ship Stardust has about 75 missions on it and has shot down over 10 enemy airplanes. The food isn't so bad now. We had pork chops for supper but I had some fried spam too and it was good. We get no real butter and very little meat. Of course there is no milk here as the cows are diseased. We are all sitting around discussing how Christmas was at home when we were little. I guess to the little ones, that is the most important part of the year. I remember the B-B gun and the sled and the electric train and stuff like that. We didn't have any money to*

149

spare but none of us kids ever were cut short at Christmas time. I guess that is one of the things that make us love our parents so much. Wishing you a merry Christmas and I'll pray for you tonight."

December 25th, Christmas Day, we flew as a crew in "Stardust" to the Udine, Italy, railroad yards. The target was covered by clouds, and we were recalled without dropping our bombs.

On the 26th or the 27th, while Ernie and Walt were in Foggia scrounging for what we needed for our tent, Bob and I were looking for armor plate to replace the cockpit armor that was removed when the airplane was repaired. After the heavy flak incident that nearly shot down Capt. Shaefer's airplane with two of my crewmembers on board, Bob and I decided to find armor for our pilot seats. We surveyed many of the old aircraft wreckages nearby to see what we could find, and finally found a wrecked German JU-88 that still had the armor plating in it. Bob stayed with the prize while I went to our squadron truck maintenance shop to borrow a hacksaw. When I told the sergeant what I wanted it for, he gave me a couple of new blades and said I would need them. He was right, as we had a very hard time removing the plating from the wreck. We walked back to the maintenance shop with skinned knuckles along with our booty.

We returned the hacksaw and thanked the sergeant for lending it. He said, "What are you going to do with them now that you have them?" We said that we would measure the seats in the cockpit and cut them to size and put them under our butts. The sergeant said to go and measure how we wanted them cut and he would cut them with a torch for us. This seemed to be a great idea, and we caught a ride to the flight line to climb up into "Stardust" to measure the length and width they needed to be.

The sergeant then cut them for us and we had a lot to thank the older soldier for; he really took care of our immediate needs. This day was well spent and we took our two finished pieces of armor back to our tent to be put in the airplane as soon as possible. The cockpit seats on the B-

COMBAT IN ITALY

17 were of the metal "bucket" type, which was common in the Air Corps. They were made to accommodate a seat-type parachute, a type which we didn't use, so we had a thick cushion in the bucket seat instead of the parachute. I had my plate cut a bit longer than the bucket, and in place of the thick cushion, I had a piece of wood 2X4 in the back of the bucket to make the plate level. On this I put a thin soft cushion. I had to lower the seat a bit for a good flying position but that was no problem.

December 28th. We flew to Rimini, Italy, again to the railroad yards. It was another easy mission. The next day I flew as co-pilot for Capt. Shaefer in #439 and we were in the squadron deputy lead position, bombing the railroad yards at Ferrerra, Italy. There was some flak but no fighter action that we saw. The P-38's had the task of escorting us lately. In North Africa, we had P-40 escorts, but now it was primarily P-38's and occasionally the P-47's for our top cover. On this mission, one of the P-38's, with one of its engine propellers feathered, tucked in under us for a safe flight home. When he left us south of the bomb line, he did a slow roll into the good engine just to say "goodbye" and thanks a lot!

I was the squadron "duty officer" on the evening of the 30th, and just after I had gone on duty, there was a terrible explosion heard. At my station as "duty officer," I soon heard that a British "Wimpy" Wellington bomber had blown up on the runway with all of the bombs on board. Many of the airplanes parked closest to the runway were damaged, including five of the B-17's of the 416th squadron. A 416th First Sergeant was killed by flying debris or bomb fragments in this debacle.

I wrote home that night using a typewriter in the squadron headquarters and used a "V" mail form. This was a good chance to use a typewriter as I had lights all night. I wasn't able to mention the earlier excitement so there wasn't anything new in the letter except that I said, "Either Walt or Ernie normally read from the Bible each night." I thought that would gladden my mother's heart.

On New Year's Day we had turkey and all the trimmings for dinner. We still had to eat in the pigpen but the food was good. We continued to have the peach half plopped on top but it didn't slow us down much from getting at the good stuff underneath.

Later that night and early the next morning, dysentery was the big thing. I heard tell of the line at the latrine with some begging others to hurry up before it was too late. Some of the crewmen had to use their foxholes as a latrine and would now have to get an Italian worker to clean it out or dig a new one. Walt and Bob had some problems, and Ernie really came down with it bad. He said that he didn't have to use our foxhole as he was lucky to get a hole on our 12-seat throne often. I didn't eat any of the dressing, opting instead for a second helping of potatoes. Everyone who ate the giblet stuffing seemed to have the dysentery to some degree or another. This would have been a problem if we had been operational the next day, which we had expected to be, as many were too sick to have flown. All were well on the 3rd when we did fly again. I did take time to write letters home and also to Dionne on January 2nd.

The latrine area that was used by the men of the 347th was located between the officers' and enlisted men's tent area, and it was over a small narrow stream that was flowing through our area. The Army engineers had apparently towed a wrecked Italian bomber to the site chosen for the latrine, and perched it with one wing slanting up and over the toilet seats. The latrine box was located over the narrow ditch. The seats were in the open with just the wing of the airplane as a roof. The latrine was a long narrow wooden box with open rectangles of about 10 by 15 inches located all along the top. There were at least a dozen of these holes in the one row and it was known as the "twelve-holer."

This area served us well as long as the rains persisted and the stream continued to flow. I am sure that when the dry season came, they connected a log chain to the old wrecked bomber and towed it to another area, and dug a new slit trench and covered it with the same old box. Would they never think of a new angle for the old "out house?"

I never have figured out why they made the seats of the latrine rectangular; I knew of a few in our squadron that this might have fit well, however. When the seats were occupied you could see the white bare behinds of all of the users exposed to the elements. It didn't take long to learn that it was not good to be the first one to use one of the seats in the early morning, when a heavy cover of dew and frost was present. Many of the tent dwellers planted a piece of drain pipe near their tent, with a foot or more protruding above the ground to serve the call of nature in the daytime. I doubt that any used the flashlight to find the pee pipe drain at night, however.

Jan. 2nd. I wrote to my sister Audrey: *"For a New Year's Eve celebration the squadron had some rum but I thought that I had to fly the next morning so I steered clear of it. As it turned out we didn't fly. We are all hoping for some fruitcake, cheese or chocolate candy. We have another fellow in our tent, a new navigator, he is on a new crew and they don't have tents for them yet and he doesn't have a cot either so he is sleeping on the floor. It isn't very comfortable but it is the best we can do for him. I guess that I haven't told you much about the Italians, they are very poor and we always have a line outside our mess area to get scraps that we don't eat. They put everything in a can and take it home to warm up to eat. It seems sort of disgusting but it is a reality. The military doesn't want us to do this but we do it anyway, who can deny a starving kid."*

On the third of January, I was scheduled to fly as co-pilot for Lt. Wardwell, but was notified at the flight line that I was to pilot Lt. McDonald's airplane, as he was sick and couldn't "answer the bell." I flew the mission in his airplane along with his regular crew. This mission was to bomb the ball bearing plant at Villa Perosa in northern Italy. We had a long mission as the target was partly covered by clouds, and we had to circle back and finally hit the target. There was some fighter activity and we saw the P-38's mixing it up with the Germans - quite a show. We had circled around looking for the target, and on our return we were getting short of fuel. I decided to land at

153

Naples, and after refueling, we made the short 30-minute flight to our home base.

A day or so later, Bob Johnson flew as co-pilot on what was to be Lt. Wardwell's 50th and last mission. Bob said that Wardwell let him fly the mission, with the exception of the takeoff and landing. Bob said that Lt. Wardwell sat there in his seat with his arms folded and a smile on his face for the entire mission. With their safe return and de-briefing over, all of our flight crews returned to the squadron and gathered around the flight surgeon. They waited to receive their normal ration of 2 oz. of "Old Overholt" Rye whiskey that was poured into their mess cup. This was a regular routine for everyone who had just returned from any mission. Normally, if one of the crewmembers had just finished his tour, some would pour their ration into his cup until it was nearly full. Lt. Wardwell drank it all down in two or three gulps and promptly fell over backwards on the concrete floor. He was carried off to the dispensary and was found to be OK, just a bad headache. I'm not sure if the headache was from the bump on the head or the big slug of "Old Overload," as we called it.

Jan 4th, 1944. My 9th combat mission was with my crew in "Stardust." We were to bomb the Sofia Bulgaria business district. The Nupnitsa, Bulgaria, railroad yards was our alternate target. Sofia was obscured by clouds and our group was the only one to find the secondary target. This was quite a long mission, owing to our wandering around Bulgaria looking for the secondary target. As we crossed the Adriatic Sea, the "ten percent remaining" fuel lights on the fuel gauges on the instrument panel of "Stardust" illuminated.

We knew that we were really short of fuel, so after advising the squadron leader, I requested permission to make a straight in approach to our home base at Tortorella. We landed with no problem, but also with very nearly dry tanks.

We had a couple of days off due to the local weather, so decided to try to get a door for our tent. Walt arranged for a truck and we piled in and went scavenging. We were told that there were doors in the damaged railroad yard in Foggia and so we headed there. We found a Pullman coach door that had a window still intact and decided that we had found our perfect door. We had the loan of tools from the motor pool and proceeded to remove the door and carry it to our truck. We then tried to figure out what we would use for doorposts and lintel. There were wooden railroad track cross ties everywhere, and we took two good ones and a good 2x6 for the lintel. We went back to the base with our loot and were anxious for a day off so we could hire an Italian laborer to complete the installation. Italian labor was cheap. We could get an unskilled laborer for around 50 cents a day or a skilled carpenter for 75 cents a day.

Nearly everyone got busy improving their living accommodations. Some were more zealous at this than others. We knew that our tent was shaping up to be in the upper tier. I am sure that when we no longer needed our tent it was passed down to another lucky crew, perhaps even passed up to a senior crew. Later I heard that our squadron gave a prize of a quart of Scotch whiskey to the best and most decorated tent at Christmas time 1944.

Our mission on January 7th was to attack the enemy aircraft plant at Weiner-Neustadt, Austria. I had my regular crew in "Stardust." The flak over the IP and the target was very heavy and the air was full of oily black anti-aircraft shell bursts residue. It was a successful mission, but this was the most flak that we had seen to date. We saw some enemy fighter planes in the distance, but they didn't attack us, as they don't like to be in heavy flak areas either. This was my 10th combat mission.

The flak from the IP (initial point to start the bomb run) and to the target and just beyond was of very great concern to all. We knew that if a shell burst in or very near the airplane, we were probably in "deep sh.., er... trouble." We knew that if our bombs were still on board and we were hit in the bomb bay area, the explosion of our bombs would more than likely take out several other airplanes in our vicinity. It was more comfortable for us (if "comfortable" is the word) if our bombs were away and the bomb bay doors were closed.

Jan 7th, I wrote: *"... at last I got your package. It was very much appreciated. The puzzles are especially nice because the time does hang heavy on our hands at times. We just got in another mission today, we are doing pretty well now. We were sort of disappointed not to have gotten something to eat but I assured the fellows that the next package would have something for all to eat, maybe fruitcake. Everything is the same here, the tent is really cozy, we have some bricks and we will soon have a brick floor all around. It gets cold at night here, just as it did in North Africa."*

On Jan 8, 1944. We flew on a large raid on the aircraft plant at Reggio-Emilia, Italy. There were 109 B-17 Fortresses on this mission and we destroyed two thirds of the facility. Our mission on the 10th was to Sophia, Bulgaria, and this time we were successful and dropped our bombs on the primary target. The flak was quite heavy, and we were attacked by enemy fighter planes. My gunners put in a claim that they had shot one down and damaged another. I was quite proud of the actions of my crew that day. On our way to the target, we saw a B-17 from the group just ahead of us suddenly go into a tailspin, and we were watching to see if we could see any parachutes come from the stricken craft. Our ball turret gunner reported that the airplane came out of the spin before it hit the ground and was now heading for home at a low altitude. Who says that a B-17 can't recover from a tailspin? I would imagine that the crew of this airplane checked their britches when they returned safely.

I would like to describe how it feels right after the bombs are "away" and the bomb doors are finally closed. The airplane immediately feels lighter when the three-ton bomb load is dropped, and we experience some measure of relief. Our group and squadron would then make a predetermined right or left turn off the target and proceed a *distance to a "rally point."* There was a turn over the rally point to proceed over a less infested flak route home. Once we settled down for the homeward trip and were again out of the area where we could expect enemy fighters, it was my pleasure to tell Bob Johnson that he "had the airplane." I would get up out of my seat and stretch my tired muscles, and take a condom out of my flight suit pocket and use the newly invented pee pouch to relieve myself. I would then get back into my seat and tell Bob to relax and do the same, if he wished.

When the formation had descended below 10,000 feet, I would advise the crew to shut off their oxygen and remove their mask and it was OK to smoke. We almost all lit up at this time; it was a good smoke and we appreciated it a lot. I usually shared the flying with my co-pilot. Bob was a good formation pilot and I was relaxed when he was at the controls. The B-17 was "heavy" on the controls and it was tiring to fly formation for a long time. I usually flew the airplane on the leg from the IP to the target and to the rally point. It was more to keep my attention on the formation flying and shut out what was happening around me than anything else. Maybe I was selfish; I was the captain of the ship, for whatever that was worth.

On Jan. 10th, I wrote in part: *"Yesterday an Italian drove up to our tent with a horse and rig with a big barrel on it. He spoke good English and said that he had lived in New York for 17 years. He was trying to sell some of his wine to buy clothes for his kids. We didn't have any use for his wine, but my navigator gave him a pair of pants that he couldn't wear anymore."* (I recall that we did get wine bottles filled and thereafter left the empty bottles out to be filled each day. The money for the incoming wine was stuck in the neck of one of the bottles. I said that we didn't have any use for the wine in the above letter because I didn't want my mother or dad to know that I drank). The wine vendor told us that he was unable to get clothes, or cloth to make clothes, for their children. He said that the children had to take turns wearing the clothes available each day, and that some of the children had to stay in bed all day, as they had nothing to wear. He was able to visually point out the village where he lived in the hills northeast of the base.

Jan 11th I wrote: *"We went to town today and got a haircut. An Italian barber, they are pretty good and they only charge 15 cents. We have to go into town for a hot shower. This is nice on a day when we don't have to fly. I wish I could tell you what town I am near. I can't even mention what town we visit like I could in North Africa. You have probably already guessed where we are anyway. We put our door up today and it makes a lot of difference. The fellow who was staying with us has moved into a tent of his own. I hope if you have one of the crew pictures left you will send it to Alice (Eakle) Marks. I promised her one and forgot to tell you. I am going to get a picture of my crew beside "Stardust" with my small camera. I can't get it developed here though so I'll try to bring the films home. Bob is working with that puzzle that you sent and he is having a tough time because he has it spread out on his bed. I feel good because I just got back from a real hot shower in town. We were lucky to catch a ride back so easy for we started back after dark and it is only 8 now. I got a new comforter from the Doctor here; he went to another town and bought it for me."*

Captain Irving "Doc" Neuman, who was our squadron flight surgeon, was a good friend who often came to our tent to visit. I had promised my uniform "great coat" (overcoat) to him if I was shot down or killed. When "Doc" Neuman came to visit us, he often had a jeep signed out for his use. He would park it out in front of our tent, and Walt and Ernie would "borrow" it to go to the flight line to get a couple of "jerry" cans filled with av-gas for the outside barrel for our stove. He knew what they were doing but said nothing about it. He also liked the warmth of our tent and came to visit us often.

On Jan 12th Walt Amundsen, decided to go around to some of the tents in our area asking for donations of old clothes so that he could take it to the wine vendor's home. He did get several pairs of pants and shirts and quite a few pairs of warm worn socks. A couple of pairs of shoes and some other warm items were also donated. I gave him a scarf along with an underwear top that had seen better days.

Walt wanted volunteers to go with him to give the stuff to the wine vendor's family. We all doubted that he could find the village that the wine vendor had pointed out, but Walt was determined to go anyway. It had rained in the night and was overcast and cold that morning and we thought that it was a poor day to be away from the warm tent. I finally volunteered when I saw that Walt was going, "come hell or high water," and no one else was overjoyed with enthusiasm.

We caught a ride on the perimeter road to an exit gate. Then caught another ride on a military truck that was going northeast on the Manfredonia highway. We knew that this would take us in the vicinity of the wine vendor's village. The truck driver dropped us off at a side road that we thought might lead us to our destination. The thought occurred to me that the truck driver probably thought that we were looking for girlfriends up the hill and we were taking things to trade with them.

We trudged up the hill on the muddy road for quite a distance with Walt and me taking turns carrying the heavy duffel bag. This whole area was lined with vineyards. Finally, we arrived at a cluster of homes and sheds that looked like it might be the place we were looking for. Neither of us spoke Italian, but we hoped that we could find someone in the surrounding homes who spoke English and would give us directions to the wine vendor's house.

We were approaching the first home on the hillside when we saw the wine vendor himself coming up the hill, walking beside his horse with the big empty wine barrel hitched behind. We waited for him and he was overjoyed to see us. We opened the duffel bag and showed him the clothes that we had brought and told him that we were there to give them to him and his family.

He took us to his home and introduced us to his wife and children. I don't know how many children there were, but I thought he must have added substantially to his family after his stint in the U.S. Their home was well furnished according to the standards that we had expected. He insisted that we stay and eat with them. It was noon and we told him that we had to get back to the base before dark. He said that his wife would have food for us within the hour and we agreed to stay and dine.

    I don't know how she came up with a couple of chickens, dressed and ready for the pot, so fast, but she did it. Perhaps she had planned to serve the chicken for their own supper. She prepared chicken cacciatore and spaghetti and wonderful Italian bread. The father ate with us while the rest of the family stood around smiling at us while we ate. Both Walt and I ate a couple of pieces of chicken and a large bowl of spaghetti. All the while we were washing it down with the good red wine. It was all very delicious and we were lavish in our praise of the cuisine and the cook.

    After we had eaten and had given the good man a cigarette, he took us outside to show us around. The sky was brightening up by then and it was a much nicer day than we had expected when we had left our tent. The man was very proud of his chicken flock. I think that the chickens were the main source of their meat, and, of course, eggs.

    We gave him a handful of cigarettes and Walt gathered up our empty duffel bag as we were about to leave. The wine vendor told us over and over how grateful they were to have the clothes and shoes. As we were leaving, Walt, almost as an afterthought, asked if he could buy a couple of the chickens. I thought that Walt was out of his mind and asked him what he intended to do with the birds. Walt said that he would use them as barter when we got back. He would keep them in our tent and get rid of them as soon as he could get a good deal. I said, "No way, Walter, those chickens will never be in our tent as long as I am the pilot of this crew." He said that he would tie them to the tent stakes outside, if that was OK with me. I said that he could do whatever he wanted to do with the chickens, as long as he kept them out of the tent and off our front gravel walkway.

    The man promptly caught and put three young roosters in a

gunnysack. He would take no money for them and Walt thanked him.

Walt put the gunnysack with the chickens in his duffel bag and said goodbye and started off down the hill back to the main road. Walt asked me to carry the duffel bag containing the chickens part of the way down the hill, and I refused. He knew that I wasn't happy with his acquisition. We caught a ride on the main road toward Foggia and were dropped off near our airfield. We caught another ride in the back of a truck to our squadron.

It was nearly dark by this time. Walt had time to tie a string to one leg of each chicken and tie them loosely to the tent stakes out back. I went inside to get warm and tell the other two about our adventures of the day. We went up to the "pigsty" to eat our evening meal and found out that we were scheduled to fly the next morning.

Jan 13th, 1944. Our mission was to Rome in "Stardust." The flak was moderate to heavy on the bomb run and over the target. There were some enemy fighters in the area but they did not attack our group. We hit the target airdrome well and it was a good mission.

Jan 14th. This morning we were not scheduled to fly so we looked forward to a morning to sleep in. At about six in the morning, the roosters started to crow right outside of the back of our tent. They woke me and everyone else in the tent with their crowing, and I got up and lit the fire. I told Walt that the chickens had to go, and I meant just as soon as he could get them out of there. We were all irritated about the early wake up and that was the end of the chicken story. Walt got rid of them that morning. I think that he gave them to his mechanic friends at the motor pool for a favor that they were doing for him, and I was happy that this episode was over.

Our "Super Scrounger" Walt had found a Ford four-door car that had been abandoned by the Aussies when they moved up nearer the front with their A-20's. The transmission and drive shaft had fallen out and it was in need of a lot of repair, to say the least. Walt had made friends with several young mechanics at the squadron motor pool and they agreed to tow it to the maintenance area and fix it up for him.

They had proceeded, in their spare time, to somehow get it in nearly driving condition and intended to paint it with U.S. Army olive drab green and put a number on it. When the car was drivable, Walt would have transportation at his disposal for his trips into Foggia and more foraging. We assured Walt that if that "right-hand drive" Ford made it out of the motor pool, it would promptly be the property of one of the "Brass" on the base, but this didn't detour him in the least. I think these mechanics were the ones that took over our chicken headache for us.

On Jan 15th, we flew in "Stardust" on a mission to attack the railroad yards at Arezzo, Italy. That evening I wrote in part: *"In one of your letters you asked if I was on that Brenner Pass mission. I wasn't but my co-pilot was on it. At night we can hear the artillery guns at the front about 70 miles north of us."* (This last sentence obviously passed the censor.)

On Jan 16th, we were on a mission to bomb the Villaroba airdrome in Italy. The target was nearly covered with clouds but we saw enough to drop our bombs. Again we had flak but saw no enemy fighters. We had overhead protection from our own P-38's as usual. We did witness one of our P-38's being attacked by a single German ME 109 enemy fighter plane. After being hit by the enemy gunfire, it spiraled down with an engine on fire. Our ball turret gunner, Sgt. Harold Rice, watched it go down but did not see it crash or see the smoke from a crash. We hoped that the pilot had made it back to safety.

After we had dropped our bombs on this mission, an incident happened that involved the 99th Bomb Group and our Squadron in particular. The target was partly obscured by clouds and there were some scattered clouds at our bombing level also. We turned right off the target after releasing our bombs to start our journey home. I will quote from one report of this incident as published in a 99th Bomb Group Historical Society newsletter that I received:

"A formation of B-24's came out of the clouds ahead and

> slightly below us. They were being attacked by a large
> number of ME-109's and three of the enemy aircraft
> were seen being shot down by the Liberators."

I believe that our squadron was the lower squadron in our group formation diamond as we were returning that day. Through the clouds, I remember seeing some B-24's passing from our left to our right and slightly below us. All of our gunners were alerted as to the location of the B-24's and were keeping an eye on them. Someone in the back of our airplane called me on the interphone and said that he could see no group or squadron markings on the Liberators. This seemed strange to me.

> And again from the newsletter…"It was later reported
> that this group of B-24's was a new squadron and aircraft
> markings had not as yet been painted on them".

Another cloud obscured them from our view, and when my gunners saw them again they were on our right side at about 4 or 5 o'clock to our position and the gunners said that they were entirely too close to us.

No one in our squadron had reported seeing any enemy fighter planes attacking the Liberators. Perhaps the B-24's proximity to us was scaring the enemy off or perhaps the clouds had been screening us off, from the enemy fighter planes. I don't believe any of the crewmen in our squadron were aware that the Liberators were being attacked by the enemy 109's.

The proximity of the unknown and unmarked Liberators prompted the gunners on several of the B-17's in our squadron to open up on the nearest Liberator and to shoot it down. There were 9 parachutes seen coming from the stricken plane when they went down into the cold Adriatic, and I doubt that there were any survivors. My gunners said that they didn't fire a shot at the plane and I believed them.

In the investigation later the count of the expended cartridges in our airplane completely exonerated our crew of firing into the unfortunate Liberator. There were reports that the Libs were still under fire from the enemy as we were firing at them, but from the viewpoint of our squadron all of this was obscured. The gunners from the crews that did fire on the plane said that the Liberator opened fire on us first. I doubt this and I think that if they did see tracers, it may have been from the attacking Germans, which we could not see because of the clouds. The Liberators were probably trying to get up under us for protection.

As we were continuing our flight home, all of my crewmembers were convinced that the Liberators were a German plant. They surmised that the Germans had repaired downed Allied bombers and were flying them into our squadron to shoot all of us down. There had been numerous reports of this happening; however, it had always been a single airplane flown by a German crew; we had never heard of six trying this in a formation.

We had strict orders that if we were trying to join up with another of our friendly group or squadron formation, we must first try to contact their leader on the radio and transmit the code word of the day, show the color of the day, and absolutely never point a gun at the squadron being approached. After you had been recognized and accepted, then you could assume a proper position in the squadron.

We gave our report to the intelligence officer at our post-flight debriefing and were informed, in no uncertain terms, that we had shot down one of our own and that there would be an investigation. I gave the report of my sighting of the B-24's and their position to us. My gunners were questioned, and they denied again that they had shot at the Liberator; and the ammo count showed that they had just fired enough ammunition to test-fire the guns, which was the normal procedure. I doubted that this "friendly fire" incident was reported in any detail until it was discussed in the 99th BG Historical Society newsletter.

Jan 18th. We took off on a mission to bomb the Poggibonsi, Italy, railroad yards, but in our climb to high altitude I was informed by S/Sgt. Frank Rogers, our flight engineer/top turret gunner, that he had forgotten his parachute pack. We had to leave the formation and return to

COMBAT IN ITALY

Tortorella with our bombs still in the bomb bays. There was absolutely no excuse for Sgt. Rogers to not have checked his equipment properly, and I knew that disciplinary action was necessary.

Of course, being the Pilot and crew commander, everything was my ultimate responsibility. Upon landing, I was called into the squadron commander's office and was put in a "brace" and chewed out royally. The C.O. finally asked what I intended to do with my flight engineer who was responsible for not following his pre-flight equipment checklist. I said that I would ground him if another man was available. He told me that he would have another assigned to my crew the next day. In departing his office, he sarcastically said that since I hadn't worked very hard that day, he would have me fly an acceptance check on an airplane that had been transferred to the squadron. It was a fairly old B-17F that had been stripped of all of its armament, so I thought it would be a good time to see how high one of these birds would go.

Lt. Lamb was my co-pilot, and one of the new replacement flight engineers was the third man. After a normal pilot preflight, we cranked up the light bird and started our tour of southern Italy. We continued to climb until we were up through 31,000 feet, and the airplane was still willing to climb higher. We were getting really cold as the cockpit heater in this "F" was not nearly as good as "Stardust," so we decided that we had had enough. It was a beautiful day and we could see all of southern Italy from this vantage point and found it awesome. The day ended on a positive note, even though I had to inform my flight engineer that he was no longer on my crew. We also found out that we had missed out on a "milk run" mission that day. On every mission after this incident, I had our radio operator, Sgt. Najarian, check out, and be responsible for, a spare parachute pack to be on board and stowed in the radio room. This was not officially authorized but we continued to carry the spare chute.

On Jan 19th we went to Rome, Italy and bombed an airdrome near the city. We now had a new engineer named S/Sgt. Ed Madigan. I didn't know anything about him other than that he was a replacement for my former engineer. Our bombing target was the airfield at Centocelle, near Rome. We did see some enemy fighter planes but they seemed intent to harass another group and left us alone. The flak was heavy and accurate and some of the planes in our squadron were bounced around by it. We felt one blast under us and I glanced at the engine gauges to see if there were any problems. My ball turret gunner said on the inter-phone, "That one was close." I asked him to see if he saw any damage on the under side of the airplane and he answered "no."

 I made a crew check to see if anyone was injured. I asked for a reply from each position and was assured that we did not have an injury. Another look at the engine manifold pressure showed that the #2 engine power had dropped a bit. I tried to advance the #2 throttle and found that I had no throttle control in the cockpit, and assumed that the throttle cable to the #2 engine had been severed. I was able to balance the power from engines #2 and 3 with the turbo supercharger controls, and I used the outboard engines to keep us in tight formation. When the #2 throttle control cable was cut, that engine had gone, automatically, into "long range cruise power" and remained at that power for the remainder of the flight. On the descent back to our base, I could keep the power under control by using the turbo supercharger control on that engine until it became apparent that I would have to shut down the #2 engine on final approach for landing. I closed the mixture control and that shut off the fuel supply to that engine on final approach, then proceeded to make a normal 3-engine landing.

 After the landing, we returned to our hardstand and I stuck my head out of the open cockpit window to talk to our ground crew chief. He wanted to know what happened, and I told him that we were hit by flak and that I thought that the #2 engine throttle cable was cut. He said that there was a hole in the fuselage right under my seat and that it probably had cut the throttle cable where it runs under the floor at that location. I got up out of the seat and removed the cushion and the armor plating that

COMBAT IN ITALY

I was sitting on. There was a jagged hole in the seat bucket, with a piece of flak almost 2 inches long and a quarter of an inch wide still lying in the seat bottom. I hadn't felt anything at the time it hit the underside of the armor plating, as we were bouncing around quite a bit from the close flak burst. I am sure that if I hadn't put that armor plating in place a month earlier, I would have had an interesting "Purple Heart."

On the evening of Jan 19th I wrote in part: *"We have a table now and it is big enough for two of us to write on at once. Walt scrounged it somewhere and we all enjoy it. We went into town and had a shower today; it feels really good to be clean. Afterward we went to the Red Cross Officers Club and sat around listening to the radio and enjoying ourselves. They have a girl working at the Red Cross who is an American. She is married to an Italian Nobleman. She is very nice, a lot of nurses come in to the club and I guess before long we will have WAC's also. I hope so anyway, I haven't had any personal contact with a woman since I left home, Love to all, Wes."*

Jan 20th. We were sent to Rome to hit the airfield, another "milk run." On the evening of Jan 20th I wrote: *"I just finished cutting some fruit cake, it was some that Walt got from his folks and it was really good. We had six fellows here and I cut it in twelve pieces so we had two each. We had a good session here tonight; we hashed over why the Army isn't running right and how to improve our bombing score. We had a nice hot fire going but it got a little too hot and our tent pole started to smoke. We had to pour water on it to put it out. I guess that we will have to move our stove a little farther away from the pole. I have some bouillon on the stove and when it gets hot it will taste good. Walt is reading scripture tonight. We always read a bit of the Bible and a prayer before we go to sleep. Either Ernie or Walt do the reading and lead the prayer. It helps, mom, I didn't realize how much power something like this has."*

Our av-gas stove was quite a GI invention. The tubing from the aviation gas storage tank outside of the tent ran under our tent wall and

167

STARDUST FALLING

under the bricks of the floor. There was a "shut off" where a brick had been removed just outside of the stove barrel proper. When the gas line tubing entered the hole near the bottom of the barrel, it had a "T" fitting which now made two lines inside the stove barrel. The two lines of tubing were coiled in opposite directions, near the bottom of the stove. There was a layer of rock on the bottom inside of the stove, and the two coils of tubing made a couple of circuits around the base of the stove just above the rocks. Then the two coil ends crossed near each other in the center of the stove just above the rocks. To light the stove, we would let a few drops of the gas drip on the rocks, and then turn the spigot off and light the gas that had accumulated on the rocks. When the fire on the rocks was going well, we would gingerly turn the gas back on, and soon the ends of the tubing would act like a blowtorch. Before long, the sides and top of the barrel would be "cherry red" hot and we'd control the heat by monitoring the flow of fuel to the burner. Where the cast iron stovepipe went out of the top of the tent, next to the center pole, we had a metal shield cone, which was meant for the oil heaters that hadn't arrived as yet. With a little tin cutting, the six-inch water main pipe fit through this cone. The pipe and cone was warm near the top but never seemed to be too warm.

In my letter of the 21st I wrote: *"I wonder how long it takes for my letters to get to you, please let me know. I get yours in two weeks or slightly more. We did a little work on our stove today, it caught the center pole on fire so we had to move it out a little and add reinforcements to our tent pole. I don't know if I told you or not but I have a new engineer now, his name is Madigan. He seems like a good boy and I'm hoping he turns out OK."*

On Jan 22nd our mission was to bomb the railroad yards at Perugia, Italy. Our bombardier, Ernie Jenkins, was in the lead ship and we all dropped our bombs on his release. This was a successful mission, and on our return flight we proceeded out over the Mediterranean, where we gradually descended. We witnessed the Allied landing at Anzio, south of

COMBAT IN ITALY

Rome. This was very spectacular, with hundreds of ships and some fires burning on shore, and several of the Allied Force boats were on fire also. I don't remember much about this bombing mission; it must have been an easy one. All that I recall about this day was the Allied Fleet landing south of Rome.

I wrote that night: *"...I had one of the greatest thrills of my life today. We saw something more spectacular than anything I have ever seen. I can't tell you what it was but if you notice the date you can surely connect this up. Well, we had a ringside seat and we listened to broadcasts on the radio going to New York at the same time. We were on our way home from a mission when this all happened. I will tell you all about it when I get home, hopefully in a couple of months. I hope to be half done by the end of this month. I am really proud of my bombardier, he did something big today. I got some stationery today; one of the fellows that is going home gave it to me. Love Wes"*

Jan 23rd. We flew today in "Stardust" to Poggibonsi, Italy, again to attack the railroad yards there. The Germans seemed to fix them as fast as we tear them up. We were unable to see the target or the two alternates because of a heavy overcast below, so we returned to base with our bombs on board. Because of our time over enemy territory, I was credited with my 19th mission, even though we were unable to drop the bombs on any target.

Jan 24th. I was co-pilot for Capt. Shaefer in a new B-17G model airplane. He was our deputy squadron leader and the leader of the second element of the squadron formation. The squadron had only two "G's," and the leader and the deputy leader had the new airplanes. Lt. Laino took over my crew and my airplane "Stardust" on this day. For one of the squadron pilots, such as me, to fly as co-pilot for one of the leaders was common, and on this we were rotated. This was my second turn to fly with Capt. Shaefer as an element leader or a squadron leader. I did much of the actual flying from the right seat. We pilots were being trained to eventually become element leaders in the formation. I was thankful that day that I was in a "G" and that we didn't have to worry about fuel. The "G" carried considerably more fuel than did "Stardust" and the other "F's." The mission, my 20th, was to Sofia, Bulgaria to bomb the railroad yards, a "maximum effort" mission for the 99th bomb group.

This mission started to unravel soon after we crossed the Adriatic. The seriousness of the mission dictated that we press on and we climbed higher than our bombing altitude to avoid the cloud buildups. We then had to descend lower than our planned altitude, again to go under some clouds. When I say this, I mean the entire 99th bomb group. It was climb and descend several times on the way to the target, which caused all to use more fuel than was planned. We also made several unplanned course changes that ran us through areas of flak, and then when the target was determined to be covered by clouds, we started for our first alternate target. There was another cloud front between us and the new target and we again descended to go below the clouds. This was just too much for some of the pilots and they were calling in that they were turning back as they were short of fuel.

Our squadron was leading the group that day and the group commander was the pilot of the "G" lead ship just ahead of us. The group commander just pressed on, and soon he could see that the secondary target was also cloud-covered. He started a turn toward the third target and the whole squadron now turned back short of fuel. Finally, the Group leader gave it up and turned toward home with us in trail. There is nothing like the leader finding out that he has only one soldier still following him into battle.

This was a real fiasco, as it turned out the airplane, an "F," piloted by Jesse (JD) Wheeler and his crew, turned back when the group started to descend after the first target was abandoned. He could see that he couldn't go any further and still make it home on the fuel remaining. He was the first one of the group to sensibly decide to turn back. In talking to his co-pilot, J.O. Grizzell, he said that they broke out of the clouds at the coast of the Adriatic on the Balkan side. Jesse asked his new navigator to give him a course to get them home. The navigator was unsure where they were and suggested a 15-degree turn to the right. J.D. elected to turn left 5 degrees instead, wanting to fly over the coast of Italy well south of the enemy territory. Luckily he did and they made landfall near Manfredonia, about 20 miles from home.

When the Wheeler crew landed, they alerted the squadron personnel that a fiasco was in progress out there. At least an hour later, the two "G's" landed at Tortorella and were the only airplanes, except Lt. Wheeler's, to make it home without refueling. In the two "G's" that flew the entire route were the group leader in our squadron lead aircraft, and us in the deputy lead position. We were both flying in airplanes that had much more fuel than the standard B-17F. I was indeed fortunate to be flying with Capt. Shaefer that day or I would not have made it all of the way home without re-fueling.

After the de-briefing at Group headquarters, we returned to the squadron and received our two ounce shot of "Old Overload." (I say two ounces; Doc Neuman always poured and history probably says that we each got two ounces if we wished. However, I am sure that he did not measure as exactly as it was prescribed in the manual. It felt like two kicks from a mule, all of this after a "long day's work at the office.") I retired to our tent to get out of the flight gear. I went back to the squadron operations office to see if they had heard anything from the crew of "Stardust." They had received no word as yet and I knew that they were down somewhere. I hoped it was on dry land.

I was getting quite anxious as we had heard the numerous "Mayday" calls and I was afraid that I may have lost my crew as well as my airplane. I went into the Officers' dining room and found it almost empty. (The squadron officers' club dining room had finally opened; no more eating in the pigpen.)

One report quoted in the 99th BG Historical Society newsletter written by a pilot who was on this mission went as follows:

> *"I believe that only two Forts got back to Tortorella; they were the group leader and his second element lead. Both were in Tokyo Forts or "G's." The crews of five Forts either bailed out over, or crash landed in Yugoslavia."*

From this same bulletin the pilot went on to say,

> *"he just barely made it to the runway at Bari and turned left off the runway as quick as he could. Another Fort went right past him, having come in long and hotter than a two dollar pistol."*

He went on to say,

> *"This guy ran out of runway, went through an opening in the boundary fence which was being patrolled by an Italian soldier. The guard, when he saw the Fort almost on top of him, threw his rifle in the air and ran in the opposite direction, the Fort continued across a pretty heavily traveled road, not hitting or being hit by any other traffic. The Fort washed out its gear in an orchard up the hill on the other side of the road."*

This report in the 99th Bomb Group Historical newsletter concludes with the writer saying that,

> *"I think that the 5th Wing (of which the 99th was just one group) lost a hell of a number of airplanes that day. Five in Yugoslavia, eight or more by ditching or other causes. None lost to enemy action. The 24th of January was a real disaster as far as i could see."*

Thanks to the 99th Bomb Group Historical Society bulletin editor and the pilot of the article for the quotes.

The evening of the 24th was our third supper meal in our new facility ("O" club dining room) and I sat with the crew of Capt. Shaefer. One of his crew-members remarked that, "I would rather fight the Nazis than the weather." Another said that we ought to fire that new group leader for needlessly leading us through all of that flak and running the squadron out of fuel. We all agreed. After we had eaten, I again went to operations and was told that the pilot of airplane #746 had contacted our squadron operations office and said that they had landed near Bari, Italy and that the airplane would be home the next day. I was relieved to hear the news but it was an empty tent that I went back to that evening. On that same night, in part, I wrote: *"I received a letter from you tonight and although I'm tired as the dickens, I will answer it right away. We had a mission today that is the reason that I am so tired. About giving some money to the church, of course give them all that you think is reasonable; take it out of my account at the bank. I owe the Lord an awful lot so please take care of this for me. We had fried chicken for supper tonight. It was really good, we are eating at an officers club now, and it is a very nice place, run by our squadron. It's going to make living here at least 50% better. I will close now as the lights just went out and I am using a flashlight to finish. Love Wes"*

Jan 25th. My crewmen returned this noon and told the story of being completely out of fuel when they landed at an airfield near Bari. They said that they nearly hadn't made it onto the runway when two of the engines stopped, out of fuel. They made it to the parking area with the other two engines still running on fumes.

Jan 26th. We heard that all of the airplanes in the group that were in a condition to make it home had finally made it back by sundown on the 25th. The 26th was a day off while the group "licked its wounds" and we went into town to the Red Cross Club. It is a nice place to relax but there are just too few girls. We poured over the copies of the "Stars and Stripes" newspaper that were available at the Red Cross reading room, which kept us pretty well up to date on what was happening at the front.

We all enjoyed the cartoons in the "Stars and Stripes." The papers were delivered daily to the Red Cross Club and the copies were kept for a week or more so we could catch up on what was going on in the world.

It was nice to have another day off after so many consecutive days of flying. We were to learn the next day, to our relief, that we had a new group commanding officer.

When we returned from Foggia after dark the night of the 26th, we checked to see if we were operational on the 27th of January. We found that we were scheduled to fly as a crew in "Stardust" on what was to be my 21st combat mission.

In my letter to my parents on the night of the 26th I wrote: *"We went into town again today and ate sandwiches at the Red Cross, it is a nice place to go to write letters and to sit around and listen to records. We missed our supper out at the base tonight so we are a bit hungry. "Joe E. Brown" was performing at one of the theaters tonight, but even though we got there an hour early we couldn't get a seat so we hitched a ride home. I wore my overcoat today for a change. It was the first time since I came overseas, not because it is colder but I thought that I'd wear it instead of my leather jacket. I just had a toasted cheese sandwich and a cup of boullion and it really hit the spot. I'll be hungry in the morning. Love, Wes."*

This was the last letter that I sent home from Italy. I wrote this letter on the evening of the 26th and obviously dropped it in the box at the squadron mailroom in the early morning hours of the 27th.

CHAPTER 7

GOODBYE "STARDUST"

Nine aircraft made up the 347th squadron normally; however, often an airplane would need to return home due to mechanical reasons. Thus on the mission of the 27th of January, we were to be in the 10th position, which was often referred to as "Tail end Charlie." We then would move up to replace any aircraft returning to base for any reason. Being #10 we were directly behind, and slightly below, the 3rd element leader of our squadron formation.

The ten men that made up my crew that day included 2nd Lieutenants Robert Johnson, co-pilot; Ernest Jenkins, bombardier; Walter Amundsen, navigator; and myself. The enlisted men were: S/Sgts. Edward Madigan, the flight engineer and the upper turret gunner; "Arky" Askanaz Najarian, radio man and upper rear gunner; and Sgts. Harold Rice, ball turret gunner; Joe Kinnane, left waist gunner; James Hoskins, right side waist gunner; Clifford Henderson, who sat on a bicycle type seat in the tail facing aft and manned the twin tail guns. (Jim Hoskins was my regular tail gunner but had traded positions with Cliff Henderson that day).

We were all quite young, as you can imagine. I just happened to be the youngest. I had just turned 20 when we formed as a crew in Texas, and flew my first combat mission about six months later. I had been raised in rank to 1st Lt. about 9 months after my 19th birthday. By November 1st, 1943, I had flown about 1500 hours as the pilot in military aircraft, with about 400 hours of that flying time in the B-17 bomber.

"Stardust" was one of the older airplanes in our squadron and was on her 85th mission when we took off that morning. The original crew who had flown the airplane overseas with the squadron had completed their 50 missions in the airplane and had returned home.

I had flown several missions in other B-17's, but "Stardust" was now considered to be "our" aircraft. The plane was in good condition, even though it had sustained considerable damage on November 30th, 1943.

On the morning of January 27th, 1944, we were awakened at about 3:30 AM by an airman driving a Jeep up to the front of our tent and honked the horn until he got a response from someone inside. The electrical generator in our area had been turned on early so we were able to use our only light bulb to get everyone out of the "sack" and ready for the day. We started a fire in the gas heater and put the bucket of water for our washing and shaving on the stove to warm. We went through the morning routine with the barely warm water, using our own steel helmets as washbasins, before going to breakfast.

After breakfast was over, it was a quick latrine visit and then back to our tent to get our flight gear. Then we all met at the squadron operations area for transportation, either to the group headquarters for our target briefing or directly to the airplane. The four officers of our crew and the radio man were required at the target briefing, and the rest of the crew went directly to the airplane to assemble and check their guns and ammunition, to do their pre-flight check list, and to arrange their gear for the flight.

The Group operation officer opened the briefing to the officers and radiomen assembled in the shed, which was used as a briefing room. He uncovered a large map on the wall that had a black cord showing our route to the target. When we saw the length of the cord that day everyone let out a loud groan, as we all realized this mission was at about the maximum range of our fuel endurance for the B-17F airplane. We knew that we would surely be "sweating" out the fuel remaining on our return trip. I was relieved to see that we would cross over Naples on the return and I knew that we could land there for fuel as I had done once before.

Next, we were briefed by the weather officer, he said that there would be clouds below us on the route but that the target, the airdrome at Salon de Provence, France, should be clear of clouds. We were told that our IP for our bomb run would be northeast of Aix-en-Provence. We would make a left turn northeast of Aix to avoid their anti-aircraft batteries and make a straight and level run for the few minutes to the targeted airdrome. The time that our bombs were scheduled to be dropped on the target was 12 Noon, local time.

We were next briefed by the intelligence officer, he said that we could expect heavy German fighter plane attacks and heavy anti-aircraft fire along the coast and over the target area. We were told that we could expect to have top cover by our P-38 Lockheed Lightning fighter escorts as we were approaching the French coast and that they should be able to engage the German fighter aircraft that were expected. The intelligence officer also said that the airport at Ajjacio, Corsica, was now in Allied hands and was operational and available in an emergency.

After this we were briefed by our new group commander. This new commanding officer had previously been with our group as its deputy commander. After he had completed his first tour, he had enjoyed a short stay in the States and had now returned the day before this mission to be our new group leader. This change was welcome after the fiasco of the 24th. He spoke to us and stressed how important it was to make this airdrome completely unusable to the Germans. They were using it as a base to re-enforce their troops at the new

Allied beachhead at Anzio, Italy. Our group and another B-17 bomb group were scheduled to completely destroy the German airdrome that day.

Our bomb group, the 99th, was the first group to be over the target. The group was to fly in a "box" or "diamond" formation to and from the target. Our squadron, the 347^{th,} was to be just to the left of the lead squadron and behind and somewhat below their level. Another squadron was to the right and above the lead squadron, while the fourth squadron was directly behind the lead and slightly below them. This made up the group box formation that looked like a diamond. After the initial point (IP) northeast of Aix en Provence, our squadron was to move to the left of the main part of the group about 1 mile. We were to bomb the southern part of the airfield while the bulk of the group targeted the northern part. The second bomber group of the 15th was to come in behind and slightly above us, and their bomb drop was scheduled to be a few minutes after our attack.

Just before the end of the briefing, each crew navigator was given a packet containing the route maps. Every radio crewman was given all of the code instructions, the color of the day, the code word of the day, and the escape packets for all of the rest of the crew who were not present at the briefing. Each of the officers picked up their own escape kits, etc. We pilots were given our takeoff time schedule. Our squadron was to begin takeoffs at 0745 hours. We were all given the correct time with a time "hack" synchronizing our watches so that we would all have the same exact time.

The briefing being over, there was a Chaplain in each corner of the room who said a prayer and blessing to each according to his religious preference. Almost everyone attended this closing session of the briefing, with their hat in their hand and their head bowed. There were exceptionally few "atheists" in our bomb group.

We then boarded the trucks to take us to our planes. We stopped at the squadron flight line supply and each checked out a parachute,

"Mae West," and throat mike. (Later crews were issued flak vests and flak helmets in addition to the foregoing. We had neither, but could use our steel helmet "wash basin" as a flak helmet, if needed.) We were then dropped off at our airplane and we stowed all of our gear aboard. The co-pilot started the "walk around" inspection of the outside of the airplane, while I checked with the ground crew chief and had a look at the airplane's log book. We both were satisfied that the airplane visually was in airworthy condition. The flight engineer had checked that the fuel tanks were full and the oxygen tanks had been filled. It was up to our armorer, Sgt. Henderson, to check the bombs in the bomb bay for security and the bombardier to pre-flight his Norden bombsight. The navigator got out his route maps and made them ready for the flight. Each gunner had already checked his guns and supply of ammunition before we had arrived at the aircraft.

Our designated armorer had made sure that the guns and ammo were checked in the nose section of the airplane and in the radioman's position prior to our arrival.

The bombardier did a second check of the bombs to be sure that the pins were in and the bombs were secure in the bomb racks so that they would be released in their proper sequence. Each crewmember saw to it that his parachute was properly stowed and handy to their position, and that oxygen was available. The radio operator checked his radios and had his position ready for flight. Then all of the crew that needed, climbed down and relieved themselves of the morning coffee. It was now "all aboard," the crew in the forward section swung up through the hatch in the nose section under the cockpit. Bob Johnson, and I climbed up into the cockpit, Ernie Jenkins and Walt Amundsen, the other two went forward to the nose section. In the cockpit, we checked to see that our escape kit was secured in our flight suit pocket and our parachute pack was nearby. All of us wore only the harness of the parachute all of the time; the parachute that we used on the big bomber was of the "chest type" (a 28 ft. parachute, known now-days as an emergency-type parachute), and we normally stored the parachute pack within arm's reach of our position. We only snapped it on to the harness when we needed it in an emergency. We did sometimes wear the pack attached to the harness when we were approaching the anticipated heavy flak areas and wanted to be prepared if the airplane exploded due to a direct hit from an anti-aircraft shell. It was hard to fly the airplane with the pack on, so Bob and I were content to have the pack very close by.

We now checked our oxygen mask for fit and turned the oxygen on long enough to ensure that we would have a proper flow when needed. We were then ready to go through the aircraft pre-flight checklist and prepare for engine start.

At the allotted time, as a squadron, we started our engines and prepared to taxi out. The leader took off at exactly 0745 and we all followed, in order, at 30-second intervals.

We pushed the throttles forward when our turn came and the takeoff was uneventful. We, who were in the forward part of the airplane, were in our normal positions on takeoff, while the remainder of the crew was in the mid-ship area or in the radio room, as was their choice. The squadron formed up quickly and then each squadron maneuvered into their proper position in the group, with the second and third squadron to the right and left of the lead squadron, and the fourth squadron behind and slightly below the lead squadron. Forming the diamond shaped box. Each squadron flew at a slightly different level than the lead squadron; the difference between the high squadron and the low squadron might be as much as 1000 feet. The lead squadron was to be at 22,000 feet and we were to be at 21,500 feet on the bomb run.

The 99th BG that morning was composed of 36 airplanes, (one squadron was one plane short and our squadron had one extra, us). As we started out, on our flight to the target the route took us across Italy to a point northeast of Naples, and then a right turn was made to head toward our target area. We were climbing gradually all the way until we started to encounter the clouds that were at our level and above us.

We were probably at 14,000 or 15,000 feet altitude and abeam of Rome when it became apparent to us and to the group leader that he was going to have to change direction to the east or west, or risk flying his entire group through the heavy clouds up ahead. It is very difficult to keep the formations together while in the cloud, so he made a fairly sharp left turn to avoid them.

We were now in the #9 position in our squadron, on the left of the rear element leader, due to the turn-back of one of our airplanes with mechanical troubles early in the flight. Our squadron was on the left side of the lead squadron, and we were one of the planes on the left side of our squadron and on the inside of this left turn. The group leader tried to climb a bit steeper to get above the clouds, sacrificing some airspeed and we, being on the inside of the turn, were even slower.

We inadvertently got into the slipstream of the airplane just ahead of us and made an uncontrolled roll to the left. We entered the clouds and it felt like we were in a conventional tailspin. I closed the throttles and eased the control column forward, used hard opposite rudder, and we came out of the spin, or whatever we were in, just below the clouds. I didn't know if we had made a full turn and a half, or perhaps just one-half of a full turn in the maneuver - in any case we had lost about 5000 feet in the recovery operation and were now headed in the opposite direction of our group. We made a quick turn back on course and started to climb back up to find our group and squadron.

One of our gunners from the back of the airplane came up front to see what had happened. They all were pinned to the floor in the spin. He said that all of them had finished eating their "K" rations and were in their work positions when the upset came. We assured him that we were now OK and that they could have a quick smoke before we had to go back on oxygen. (My crew in the back ate their "K" rations before we went on oxygen. They said that they didn't want to be hungry if we were to go down.) This unexpected chance to have another smoke was probably appreciated.

The second wave of bombers was just behind us and above us. I considered the idea of joining this group for the bomb run but at about this time I saw our group off to our left and thought that if we kept climbing, we could catch up with them. They had made the wide turn to the left and were now returning to intercept the original course. We were still trailing them by some distance when they leveled off at 22,000 feet. We maintained climb power and soon caught up with them. This wide turn by our bomb group put the two groups of the 15th very close together, maybe only 2 or 3 minutes apart on their route to the target.

We rejoined our squadron in the same position as we had before the upset and were still number 9, and were flying on the left wing of the third element leader, 1st Lt. Ralph Campbell. We had burned considerably more fuel on the second climb and I was now not sure that we had enough fuel left in the tanks to even make it back to Naples on the return. Fortunately, we had the alternate at Ajjaccio, Corsica that we could use for an emergency refueling stop. Under no circumstance did I want to have to land in the cold water of the Mediterranean Sea at that time of the year, or at any time for that matter. Our chances of survival would be nil to none in the frigid water.

As the war diary states (as quoted in a 99th BG Historical Society newsletter) 62 B-17's of the two heavy bomber groups dropped 186 tons of 500 lb bombs on Salon de Provence airfield that day. The bombers were escorted by P-38 fighters on this mission.

We had been briefed to hit our target at Salon de Provence at 12 Noon. As I stated earlier our squadron, the 347th, was to move to the left of the main part of the group on the bomb run so that we could target the south end of the airfield. The other 3 squadrons concentrated on the main northern part.

We crossed the French coast somewhere east of Marseille and west of Toulon, France heading directly toward our IP northeast of Aix en Provence. From there we would turn left and make our level bomb run directly toward our target. The bombing altitude of our squadron was 21,500 feet. The actual time that our group (99th BGH) was over the target was at 1223PM, according to the war records. The turn to avoid the clouds made our group 23 minutes late. The second group was also a bit late, or they had possibly slowed down so as not to overtake us. Their bombs started dropping at 1225PM. This second group dropped their bombs from an altitude of 22,750 feet. It must have seemed to be one continuous series of explosions for at least four or five minutes on the ground.

The move that our squadron made to the left of the main group left our squadron quite vulnerable to German fighter aircraft attack. Our airplane ("Stardust" #25746) was the most exposed as we were on the farthest left side of our squadron formation. Our squadron was in the process of moving into what we called a "company front" formation immediately after we had completed our turn over the IP. This formation change meant that one of our squadron elements was moving to the right, and the other to the left of the leader of our squadron in order to get the widest coverage possible over our target. We were on the far left side of our element, which made us the farthest to the left of our squadron leader and also of the main group as we started our bomb run. This type of bombing formation, with the second and third element almost abreast of the leader of their squadron, made for the widest bomb drop pattern.

The first two enemy German fighters that we saw, were ME 109's coming towards us from the 11:30 position just slightly above us. They were in a shallow dive as they were firing at us, both doing a half-roll while still firing into us. The navigator was firing his gun on the left side of the nose of the airplane as he could see his target. As the German fighter planes came toward us, the hammering of the heavy twin 50's from the upper turret just above my head was deafening. The Germans passed just below us and they were now both completely inverted. We immediately realized that we had been hit in the #2 engine (that is the nearest to the fuselage on the left side of the airplane.) The oil pressure dropped on that engine and I ordered the engine to be "feathered." By pushing a red button on the instrument panel in front of us, we could turn the propeller blades on the damaged engine so that they offered no help or resistance to the flight and the engine could be stopped completely. I ordered the fuel and ignition to that engine to be turned off, and the engine was secured and was completely inoperative. When the propeller stopped, I could see a bullet hole in the blade that had stopped straight up and streamlined to our flight. The bullet had made a large hole and the rear part of the propeller blade was broken out, making it look something like an old fashioned horizontal keyhole.

We fell back and turned a bit to the left after the first attack. We increased the power on the three good engines and again made our way back into a good formation position in the squadron.

After we had completed our engine "shut down" and regained our position in the formation, the second German fighter attack began. This attack was made by two FW 190's on the same path (11:30) as the first fighter attack, but they started the attack slightly lower than our level. The FW-190's were in a shallow climb as they fired at us. I could clearly see the red blasts from their guns as they were firing them into us. They also did a half roll, still firing at us as they were passing beneath us. We could feel the bullets hitting the airplane and now our #1 engine was badly damaged. It was vibrating severely and we tried to "feather" that propeller but were unable to do so, apparently because of the damage to the engine. The engine RPM's on that engine went higher and higher and went off the scale and "ran wild." The engine was totally uncontrollable and was now on fire.

This engine was now of no help and was creating a heavy drag on that side of the aircraft. The spinning propeller was like a solid disk on the left wing, and this increased drag was turning us more and more to the left. We tried to position the control surface trim tabs to help us fly a straight course and to keep our wings level, but we ran out of trim tab control as they were now at their limits. We were turning slowly to the left and falling farther back from the protection of the squadron and losing altitude. Even with full power on engines #3 and #4, we were losing altitude and the squadron was leaving us far behind. I decided to lighten our load and pulled the red "bomb salvo" handle just to the left of my cockpit seat, which opened the bomb bay doors and released our twelve 500 lb bombs.

Dropping our bombs helped to decrease our rate of descent, but we still could not keep a straight course with full power on the engines on the right wing with the drag of the runaway propeller on the #1 engine. The bombardier was told to close the bomb doors to reduce the drag that they made, but it didn't seem to help much.

I was thinking of the long over water flight that we would have to make to get to Corsica when the third attack came. This was a single German FW 190 coming in from our right side. I saw it at the 1 o'clock position and just about at our level. Some of the bullets must have hit in the fuselage and also the underside of the right wing and the #3 engine. This engine, which was the nearest to the fuselage on the right wing, was still running, but the turbo-supercharger on the bottom of that engine was now inoperative and we could only get about 15 inches of manifold pressure out of that engine without the supercharger. This was about 1/3 of the maximum power that the #3 had been putting out before the third attack. The #4 engine was still undamaged and we were getting 45 inches of manifold pressure and 2550 RPM out of it, which was full rated power at that altitude. We were now sinking below 20,000 feet and still losing altitude. We could not keep the airplane going straight without reducing the power on the #4 engine and by increasing our airspeed, which increased our descent rate. This was definitely a "no win" situation.

I remember that the left waist gunner, at sometime in this encounter, said "Waist to pilot, #1 is really burning." The ball turret gunner said after the third attack that "there is white smoke coming out of the #3 engine." (This may have been raw fuel coming out of the damaged right wing fuel tanks.) I acknowledged by saying "Roger" to both. I was now most concerned about the #1 engine as I could see that it was burning fiercely and could feel the heavy vibration that the damaged engine was putting on the airplane. I was fearful that the left wing would separate from the airplane because of the fire and the vibration.

I made the decision at that point that we would have to leave the ship. The fact that we were on fire and with only 1 and 1/3rd engine power made it doubtful that we could even make the 220 miles (355 km) to the emergency airport at Ajjaccio, Corsica.

It was an easy decision to make, as I surely did not want the airplane to lose a wing or have to ditch into the Mediterranean. I rang the "bail out" bell and announced on the intercom system for everyone to "bail out" of the airplane. We were by now heading in a southeasterly direction, 90 degrees away from the bombing run course and far behind and several thousand feet below our squadron. My co-pilot and I were trying our best to keep the airplane straight and level.

After the second German fighter attack, my flight engineer/top turret gunner, S/Sgt. Edward Madigan, had notified me on the intercom that the upper gun turret was inoperative and that it would not move. He got out of the turret and snapped his parachute onto his harness. Bob Johnson and I had our parachute packs still stored on the left and right of our seats. When I said "bail out," S/Sgt. Madigan, with his parachute already snapped onto his harness, went to the escape hatch in the tunnel below the cockpit seats and tried to pull the pins that would release the bottom escape hatch. This was the escape hatch that all of us in the front of the airplane would normally use for our escape. Bob and I were both busy trying to level the airplane. We reduced power on #4 and got some amount of control by increasing our descent rate and increasing our airspeed.

Madigan couldn't get the hatch pins to release so he came back up into the cockpit, saying that he was going to the back of the airplane. That is the last time that we saw him. The navigator and bombardier came out of the front compartment and proceeded to tug hard and remove the pins holding the forward hatch door and it was jettisoned. I leaned to my right and looked down into the tunnel where the open hatch was located, and saw that the navigator was just sitting near the back edge of the opening and was hesitating to leave. I unbuckled my seat belt and stepped down into the tunnel and pushed the navigator (Walt) out. Ernie Jenkins, the bombardier, was kneeling just forward of the open exit and I stepped back and stood up to get back into the cockpit.

I had intended to get back into the pilot's seat, but before I did so, I reached across and grabbed my parachute pack and fastened it onto my harness. The co-pilot unfastened his seat belt and, as he already had his parachute snapped on his harness, indicated for me to go out and he would follow. I left the airplane thinking that Bob was right behind me.

I later learned that Bob Johnson had decided to again sit in his seat to attempt to level the wings one last time before jumping. Bob looked back through the airplane and seeing no one, and believing everyone else was gone, exited the aircraft through the open forward hatch. Bob later related to me that during this time he saw two enemy fighter planes coming in at our level on our right side. He thought that they had raked the airplane with bullets from the front to the back but by the Grace of God, he was not hit in this final attack and was the last to leave our great old bird.

187

In the meantime, the other enlisted crewmen that were assigned to their positions in the back of the airplane were able to "bail out." Sgt. Jim Hoskins was the last to leave from the back of the airplane, and he said that he saw no one else back there and was pretty sure that they had all gotten out.

That leaves the question of what happened to S/Sgt. Edward Madigan. He wasn't seen from the front or the rear of the airplane; we speculated later that he may have been hit by the enemy gunfire and that he fell from the cat walk into the closed, empty bomb bay area or in the radio room, which was not completely visible from either the front or the rear of the airplane. We will never know. He did not "bail out" and did not survive the airplane crash.

I was, apparently, the third crewmember to leave from the front of the airplane and Bob Johnson was the last to leave. This all happened very rapidly, of course.

As I dropped through the escape hatch, I had the sensation of the airplane passing over me and of my descending softly. I was falling on my back turning slowly in a horizontal attitude. I felt a sense of relief in being out of the doomed aircraft. Under my parachute harness I was wearing my yellow "Mae West" floatation life preserver. The top part of the life vest went over my shoulders and around my neck, flapping wildly. I reached up with both hands to hold it down. By turning my head to the left and right I could clearly see the ground, the coastline and "Stardust" going down on fire and in a steep spiral.

We had heard stories of the German pilots shooting at our crewmen as they were drifting down in their parachute, and I was determined to wait to open mine so that I could be as close to the ground as possible. I thought that I could wait until I was at or below 2000 feet before I needed to open the chute. Somewhere in this long "free fall," I looked at my wristwatch and remembered that it indicated that it was 1226. We had apparently spent at least eight or ten minutes from the time of the first enemy attack and the time that we had left the airplane, although it seemed to me to be a much shorter period of time than that. I must have given the orders to "bail out" a couple of minutes before our group actually released their bombs on the target.

In my "free fall," I began to see electrical transmission towers below me, and then on my next horizontal rotation I could clearly see the wires of the transmission lines. I decided that I was probably low enough and I pulled the handle of the "ripcord" that opened the parachute. It opened with a loud report that sounded much like a gun being fired over my head. Since I was on my back when the chest pack opened, it gave a great strain on my back. It was quite a jolt, much more severe than my ground contact.

When the "chute" opened, for an instant I felt as if I was going back up and then the sensation of falling slowly reappeared. As soon as the chute opened, I saw that I was turning slowly and oscillating, but was now on a vertical rather than a horizontal plane. I saw that I was going to land very close to the electrical transmission lines due to the strong wind drifting me toward the wires. I was afraid that I might be entangled in the high-tension lines.

I had been able to get a glimpse of the airplane finally going straight down while I was in the final stage of the "free fall," and it was burning brightly and trailing smoke. I knew that the airplane would crash between me and the coast and I felt that it would crash quite close to my landing place.

Just as I made the last turn in the parachute before my landing, I saw the airplane pass behind a hill followed by a bright flash as it exploded. Just like in the movies but a *lot* more disturbing. I had missed the wires on my last forward swing and then landed heavily on my back against the rocky hillside. I then heard the noise of the explosion of the airplane crash. I again looked at my wristwatch and it was 1229.

I have since estimated that I probably opened the parachute at between 2,000 and 2,500 feet altitude above the ground. The last altitude that I had seen in the cockpit when I stood up to snap my parachute into place was 19,000 feet, so I believe that I left the airplane at about 18,500 feet. My "free fall" was at least 16,000 feet. It has been calculated that my free fall probably took almost 1½ minutes. The free fall was a wonderfully soft feeling, probably something like being weightless, and was marred only by the flapping action of the life vest.

As soon as I stood up, I saw an automobile passing about a kilometer or more distant on a road somewhat above my position and on a bluff above me. The automobile was between my position and the smoke of the crashed airplane. In looking at recent maps of this area, this would appear to be the road that parallels the ancient Roman road or ancient Roman aqueduct (see the map in the picture section). The automobile was traveling in a southeast direction and didn't stop. The occupant or occupants of the auto were probably looking at the smoke from the downed airplane. No doubt absorbed by the crash, I doubt that they even saw me land in the barren and rocky area. I tried to count the number of parachutes that I could still see in the air although they were quite far away; I counted five or six for sure. I felt then that perhaps not all of my crew had escaped the airplane.

The parachute had caught in some thorny brush, making it difficult to gather up and bury. I wanted to hide it and my lifejacket and other gear that I was to leave behind but there were only bushes and rocks all around. Finally, I stowed it all under the largest bush that I could find and covered it with rocks.

I knew that "Stardust" had crashed between my position and the coast, so I ran and walked with my back to the smoke of the crash to put distance between me, and the heavily fortified coast of southern France.

After passing under the electric transmission lines, I started to climb a steep and rocky hillside and found that I was soon quite exhausted. I sat down and started to pray for my deliverance from the enemy and gave thanks for my survival from the doomed airplane. I finally caught my breath and then noted that I still had my fur-lined flying boots on, which were quite heavy and part of the cause of my exhaustion. I took them off and tied the thongs together and carried the boots around my neck. I was wearing my regular shoes under the flight boots so now it was much easier going.

I had the impression that I was walking generally north or northeast. I still had the smoke from the burning aircraft as a check of my desired direction. (I didn't think to check my direction with the little compass in my escape kit.) I soon left the barren rocky area and entered a spread of woods. The walking was much easier here than on the steep and rocky hillside.

I eventually heard the sound of someone using an axe, which sounded like someone either chopping wood or cutting a tree down. As I got closer to the sound, I could hear several men talking but I couldn't see them. Their voices didn't sound like they were speaking French but more like German to me. I was somewhat familiar with French, as we had been stationed near Tunis before moving up to Italy. I thought that if they were Germans, they were probably gathering firewood. I made a large detour around this area so I wouldn't be detected.

I soon passed a small stream where I washed my face and hands and filled the small bladder from my escape kit with water. I moved away from the stream and sat where I didn't think that I could be observed and surveyed the content of my escape kit. I also checked my pockets for any unwanted items just in case I was captured. I had several condoms in my flight suit knee pocket and I discarded them. I probably shouldn't have, as they could have served as extra drinking water storage bladders later if I needed them.

I was hungry, having not eaten since breakfast, but at least I had water. I continued through the woods until I passed near a small farm. A dog barked at me but no one came out to see why the dog was barking. With the exception of the men chopping wood and the barking dog, it was a silent world. There was no traffic noise, no sound of anyone engaged in any activity. I continued across a dirt road into another wooded area for some distance, and sat down to try to figure out what to do next. After I had "bailed out" and started my trek across the French countryside, I had been mostly just thankful that I had gotten out of the burning airplane alive and that I was still free and not an instant POW.

I was now beginning to realize what a serious situation that I was in. I didn't want to spend the rest of the war in a POW camp and I firmly decided to remain free as long as I possibly could. It started to get dark early that time of the year and I was thinking of where to spend the night. I sat there and again prayed that I wouldn't be captured and gave thanks for my escape from the burning airplane.

I remembered that I had seen a haystack in a field not too near the house and barn where I had encountered the barking dog. I decided to backtrack to that area and hide in the haystack as soon as it was dark. I found the farm again and circled behind it to get in the haystack where I couldn't be seen from the house. I put my flying boots on my feet again to keep my feet warm, and took a good drink from the water bladder and settled in and tried to go to sleep.

I slept some of the time, but mostly I was cold and miserable all through the night. I wanted to remain free from capture but I felt that any chance of escaping from France was quite remote. Since I was from the 15th Air Force in Italy, I knew of no one who had been able to escape from France. At this time, I knew nothing of the escape routes that had enabled some of the 8th Air Force airmen based in England to be routed out of France by the French Resistance people. I lay there in the haystack thinking that I would just avoid capture as long as possible. I was worried that when I tried to leave the haystack in the morning I would wake the dog and would be seen and reported. This, thankfully, did not happen.

Early the next morning, January 28th, I decided to return to the stream and refill the water pouch and wash my face and hands. After filling my pouch, I started to follow the stream. Soon, I came to a small walk bridge over the stream, which I used to cross over and then followed a path that was still taking me in a general northeasterly direction. I soon came to a hill on my right that was partly covered with trees and shrubs, and I started to climb the hill to see what was on the other side. When I reached the summit I could see cultivated land in a narrow valley below. Grape orchards lined both sides of the valley. There was a large home at the far end of the valley with several large outbuildings near it. A road down the middle of the valley led to several smaller homes spaced on each side of the road. I assumed that these smaller homes were for the workers or tenants who took care of the grape vines and probably worked for the people in the large house at the head of the valley.

While still in the shelter of the trees and shrubs, I crept down the hill and sat there for some time watching a man working in the vineyard nearest to me. There was a low rock-wall dividing the vineyard from the rocky hillside.

When the man had worked his way to the end of the row, I stood up and came the short distance down the hill to the rock wall. I could see that he was startled to see me and while he appeared to be as large as a man, it was apparent that he was really just a boy. He could tell that I was in the military by the way that I was dressed, as I was still in my flight suit and heavy fur-lined jacket with my rank and wings sewn on the jacket. He just stood there as I tried to tell him, in my halting try at the French language, that I was hungry, thirsty, and that I was an American.

Without a word he dropped his tools and ran toward the nearest house, which I took to be where he lived. I retreated back up the hill where I wasn't so exposed but where I felt that I could still be seen from the small house.

   Soon a man and a woman carrying a basket emerged from the house and hurried up to the vineyard wall where I was now standing. The man and woman shook hands with me and through a French-English translation dictionary that they had brought, they did their best to converse with me. The first word that they pointed out was the translated word friend (ami). They then pointed to the French/English word for resistance, followed by the word safe. I now knew that I was with friends. I watched as the lady spread a thin blanket or tablecloth out on the ground near the rock wall. She opened the basket and took out three wine glasses and a long loaf of bread, a roll of hard sausage, and some hard cheese. The man had brought along two bottles of wine from which he generously poured. My "hostess" cut the bread, the sausage, and cheese and we each took some. I started to take out my pouch of water but the man indicated no water, just wine. I enjoyed the wine and ate quite a bit of the sausage, as well as the cheese and bread. I was very hungry and ate hurriedly as they watched me. This may have been too early for their noon meal and they seemed content to see me fill up.

   The Frenchman and his wife continued to look up words in the dictionary so that we could communicate. He finally told me through this method that I should stay there until dark and that someone would come to take me to a place where I would be safe. I gratefully thanked them for their kindness as they smiled and shook my hand.

   They had left the basket with the leftovers from lunch for me to eat in the afternoon. I went back up to the place where they could see me but I wasn't so exposed, and sat down to rest and wait. Later on, I ate what was left of the lunch and finished off the rest of the wine. I felt very encouraged by what had happened and extremely appreciative to these wonderful people.

   In the afternoon sun, I had begun to fall asleep but was awakened by the tinkling of a sheep bell. There was a flock of sheep grazing all around me. I sat up as the sheepherder passed within 30 or 40 feet of me on the hillside. He saw me but did not stop or make any indication that he was curious about me.

As it became near dark, I took the basket and the empty wine bottle and moved down near the rock wall to the place where we had eaten earlier. In a few minutes, two men came out of the little house and came up the long row of vines to where I was waiting. One was the man that I had met earlier. He was accompanied by a man I was to learn later was his brother. They had come to take me to a safer place. They indicated that I was to come with them. We stopped off at the house to leave the basket and I also left my fur-lined flying boots in the house. I thought that I would not need them anymore and was glad to be rid of the load. The man of the house took time to look up a few words for me. He indicated that I was to follow them quietly and that I would be safe. I then had a chance to thank the lady and their son, who I judged was probably 14 or 15 years old, for their kindness. She gave me a kiss on both cheeks and we were off.

We walked through the vineyards, over another fairly steep hill, and through even more vineyards. It was very hard walking through the vineyards at night, as the dormant vines caught on our clothes and we often stumbled. We came to a main road and the brother went on ahead to see if there was any traffic or anyone to be seen on the road. He whistled softly that it was clear and we hurried on across. We crossed another large vineyard and came to a lane leading up to a large house. One of the brothers went up to the house while the other brother and I hid behind the trees lining the lane. Again there was a whistle and we moved toward the house. The shades were drawn and it looked almost dark from the outside. When we entered, however, it was surprisingly well lit inside. Seven or 8 people were waiting to greet us.

It was warm inside and I took off my heavy flight jacket and flight suit coveralls for the first time since the morning of January 27th. I still had my officer's gray gabardine pants and shirt on that I had worn beneath my flight gear on the morning of my last combat mission. The military insignia on my shirt indicated that I was an officer and the silver wings identified that I was a pilot.

Some of the people in the greeting party spoke a little English, and I was able to convey to them that I had been shot down the day before on the raid on Salon de Provence airdrome. I had a nearly full pack of American cigarettes in my shirt pocket and was able to pass them around to all who wished to smoke. It was probably after 9 PM by the time that we arrived and the women had prepared a fine dinner for us. First there was a wine glass toast to my survival and then I toasted them for their kindness.

The women set before us a dinner of fried rabbit with oven-browned potatoes and a spinach casserole, followed by cookies and apples for dessert. The wine flowed freely all through the meal, and after the dessert there was a kind of colorless, thick, and sweet liqueur for an after-dinner drink.

Later, I was given some civilian clothes and told to take my uniform off and dress as a civilian. I went into a bedroom and changed clothes. I kept only my two-piece "long johns" underwear, my socks, shoes, wristwatch, and dog tags. The dog tags hung around my neck on a chain and were worn under my shirt. They identified me as a U.S. Air Corps officer and included my identification number.

All of my uniform clothes, my officer's insignia and wings, along with the flight jacket and flight suit and escape kit, were given to my hosts as souvenirs, or to their guests or others assisting the Resistance. I also gave them what was left of my cigarettes and my Zippo lighter, which had a military insignia on it. They asked me if I had a gun or had hidden a gun somewhere that they could retrieve. I informed them that I wasn't carrying a sidearm on my mission that day. It had been our option whether to be armed on a mission or not and we, as a crew, had decided against including guns on any of our missions.

The clothes that they had given me were a pair of dark trousers and a plain black belt in place of my uniform belt, which had a buckle with the propeller and wings insignia on it. I was given a long-sleeve shirt and a French navy-issue sweater, which we call a "turtleneck." This sweater was warm and heavy and proved to be very comfortable when outdoors. The next morning, I was also given a heavy navy-type Pea coat with ordinary buttons, and a heavy black knit cap that could be pulled down over my ears if it was cold enough to be necessary.

The only thing of my new attire that stood out as odd was the pair of brown shoes that I was wearing. I wanted to keep my shoes so they said that the Resistance would have them dyed black before long. I asked if anything was known of my crew and they said that they hadn't heard that any others had escaped, although they knew that many had parachuted out. They also told me that several of the German fighter planes had been shot down. I asked where the bombs that I had dropped to lighten the airplane had landed and they said they didn't know.

Everyone said goodbye at about midnight and left me with the homeowners, my new hosts. I was shown to the bedroom where I had changed my clothes. There was a modern bathroom across the hallway from my bedroom, and I was provided with a toothbrush and I made ready for bed. A flannel nightgown was provided but I elected to sleep in my long underwear instead. I later wished I'd taken advantage of the night-wear offered, as I was to sleep in those same "long johns" for many nights to come. The bed had a feather mattress and a feather pillow. I immediately sank into both for a good night's sleep.

At about eight the next morning, my hostess knocked and came in with a tray on which there was one soft-boiled egg in an egg cup, and several slices of bread and jam. She apologized for the coffee as she said that it was "ersatz," whatever that meant. I occasionally drank coffee in the military that was very nearly as bad as the coffee served to me that morning. I nevertheless assured her that the coffee was fine. All of this happened to me in less than 48 hours and was a tremendous experience. I was pleased that nearly everyone that I had met the night before, including my hosts, spoke at least a little English, and I understood most of what they were trying to tell me. Pantomime and French/English were sufficient. Many of the French that I met had studied some English in high school. I now wished I had learned French.

After breakfast and shaving that morning, I felt pretty good. I had understood the night before that someone from the Resistance would come and get me and I would go with them to a safe place. It seemed impossible to me that I had spent my first night in France in a haystack, cold and scared. By the next day, I had enjoyed a picnic lunch in the afternoon, and later that evening had a fine dinner with friends. Then to "top it off" a restful night's sleep in a real feather bed and pampered with breakfast in bed the next morning. What a contrast. This seemed like a dream. (A nightmarish, somehow surreal "good/bad dream".) Could Hollywood top this?

I had asked several times if they knew how many of my crew members had parachuted out of the plane. I was told that they thought that at least 6 or 7 parachutes had been seen floating down. I now thought that most of my crew had safely escaped the doomed airplane.

After I had dressed in my new clothes the next morning, the host wanted to show me around his large estate. There were numerous tenant homes bordering his fields. He had a nice fruit orchard, and hidden away in one corner was at least a dozen cages for rabbits. I knew then, more than likely, the rabbits that we had eaten at dinner the night before had come from those same rabbit hutches. He told me that the Germans didn't know that he was keeping the rabbits and he seemed quite proud of that fact. He told me again that in the afternoon, someone would come for me and that I would be moved to a safer place.

After a late lunch, perhaps at 2:30, three men came for me in a small covered van. I was instructed to ride in the back with one of the fellows. I noted that my companion had a small machine gun by his side as we rode. This van was a strange vehicle as it had a tank standing in a vertical position on the left side near the engine, ahead and to the left of the driver's seat. The engine of the van was powered by a charcoal fire in the bottom of the vertical tank. Apparently it was powered by lighting the fuel and using the gas emitted from the burning charcoal as fuel for the engine. I have never quite figured out how this little car actually was powered. It didn't seem to me that it was powered by steam. I had never seen anything like it before (or since). I do know that it didn't have very much power, as the two of us in the back had to get out and push several times to help it get over the hills. This is how I left the Salon-de-Provence area and headed to the region around and east of Aix-en-Provence.

CHAPTER 8

THE MAQUIS AND MARCEL

After we left the Salon de Provence area, I was driven to a section that I believed to be near the city of Aix-en-Provence. We stopped at dusk at a commercial garage, which was closed for the night. This was Saturday, the 29th of January. We went through the darkened garage and into a lighted office near the rear of the building. There were four people in the office waiting for us.

I was invited to sit in one of the office chairs and was greeted by everyone with a handshake. A small box of cookies was passed around. Before I could eat one, I dropped the cookie on the very dirty floor. I started to toss it in the wastebasket, intending to get another. One of the men stopped me with a loud "non," and promptly brushed off the dirt and handed it to me to eat, which I did. Lesson learned - we do not waste anything here.

One of the people waiting for me in the garage office spoke excellent English, and she had some questions to ask me and wrote down my answers. Although I did not realize it, she was apparently questioning me to compare my information with other known facts that she or someone else had obtained. She questioned me as to my name, rank and serial number, my hometown in the U.S.A., my squadron and group number, where I was based, and from where I had taken off on the mission. She asked me to list the other men on my crew on this mission and I was able to give her the names. She asked if I was the pilot and I replied "yes." Then she requested the names of

STARDUST FALLING

the American hometowns of any other crewmembers that I could recall.

I provided answers to everything that I could, and she left with her clipboard accompanied by one of the men who had driven me from Salon. He returned alone in a few minutes and indicated that we would leave. I had asked the lady if she knew of any others of my crew that were still not taken prisoner. She said that she didn't, and perhaps this was true. I asked her if anyone had been killed in the crash of our airplane, and she said that she didn't know that either. Although I didn't know it at the time, I was apparently being judged from my answers as to whether I was who I said I was, or if I was a German plant inserted to trap the Resistance. If they had any doubt as to my authenticity, the men who were transporting me would surely have executed me as soon as we were out of the area.

It was pitch dark by this time, and we drove in the little charcoal-powered van for some distance. There were only two of the armed men now, one of whom rode in the back with me and I soon found out the reason. Every so often we would come to a hill that the little van would not have enough power to conquer. My protector would set his machine gun on his bench seat and raise the back canvas while we got out and pushed the van over the hill, then run to catch up and jump back in.

After a period of time, we turned off on a side road and started up a fairly steep hill. We again jumped out and pushed until we ended up parking at a house, which appeared to be unoccupied. They led me to the door and, upon entering, made sure that all the blinds were closed before the lights were turned on. The house was furnished quite well and appeared to be a vacation or summer home. I knew that we were in the mountains and that there was a creek very near the house, as I could hear running water. We had something to eat, but it was not nearly as good as the scrumptious dinner I had eaten the night before. I was just trying to figure out where to sleep when another man whistled from outside and was let in. He too had a machine gun and seemed to be the boss. He greeted me and apparently gave orders for one of the men to stoke up the charcoal burner on the van, and it was apparent that someone was to use it that night.

It was at least 10:30 when the boss first spoke to me in English. He said, "Come with us" and told me to get back in the van with them. There were three of them plus myself this time. Each of them had their Sten guns with them, as we got in the van and drove for some distance, mostly down hill. After getting the little van over one big hill, we coasted through the valley below and into a little village making the least noise possible. They parked the little van in an alley behind a brick building. The night was quite dark. The boss man, who had been riding in the front seat, and the one sitting in the back with me, got out carrying their machine guns and left the driver and me in the van. Within minutes, they came back carrying a box, which they put in the back of the van, and my companions and I drove out of the area nearly as quietly as we had come. I thought that they had picked up supplies for the hideout.

We retraced our route, getting out and pushing the little van when necessary. We were now on the main road, which we had to travel for a mile or more before turning off to the vacation hideout. An automobile came up fast behind us. The man in back of the van with me peaked out through a small hole in the back canvas and said just one word, "Gestapo." I knew exactly what he meant. I knew these men would not be taken without a shootout and was really frightened. Through the back window of the cab of the van I could see that our driver was waving his arm out the driver's-side window, shouting something that sounded like "passay, passay." I was sure that he was signaling the big car to pass us, which it did. It was soon out of sight ahead of us, much to our relief.

We turned in at our side road and onto our lane, and then began the long uphill climb to the house. We again had to push all of the way up the lane to the house, but tonight the three of us had the pushing duty and it was not nearly as hard as it had been earlier in the evening.

When we entered the blacked-out house, the lights were turned on and the box that we had gone out for was opened. It wasn't a large box but it contained food ration coupon books - many, many of them. The three men were overjoyed at their haul. They apparently had stolen the coupon books from some village town hall, and would use them for themselves and give to Resistance helpers. At first I was disgusted that they had taken me on this dangerous mission. I felt that they wanted to show me some of their bravado. It may have been that they didn't want to leave me alone in the house unattended and unprotected. In any case, I was tired and they made a bed for me on a short couch.

My three companions of the evening, who I was later to learn were the Maquis, each retired to a room and as usual, carried their Sten gun as their sleeping partner. In the morning there was bread and a chunk of cheese and jam for breakfast, in addition to what was again called "ersatz" coffee. It was black and bitter and in no way resembled coffee at all. I think it was made from burnt oats and chicory, and perhaps a *hint* of coffee bean.

The leader took me outside in the morning to show me around. The home was quite substantial with a walled-in courtyard that at one time had well-tended gardens. It was probably vacant in the winter months and could be used as a hideout for the Maquis.

A gurgling creek flowed under a small bridge in the walkway to the house. This running water was the source of the sound I had heard the evening before when we approached the house in the dark. The little van was parked in the drive in the courtyard and was fairly well hidden. I had a chance to inspect the little van in the daylight. It seemed to be powered by gas fumes coming from the charcoal fire directly below the upright tank. The tank stored the fumes to be metered to the engine to power the auto. This whole contraption

THE MAQUIS AND MARCEL

looked like a small hot water heater in a home. It was about one foot in diameter and perhaps three feet tall. It was located on the left running board ahead and to the left of the driver. In retrospect, this auto may have been steam powered, but I didn't think so at the time and have continued to wonder about this mysterious contraption.

(Upon doing a little internet research for this book, regarding the "van" with the strange charcoal burning engine, I believe it might have been a "producer gas" type of contraption. These were popular in Europe in the late 1930's and early '40's due to the almost non-availability of gasoline. "Producer gas" is made by sucking a small amount of air through a bed of red-hot carboniferous fuel, such as charcoal, in a closed furnace, called a generator. The result, after a series of intricate chemical reactions, is carbon monoxide. This then, can be mixed with about the same amount of air and burned in an internal combustion engine, much the same way as gasoline. If you wish to read further, a most informative web site can be found at: (www.motherearthnews.com).

The leader said that someone would come and get me that morning and would take me to another place where I would be safer. This was Sunday morning, January 30th. At about 9:30 AM, a car arrived with two men to pick me up. I was introduced to them and both newcomers spoke a little English. The driver of the auto, Jean Juvenile, conversed at length with the Maquis leader, who I later learned was his younger brother. The young leader had been a lawyer in Aix-en-Provence and was now in hiding. Jean, the older brother who was to transport me that day, was a court recorder in the city of Aix-en-Provence and was one of the Resistance leaders in the area.

I said goodbye to my Maquis friends and climbed into a spacious, four-door automobile. We drove down the lane and side road, and onto the main road heading away from the house. From the main road, due to the trees, I could hardly see the house where I had spent the night. We drove for a distance east or northeast and the terrain was quite hilly, like the foothills of some further mountains. We finally turned off the main road and up a side road. We entered a long lane to a farmyard that was situated at the base of a steep bluff. We got out of the car and greeted the farmer. This Sunday morning, the stillness and quiet of the day was broken only by the church bells ringing in the distance.

The farmer led us to a corral in back of the barn where he had tethered two donkeys loaded with sacks and a small keg was perched on top of one of the packs. Both animals looked grossly overloaded. The farmer and a friend led the way with the pack animals. We three, Jean Juvenile, his friend who he introduced as Pierre, and I followed along up the steep and winding path. It took an hour, or so it seemed, of climbing with a number of switchbacks to make it to the top of the bluff. When we reached the top, we paused to catch our breath, and it was there that I was told in broken English, by Jean and Pierre, that I would soon meet up with some of my crewmembers. They didn't tell me who or how many. After our climb up the bluff, the terrain flattened out somewhat and we were following a path through the trees and brush.

After some time of walking, still following the donkeys and their leaders, we came to a clearing where our group paused. We were to wait for another group coming by a different path. When the new group of people arrived, I was reunited with my crewmembers - Bob Johnson, Ernie Jenkins, and Joe Kinnane. Of course we were overjoyed to see each other and asked a lot of questions as we proceeded along a new path. We now made up a single group of seven or eight, including the guides with the animals. Several of the fellows guiding my companions had turned back when we finally connected. In this same clearing, we were told by Jean Juvenile that one of our crew had died in the crash and that he would find out his name.

THE MAQUIS AND MARCEL

It wasn't too far, perhaps a mile or so along the path, when we came to a stone building situated on a hillside. This farmhouse had two levels - the lower level of the house was the home of the animals (in this case, sheep.) The upper level, which was at ground level in the front, was the farmhouse living quarters. This was where we were to live with the sheepherder, whom we knew only as Marcel Berger'. Only later did we learn that, in French, Berger' meant sheepherder, so as far as we knew his name was only Marcel (pronounced, Marseal).

The pack animals were unloaded. The two very large sacks on the one animal turned out to contain straw and two heavy blankets for our bedding. The keg on top of this pack was the wine for us and for Marcel. The other pack animal carried a sack each of potatoes, beans, long French bread, and another smaller sack with a round of cheese wrapped in gauze and a couple of jars of homemade preserves.

The farmhouse had one large room that was probably 12 feet wide and 15 feet long. It had a large fireplace at the one end. The fireplace took up most of the 12-foot width of this end of the room. A doorway at the opposite end of this room led to a kitchen, which was probably 6 by 8 feet. Another doorway out of the main room led to a small area that was used for storage. This room had probably been the bedroom for the farm couple. It would also have been about 6 by 8 feet. The walls were of stone, inside as well as out, keeping the temperature evenly cold and suitable for Marcel to store the covered portions of freshly slaughtered quarters of mutton for his and now, our meals. There was an old wooden front door and a dusty window that looked out front onto the path to the house. There was a small window in the kitchen that was at the back of the house and overlooked the sheep pen and the watering trough. A door in the kitchen opened to stone steps that led down to the sheep pen and the back of the structure.

The sheep were housed at night in an area of about 12 by 20 feet and there were thick stone walls that not only made the foundation for the building above, but walled in the sheep area. On one end of the sheep enclosure there was a bench of stone running along the wall, about 2 ½ feet wide and about 3 feet high, and it was here that Marcel slept at night.

If the house still had a decent roof it would have been quite adequate. The problem was that for us to sleep in the only room with a fireplace for heat we had no roof. At least we had no roof over the end with the fireplace. Only the ridgepole was left after an obvious fire had gutted that end of the abode. A patchwork of old blackened tiles remained over the part of the room nearest the kitchen. At some time after the fire, the area above the kitchen had been covered with corrugated metal, and while dry, it was always cold.

On our first night out in our mountain hideout with Marcel, we investigated what the pack animals had brought for the four of us. Two of the sacks contained straw for bedding. There were two heavy blankets that we were to share. We tried to arrange the straw and blankets close enough to the fireplace to get some of the heat. After a dismal first night, we figured out that we couldn't sleep close enough to the fireplace without some adjustments. We found four poles near the house that probably were to be used by someone to make rafters for a roof repair, that never had been done. We used the poles to line the area in front of the fireplace into a box square, and then put all the straw in this box. We kept it far enough away from the fireplace to keep the embers from igniting the straw and destroying our bed. We tried to stoke enough fire in the pit for heat and light at night, such as it was. The winter was quite cold, especially at night, and there was often a skim of ice on the sheep's drinking trough in the morning.

We started out putting one blanket on the straw and the other over us, but sleeping this way was just impossible; the two on the outside were freezing cold while the two in the middle were warm enough. We decided to sleep on the straw and have a blanket for two rather than four. This worked out much better. On several of the evenings,

THE MAQUIS AND MARCEL

we had to move the straw into the tiny roofed kitchen to sleep because there was rain falling, which later turned to a dusting of snow.

Although I was the senior member of the crew, we dropped all thought of rank and were just four guys in a mess together. We shared the chores equally and tried to stay upbeat. We were on a first name basis with the exception of Joe Kinnane. We all simply called him Joe while he insisted on calling us Lieutenant, with a long emphasis on the "Loo." I never heard him address me as Wes or Wesley during the entire ordeal. It was always "Loo-tenant."

Most of Marcel's dry food supplies were kept in a small overhead cabinet in the kitchen. This was to protect them from the mice and rats We prepared the food in the kitchen but all of the cooking was done in the fireplace. We also placed a pot beside the fire inside the fireplace to have some warm water for washing and cleaning our eating utensils. The pots and pans were difficult to keep clean. There was a large black iron pot and a smaller tin pot, and a large iron frying pan with a long handle. There were adequate eating utensils with cups or mugs and assorted plates, some china, and some tin. There was a rack in the fireplace that was used to put the iron pot close to the fire so that we could heat water before we started to cook the mutton and beans and potatoes. Ernie Jenkins was the official cook and we all tried to help him as best that we could. Marcel would sometimes snare rabbits on his daily trek with the sheep. When we had rabbits for supper, we fried them in the long-handled skillet, although we had a limited supply of olive oil to use for frying.

Marcel would use snares to catch the wild rabbits and he seemed to have some skill at this endeavor. He brought the rabbits home when he returned with the sheep in the afternoon. The dead rabbits were kept in the deep pockets of his ankle-length overcoat, which was as filthy as the rest of his clothes. He would usually get a basin of cold water out of the sheep trough when he returned in the afternoon and try to wash his hands and face, but they never seemed to be really clean. And of course, his clothes smelled of sheep and dirt. When we would eat, he would take off his overcoat and beneath it he had a dirty sweater and baggy pants.

His hair was long and shaggy and looked like it had never been combed. Several of his front teeth were missing. I would judge his age to be about 50 but his appearance defied any accurate determination of age. He was about 6 feet tall and was of a rather thin build. He had a sallow-type face with a stubble beard. I don't know how he kept the beard or stubble short, as there were no scissors or razors anywhere to be found. He did have a couple of very sharp knives, one of which he carried on his belt. I suppose he could have somehow shaved with his knife. He would use it to skin and cut up the rabbits before we fried them, so we often speculated that he dry-shaved his face in the same manner. Who really knew?

He would bring us chunks of rock salt that he would break off from a salt lick that was located somewhere on his route with the sheep. This would be in his dirty pockets along with the dead rabbits or whatever else was in there. We would scrape off the worst of the dirt and try to get down to white salt, and then crush it up as fine as we could to use as seasoning for our beans and potatoes, mutton, or rabbit. For the first few days, Marcel had a decent supply of mutton stored away so we could put some bone and meat in the pot with the beans and potatoes. Rabbit was always a welcome change from the mutton.

For breakfast we had bread and sharp Roquefort cheese, along with preserves. We soon ran out of the preserves for our morning bread, but always had a supply of the cheese. The Roquefort was an acquired taste, but I learned to enjoy the *bite* of this delicacy. Jean Juvenile told us that the Roquefort came from a dairy farm locally, and that the farmer cured it in a cave near us. It truly had a sharp bite and I have always enjoyed Roquefort cheese from then to this day.

THE MAQUIS AND MARCEL

    We had wine every evening with our supper, often a couple of glasses. Marcel would try to educate us in French with a few words. He would go and shut the door and say something like "famay la port." Little things such as this helped us recognize his commands. One that threw us though, until Joe Kinnane figured it out, was "pid-pore." He used this when he was mad at us or he thought we had done something wrong. We thought it was French for something bad, but Joe thought he was saying, "piss-poor." When we used those words, he brightened up and we were sure that he had heard it from our American troops in WWI. We tried some other "bad" words and sayings of the GI's of WWI, and he would repeat them and smile and slap his leg. Finally, we had found a kind of common language that we all understood, even though it was pretty vulgar at times. When he would come in from herding the sheep, and having no "lapins" (rabbits) for us for supper, we would say "piss-poor" and he would start in a tirade of half French and half WWI words that would convey to us we could "go to hell" as far as he was concerned.

    On Thursday afternoon of the first week, we got into the wine and drank it all. We were loud and noisy and enjoying ourselves immensely when he returned with the sheep. To say he was "pid-off" would have been putting it mildly. He berated us for making so much noise and said that we would alert the "Bosch" (Germans) of our presence. Most disgustingly, we didn't have a drop of wine for that night or the next until a new supply arrived on Saturday. He was sad, sorry, and angry with us. I am sure that he would have kicked us all out if he could. He stayed grumpy until they brought out more wine with the usual supplies on Saturday.

    We ate two meals a day - breakfast after he had left with the sheep, and supper when he got home with the sheep and had put them away for the night.

    We were running out of mutton at the start of the second week of our stay. The Resistance people made arrangements with the owner

211

of the sheep to have Marcel slaughter one of his charges to supply meat for us.

On this day, he delayed taking the sheep out in the morning to select one that was to be slaughtered. He had a hard time selecting which one it would be. He finally picked one of the oldest, scraggliest, dirtiest ones in the flock to be killed. He tied the sheep up, front and back legs, and had Joe help him drag it out in the yard and down the hill a bit to a tree-lined area. Then, with Joe holding the sheep down, Marcel cut its throat and hoisted the carcass vertical from a tree limb.

Marcel sharpened his knife and began skinning the carcass, laying the hide and wool aside, I assume to be scraped and cured later. Next he cut off the head and disemboweled the carcass.

He then did a strange thing. He got a bucket and drew water from the sheep trough, rolled up his sweater and shirt sleeves, and surprised us by washing his hands and arms thoroughly - something we had *never* seen him do prior to this. He went back into the house and brought out a package tied with string containing several clean white cloths, each about a meter or more square. He cleared an area on the grass and carefully laid out the sheets.

He began to cut up the carcass and lay each piece on a clean sheet. When he had the proper amount on a sheet, he would carefully wash his hands again and fold and tie each bundle. He kept ten muttonchops out for our night's dinner, with instructions not to put them in the bean and potatoes stew pot. After the work was over, we helped him take the bundles back to the house and put them on a shelf in the cold storeroom.

Before he left to tend his flock for the day, Marcel instructed us to dig a hole to bury the remains and off he went. That evening when he returned, he told us to build up a good fire in the fireplace. When he was ready to cook the muttonchops, he spread the glowing coals from the fireplace on the hearth and put the muttonchops directly on the

THE MAQUIS AND MARCEL

coals. Ernie sprinkled them with salt and when they were seared on one side, Marcel picked them up with his fingers and turned them over. When he decided that they had cooked enough, he took them off the coals and put two on each plate. We picked each chop up by our fingers and, using our fork, dusted off the charcoal and ash, and then they were ready to eat. They were truly delicious and really memorable. With beans and potatoes, the fresh chops made for a really good and filling supper, with wine and bread, of course. If we were still hungry after each evening meal, which we weren't that night, we would dip our bread into the remaining juice from the beans and potatoes and fill up that way. Food was never to be wasted.

After our first few days we had settled down to a pretty good routine. We were kept busy every day foraging for dead, dry wood. We decided that we should burn no green wood so as to keep the amount of smoke from the fireplace chimney to a minimum. We usually would go in two's foraging for dry limbs to burn each day. We would stop and listen often to hear the noise of anyone else in the woods. Sometimes we would hear the other two, on they're foraging, cracking a limb into pieces that they could carry. We commented on the fact that we had to be as quiet as was possible.

The water that was fed into the sheep trough was alright for washing but was not drinkable. On our first day with Marcel, he had shown us the path to the nearest well that had acceptable drinking water. It was more than a quarter of a mile from the house and slightly down from our elevation. I think perhaps that the well was spring-fed and it looked ancient. We had to be very careful descending along the path to it, as it was sometimes slippery. We needed water for drinking and cooking, so two of us would make the trek each day and carry one bucket each back to the house. There was a rope tied to a log over the well opening and, with our bucket tied to the rope, we would lower it down to fill. The well was only partially covered so it had lots of leaves and twigs in it, which would come up with the water, and we would fish out the debris on our way back. We circled around the well as we approached, and left it so we wouldn't kick dirt in it, and also because there was the danger of sliding into the well from the high side.

We picked up dry leaves each day and tried to roll them for our smokes. We had a supply of cigarette papers, and no matter how futile, it was worth a try. Sometimes we would get a gift of a cigarette from a Resistance visitor. Someone had supplied each of us with a small, thin tin box, like an "Altoid" box. We put our cigarette butts in the box. The boxes were called "meego" boxes, or so it sounded to us, and forever became the name we called them.

On one nice day during our second week, we were sitting under some trees on the hillside. The four of us watched the ME-109's takeoff and land at the auxiliary airfield in the valley below us, when a German JU-88 came in very low over the trees where we were sitting. Being early February, the trees were quite bare and we were immediately afraid that we had been spotted. As soon as the airplane passed over us, we took off running for the safety of the house. We didn't build a large fire in the fireplace that day, or the next for that matter, until we needed it for cooking, for fear of attracting a German patrol. This JU-88 incident shook our confidence as to our safety deep in the woods. We were much more wary of our movements and of our surroundings after this incident. The Resistance people kept telling us the Germans wouldn't dare mount a patrol in this mountain territory, but we weren't as certain about that so we became much more cautious.

We had become quite adjusted to our daily routine. Although we slept in our clothes and were dirty all of the time, we did have a fair supply of soap and with the water from the sheep trough, we could heat water by setting the iron bucket near the fireplace. We kept a fire burning in the fireplace continually. The water for the sheep trough came from an artesian source near the house. It was gravity fed

THE MAQUIS AND MARCEL

through a rusty old iron pipe. Thankfully, we could draw our water before it went into the trough where the sheep drank. The overflow water from the trough ran in a small stream, down the hill away from the house. On good, warm days we would strip down and lather up and try to keep clean. Our hair was getting pretty long and we grew beards, especially Joe Kinnane, who had dark hair and quite a growth of facial hair. I was the most fortunate, having light hair and only fuzz on my face, but not enough to call it a beard.

Sometimes, Bob Johnson and I would venture further down the hillside to where we could see the German fighter planes practicing takeoffs and landings in the flat of the valley below. We debated the possibilities of any airplanes being kept there overnight and if we could steal a couple and fly them to Corsica, which we thought was about 250 miles south of us. We wondered if we could fit two in each aircraft so we could take Ernie and Joe with us. We discussed all the things that might be possible to make our escape.

We had been told that when the time was right, we would be smuggled into Spain and freedom. We sincerely doubted this, as we hadn't heard of anyone being rescued that way. We knew that some of our crews had come safely out of the Balkans, but we knew that there were partisans there and that the Germans did not control all of the countryside all of the time.

I, at least, felt that any plan to get us out of France by boat or over the Pyrenees into Spain was quite remote. However, we continually heard from our benefactors that we would be taken out of the country and to Spain soon. They certainly knew something that we didn't. We felt that Marcel was more than ready to be rid of us.

We had quite a few Resistance visitors. They usually came into our area and whistled to alert us before approaching the house. When we were made aware, one of the visitors would come into camp, shake hands, and go out and whistle again for his companions. Jean

Juvenile came to visit us several times and was always accompanied by his friend Pierre Dudet.

On our first Saturday at the hideout, Jean and Pierre brought an American lady, perhaps in her 40's, to meet us. She said that she was from Patterson, New Jersey, and that she was somehow related to the Winthrop family and had originally come to France to study. Marrying a Frenchman, she stayed to live and raise a family. It was very nice sitting on the ground outside of the house talking in English to someone who was familiar with our situation. She told us that we would probably be moved into the city of Aix-en-Provence as soon as the intensive German hunt for us was over. They were still searching for four airmen that they thought were hiding somewhere between Salon de Provence and Aix. She also told us that we would eventually be moved to the area near the Spanish border, and then into Spain and freedom.

This was still hard to believe, but hearing it from her gave us added hope. She asked what we wanted, and of course we said cigarettes. She told us that they were almost impossible to get. Then, we asked for a razor and blades so we could shave and get rid of the beards.

She talked at length about America but didn't seem to want to go back as she loved France. She also talked about her husband, who was a teacher. When she left she said she would get a razor and blades to us, and that she wanted to come back again and take pictures of us.

Sure enough, the next morning a young man came with a package that had a towel and a razor and one single-edge razor blade. We were disappointed that he hadn't brought a pack of blades, but we would make do with what we had. This was Sunday morning, so we heated water to clean up and shave. The clean up with soap and warm water was easy. The shaving ordeal was anything but easy. We decided that Joe Kinnane, with the heavy beard, should go first. Then

THE MAQUIS AND MARCEL

either Bob or Ernie would be next, and since I had the least to shave, I would be last.

We heated water in the iron pot in the fireplace and Joe lathered up using the bar soap. With the help of a piece of mirror propped up near the sheep trough, he had a fairly comfortable shave. He actually looked normal for a change. Bob came next and he immediately complained about the razor being dull; he had to go over some areas several times to get a smooth shave. Ernie and I reheated the water, thinking that if the water was hot enough, it would soften the whiskers and we could shave easier. I remembered that my Dad, being a barber, always put hot towels on his customers' faces to soften up the beard for a better shave. So much for that theory! Dad had a sharp, straight edge razor and we had only a dull single edge safety razor.

Ernie started to shave with the much-used blade and had an awful time getting a decent shave. He pulled and scraped and cut himself several times, all the while adding extensive vocal color about the dull blade. As previously decided, I was last. I lathered up good and took one pull with the razor and concluded that this was going to be impossible. I considered asking Marcel for his sharp knife when he came home that night, but then thought better of that idea. I continued to scrape away and the razor somehow gave me some semblance of a shave. Naturally, I cut myself while trying to bear down on some spots, and this became a memorable ordeal that I am sure none of us ever forgot.

Again that same day, Sunday afternoon, the American lady from Patterson returned with several people, including her husband, with the intention of taking pictures of us. We speculated that perhaps these photos would be hidden until after the war to prove that they had helped the Allied airmen escape. This would no doubt assist them in the post-war era. Some close-up head shots also were taken that we assumed might be used for ID papers, however I don't believe that they ever were.

Her husband was extremely nervous about being in our presence. He was afraid that the Germans would catch them with us and they would be executed. She began to berate him to us in English, calling him a "scared little mouse." She carried on about him to the point that it was embarrassing to us. He kept urging her to leave and she finally said her goodbyes, gave us a hug and a kiss on each cheek, and that was the last we saw of her.

Our daily routine, after getting out of our straw pen, would be to put more wood on the fire to warm a bucket of water for washing. Then we would cut several pieces off one of the long loaves of the bread, and then cut a nice thin slab of the Roquefort cheese to go on the bread in place of butter. We had some ersatz coffee that tasted awful, and we even tried to brew some leaves in the coffee attempting to make it more palatable, although this added effort was never successful. After breakfast, two of us would go to the well for more drinking water, while the other two would wander around the woods looking for dead limbs and twigs that we could use in the fireplace. We did not eat anything between breakfast and supper.

Ernie would start preparing the potatoes and beans right after the noon hour, as the fireplace cooked very slowly. An hour or so before dark, Marcel would return with the sheep. We would then know if we were to have fresh fried rabbit, or the mutton already cooking in the pot with the beans. Sometimes he only had one rabbit, so we would eat the rabbit first, and finish with a piece of mutton. When we had wine, we always drank it with our supper (no more afternoon celebrations). After supper we would heat water as hot as possible, and try to scrub out the bean and potato pot in the light of the fireplace. We all helped Ernie with this, but often we just got off the big pieces and had to leave the pot to soak overnight filled with sheep trough water. Then, early the next day, we would heat water to thoroughly clean the pot. This was a big chore as the beans and

THE MAQUIS AND MARCEL

potatoes often burned in the bottom of the pot, and we had to scrape hard to get the pot clean.

The afternoons were usually spent sitting in the sun and quietly talking while we waited for Marcel to return. Of course, when the "haricot" and "pommes-de-terre" (beans and potatoes) and mutton was in the pot cooking, one of us had stay near the fireplace to stir the pot frequently to keep it from sticking.

The afternoons gave us ample time to inspect the premises and to see what Marcel used for a bed in the sheep pen. The ledge on which he slept had several layers of sheepskin and a dirty old WWI blanket over the sheepskin. We never did figure out what he used for a cover at night. Perhaps he wore his equally dirty overcoat, or he took it off and covered himself with it. He said that it was warm down there, even though one side of the enclosure was wide open to the elements.

About smokes, I know that I came to Marcel's abode with no cigarettes, having given all away on the previous days to my benefactors. Either Joe, Bob, or Ernie may have had a few, I'm not sure. I remember that someone traded their remaining cigarettes for a full pack of some local brand, and that they were horrible.

As I said earlier, we had cigarette paper, so we could roll a cigarette if we had tobacco. This was in the days before filters, so any remaining butts contained some tobacco, no matter how short the butt. The little tin "meego" box was in use every day. We never smoked a whole real cigarette. We would smoke perhaps half, and then we would mix the remaining tobacco with whatever leaves we could find with what else was in our tin box, and rolled a new cigarette each time.

When visitors came, we often would ask for, and got, a local cigarette from them. Although they were scarce, we would promptly put the cigarette in the "meego" box to be mixed with dry leaves. This would be rolled into another smoke - maybe two or three.

I had given my Zippo lighter away that night in the farmhouse when I was stripped of my military uniform. We must have had access to some matches or a light from a twig from the fireplace, as I don't remember any problem lighting the cigarettes.

After the scare of the low-flying JU-88, we laid quite low and out of sight for days. We often stayed in the woods some distance from the house, but kept it in sight. We still expected a German patrol visit. On Friday, some of the Resistance people visited and brought a full pack of French cigarettes, which was most welcome. We were now quite aware of the scarcity of smokes, and the four of us shared two and secreted away at least one each so that when Marcel returned with the sheep, there were only three or four remaining for him.

The visitors this day told us that the Germans were no longer searching for us as they thought that the Resistance had gotten us out of the immediate area. They told us that we would soon be moved into town. Which town, we didn't know, but we assumed it would be Aix, and we would finally be out of the sheepherder's nest. We were certain that Marcel was anxious for us to leave. He had become less friendly by the day, and it was clear that we had overstayed our welcome.

On either Friday or Saturday (this would have been February 11 or 12th, Jean (John) Juvenile, Pierre Dudet, and a couple other men came to pick us up. As we were leaving, Marcel again seemed friendly but immensely relieved that we were finally going. We shook his hand, said goodbye and thanked him. I felt that I should give him a souvenir, but the only thing that I had to give was my GI watch. I gave it to him, and with the gift of the souvenir he had a broad, toothless smile for me.

When we were out of sight of the house, one of the Frenchmen berated me for giving him my watch, saying that he had no need whatsoever for a timepiece, which was probably so. He said that I should have given it to the Resistance to be used as a reward for some future help. I was told that someone went back for the watch the next day and I hope that, at least, he was given a full pack of cigarettes for the wristwatch.

We four accompanied the men back to the farmhouse below the bluff the same way that we had climbed up about two weeks earlier. Joe and I got in the car with Jean Juvenile and his companion. Ernie and Bob got in a car with Pierre Dudet and another man who was Peter Duindon, a shoe manufacturer in Aix en Provence. We drove to Aix, where Joe Kinnane and I were taken to the second floor apartment of Mr. and Mrs. Jean Juvenile and their young daughter. Ernie was taken to live with the Dudet's and Bob stayed with the shoemaker, his wife, and son Robert.

CHAPTER 9

AIX-EN-PROVENCE

The drive into Aix was interesting. When we left the main roads and went into the residential part of the city, the homes and apartments were quite close together. The streets were narrow and the front steps of the dwellings protruded into the street in some places, making it difficult for two opposing cars to pass. To further make this part difficult, there were patches of ice in the shady areas nearly everywhere. The Juvenile family's apartment was a two bedroom, second-story flat just off one of the main streets. Their little girl of nine or ten, slept on the sofa or in her parents' room, while Joe and I were given her room. Although we had to share a full sized bed, it was a lot better than our miserable straw pad.

As soon as we arrived at the apartment and were introduced to his wife and daughter, Mrs. Juvenile saw how dirty we were and how much we needed a bath. She had Jean light the benzene water heater on the wall over the bathtub, and told us that she wanted to provide clean clothes, underwear, and socks for each of us. We were to dress in the clean clothes that she provided so that she could wash our clothes the next morning. I was the first to get into the bathtub. This was the first time I had taken my long underwear completely off in more than two weeks.

The hot bath was wonderful. Soap and hot water was such a treat. While I was bathing, another tank of water was heating for Joe. When

STARDUST FALLING

I let the water out of the tub, there was an ugly ring where the water had been and I took some time cleaning it up for Joe. I hadn't realized how really dirty I had been. I put on a pair of Jean Juvenile's underpants, along with a pair of his trousers, a shirt, and slippers that Mrs. Juvenile had provided for me. I didn't wash my hair at this time but the next day I washed it in the sink with Mrs. Juvenile's help. After my hair was clean and dry, she trimmed it and did a good job. When she had finished with me, Joe went through the same process and we both thanked her profusely for her kindness.

The next morning, our GI brown shoes were taken to Peter Duindon (the shoe manufacturer) to be dyed black. The people of the Resistance thought the shoes were far too conspicuous in their present color. While the shoes were taken to be dyed, Mrs. Juvenile took some of our clothes to the basement of her apartment building to wash them for us. This process took several days, as she didn't want her curious apartment neighbors to know that she was doing extra laundry. I suppose if anyone had seen our GI long underwear, they would have been suspicious. She dried everything on a wooden rack in her kitchen. My pants, shirt, and sweater were thankfully in good condition, and in a few days we finally had all of our civilian clothes back again, and clean.

On Tuesday, our third day with the Juvenile's, we were advised that she was having a small group of women in for the morning to plan a women's group that was to meet there later in the week. We would have to stay in our room while these women were there, as well as be perfectly quiet so that none of them would be suspicious that she was harboring anyone in the closed room. We were still wearing the slippers and were very careful not to make any noise. The wooden floor squeaked, so Joe sat in a chair and I sat on the bed. About mid-morning, we could hear the ladies chatting and someone using the bathroom next to our room. Suddenly I had a very strong urge to cough. I tried to cover my face with a pillow and cough lightly, but

AIX-EN-PROVENCE

this just brought on an urge for a heavier cough. I finally got up, took two pillows, and quietly made my way across the room to a closet that was farthest from the women. Shutting the closet door and using the pillows, I was able to cough until my throat cleared. I hoped that if any of the women heard the coughing, they would think it was coming from another apartment.

The meeting finally ended and Mrs. Juvenile let us out of the room. When I told Jean that night what had happened in the coughing incident, he asked his wife if she had heard me cough, and she said that no one had heard anything.

On Wednesday morning, a man came with our shoes freshly dyed black. We still wore the slippers in the apartment to keep the noise down as we went from room to room. Early that evening, a man came and said that he was to take us somewhere in his car. Jean said for us to go with the man and that we would return in time for the evening meal.

The man took Joe and me on a short ride through the winding streets to an alley, where he parked the car. He took us down several steps into the back of a store, which smelled like a printing shop. Although it was dark inside, we could see a bit of light from a crack beneath a door ahead of us. The man knocked on the door, and we were led into a well-lit room where there were no introductions. We were told in halting English that French identification papers were to be made for us, and that we were to pick a French name for our new ID card. Earlier, when Jean learned that my name was Coss, he had mentioned an early-day flyer by the name of Costa. I thought that it would be a good name for me and added the first name of Rene to go with it. The man had me write Rene Robert Costa for him several times on a piece of paper, and then he took me into a small curtained area and took my picture. He repeated the same for Joe and we were taken back to the Juvenile apartment in time for a late dinner.

Friday the 18th was to be a very interesting day from start to finish.

225

Joe and I were moved to another location, as Mrs. Juvenile was hosting the women's club gathering and she wanted us out of the apartment for the day. Someone with a car came at 7:30AM and picked Joe up. At about 8:00, there was a knock at the door and a very pretty young woman of eighteen or nineteen years of age, came to get me. It was a beautiful morning, crisp but bright. She took me by the hand and we started across the city just as two young lovers would. I was quite attracted to her and she spoke fair, high school English.

She seemed to delight in taunting the occasional German soldier we passed by singing bits of any American song that she knew. This really upset me and I told her so. She just kept chatting with me in English as we made our way through the city of Aix-en-Provence. This was the first and only time that I could enjoy the beauty all around me.

She said that she was taking me to the home of her grandparents on the outskirts of the city. We had walked quite a distance and I felt that I needed to use a restroom. I told her about the situation and she led me across a tree-lined park where there was one of the French outdoor urinals for men.

I was not familiar with this type of outdoor facility but I had to go so badly that I gladly went in. The urinal was a trough going around three sides of the open-air enclosure. There was a 2 or 2½ foot iron plate that the trough was mounted on, with decorative wrought iron above and below. She was standing just outside, not two feet from me, chatting merrily away in English through the wrought iron fence.

I was supposed to relieve myself with her standing there facing me. I was feeling rather shy and had some trouble getting started, but finally the urge got the best of my modesty. The noise must have sounded like Niagara Falls and almost drowned out what she was saying. When I finished, I went over to a fountain basin in the middle of the enclosure, washed my hands and finding no towels, dried my hands on my pants and left with her. We continued to gaily move along hand-in-hand.

We were soon in an older section of modest mansions, rather than row after row of apartment buildings. We came to a rather stately home set back from the street, and she announced that we were about to meet her grandfather, "The General." I really didn't know what to expect, as we were welcomed into the home by a maid. She slipped her shoes off, and I followed suit as we were ushered in. My socks, although well worn, were serviceable, thank God.

My young guide introduced me to each of her grandparents and we were provided with slippers for the day. She told me, in her schoolgirl English, that her grandfather was a retired military officer and had been a general in WWI. He certainly had the bearing and look of an elderly military officer, being tall and rather good looking with snow-white hair and a large white mustache. He spoke no English, and she acted as our interpreter while he asked many questions and seemed to be genuinely interested in my background and military profession. He asked the size of my crew and how many bombing missions we had participated in. At lunchtime, the maid provided a light lunch of sandwiches, fruit, and wine. The general toasted the Allies and me and exhorted us to kick the "Bosch" out of France!

The afternoon was spent looking at the general's memorabilia and scrapbooks of WWI photos. The scrapbooks were quite large and were put on a table, where he sat pointing to the pictures while she and I stood on each side of the chair, with her interpreting what he said.

Her English was quickly improving and it was obvious that she had studied it in school, perhaps rather recently. I was studying her and certainly judged her age as close to mine. I was twenty at the time, and it was probably obvious to the general that we were somewhat attracted to each other. Some of the photographs he showed us were taken with other generals. One that I remember well was taken outside of the railroad car in which the Germans had surrendered at the end of WWI. The photo was signed by General "Black Jack" Pershing. My host was with several other French generals surrounding our General "Black Jack" in the photograph, of which he seemed particularly proud. There were many more pictures of the general, staff, tents, mud, old cars, and artillery, as well as a floor-to-ceiling case of memorabilia to show us. He had many battlefront souvenirs, and of course, a large section showing his numerous medals.

    I was a little overwhelmed by all of this. I was still a country boy who felt very comfortable in the cockpit of an airplane, but who was quite awed by being in the presence of this great military man. I wondered how fate had placed me this afternoon in the presence of a very high ranking French general and his beautiful granddaughter. What was to become of me? Would I be allowed to fly again and get a new crew and airplane to finish my missions? Would I survive the war? So many unfamiliar questions swirled within my head.

    The afternoon flew by and the general excused himself by saying goodbye to me and kissing his granddaughter good day and I assumed he was to take a nap. We went into the kitchen where we had tea with her grandmother, with whom she chatted. I think they talked about me being the pilot of the bomber shot down at Salon-de-Provence. Being mid-February, the sky was getting dark as we said good day to her grandmother, put on our shoes, and left.

    We went back a slightly different way and sort of melted in with the crowd of people on the street. We still held hands and she chatted with me in English when she could not be overheard by the people passing by or near us. I was more relaxed now than I had been in the morning, and really had a chance to look at the girl and realized how fun-loving and light-spirited she was.

    I was starting to enjoy our stroll when we arrived at the Juvenile's apartment all too soon. We went up the stairs and she knocked at the

AIX-EN-PROVENCE

door which was promptly opened by Mrs. Juvenile. We kissed on the cheek and I said "merci beaucoup" (thank you), and "au revoir" (good-by). I went inside, the door was shut, and I was never to see her again.

I was obviously struck by this beautiful young girl, her demeanor, her vivaciousness, and most of all by her taking the supreme risk to herself in guiding me across the city for the day. This day with her grandfather, the General, I will remember forever. I knew full well that she understood the risk that she was taking, but she did it with panache.

I have long wished, especially right after the war, that I had slipped her my home address in Illinois and asked her if she would correspond with me when she could. I never did know her name and Jean Juvenile wouldn't give it to me. He said that it was better that I didn't know, while adding with a smile that he thought that I would enjoy the day with her.

In the Juvenile household, we had ersatz coffee, and bread or croissants and jelly for breakfast. We ate a light lunch at one o'clock when Jean came home from his work at the court. He frequently took a short siesta before returning to work. He came home at 7:30 for the evening.

We would have our main meal at 9:00PM, where there were constant visitors to the dinner table. Among these were Jean's Resistance workers who wanted to meet and break bread with us. We no longer had any souvenirs to give, but this definitely was a jolly time. Joe and I spoke very little French, and what little we did speak we had picked up in Tunis or from Marcel, which was definitely not useable in our current surroundings. Most of the Frenchmen had taken the two years of compulsory English in high school, and although they claimed that they could remember very little English, they could converse with us. They attempted to teach us French; I seemed to pick it up fairly rapidly, and we were soon carrying on a fairly decent conversation. Joe and I also looked through the daily papers and could see how the news seemed to be slanted toward the Axis point of view. We felt certain that this news was controlled by the Germans.

There was one particular fellow who came often and was reputed to be a fine artist. He only had one hand, as his right hand was missing. As the story goes: He was captured by the Germans during WWI, and when they asked him his occupation, he said that he was an artist. They then asked if he painted with his right or his left hand. When he replied that he was right-handed, the Germans promptly cut off his right hand. He had since taught himself to paint quite well left-handed, and surprisingly made his living as a portrait painter. He had lived with a wealthy American woman near Nice before WWII, but had sent her and their three children on a plane out of Lisbon to the United States while they could still leave France.

Understandably, he had a supreme hatred for the Germans, which he called "The Bosch," and was the appointed assassin for the local Resistance group. Jean Juvenile told me they would have a secret trial for anyone who collaborated with the Germans or for turning someone in to the Gestapo, for instance. If sufficient evidence was gathered to convict the culprit, the one-armed man would be ordered to assassinate the collaborator. I was told that this procedure was not used against the French women who were dating and sleeping with the Germans. The resistance people said that they would deal with them after the war was over.

There were many spirited conversations at the dinner table, and the women would join in and argue vociferously about politics and the good and bad of communism and such things. As a country boy, I was totally unaccustomed to women being so involved in political matters.

I would like to make some reference to the Maquis and the Resistance. The Maquis were those in hiding and always armed.

AIX-EN-PROVENCE

They lived outside of conventional civilian life; whereas the Resistance consisted of everyday citizens that would help out in any way that they could. They would help anyone, if possible, who was against the Axis enemy.

During our dinner table conversations, we often heard that if the Allies did not do more to liberate southern France or supply the Resistance with guns and other supplies, the electorate would probably go communist after the war. This was a common theme and probably stemmed from their frustration with the slowness and lack of progress of the Allies in confronting and defeating the Axis powers.

In the evening when our host uncorked a bottle of table wine, I noticed that he always poured a partial glass for himself first and then filled his guest's glasses. I asked him in English why he did this. He replied, in what I thought was French, for "zee flies." Everyone laughed when Joe and I didn't "get" it, and I asked him to repeat it, getting our same negative reaction. He finally made a motion like a fly flitting around. I finally figured out that he put what was floating on the top of the bottle, like flies, pieces of cork, and other debris, in his glass so his guests would not have the indignity of dealing with such.

Sea urchins, a French delicacy, were served at one of the evening meals. I had never seen them before and didn't know quite how to handle them. As I observed, they just spooned the juice out of the urchin halves and I found it tasty, although quite salty. Mrs. Juvenile was an excellent cook and we often had baked casseroles with lots of cheese and sauce. There seemed to be a fair supply of meat for us and the guests, perhaps this was because the Juvenile's were supplied with extra Resistance procured food coupons.

Their daughter had to do her school homework before dinner but always ate with us. When Jean would give her wine with her dinner, he would cut it in half with water. Occasionally, some of the women at the table would ask for their wine cut with water also. After dinner, the Juvenile's daughter would go into her parents' room to sleep until everyone was gone. I wondered how anyone could immediately go to sleep after eating such a meal, but soon reasoned that no longer being 8 or 9 years of age was my answer. The after-dinner drink was cognac or clear liqueurs mixed with water.

Joe and I had a toothbrush and razor now so we kept clean and well shaven. Sometime in our stay with the Juveniles, I had begun to cultivate a mustache. It wasn't very much of a mustache but it was a start.

The room that Joe and I shared had a bed, a chair, a dresser, and a small carpet on each side of the bed. We had pretty much the run of the house in the daytime, but were cautioned to stay away from the windows. We were often assured that we were safe there. Jean Juvenile spoke of the fact that he had people guarding the area and had a personal bodyguard. I don't know if this was true or not.

There was some sort of hierarchy in the Resistance involved here. Jean was often addressed as "Chief," and I was sure that Pierre Dudet (who Ernie Jenkins, my bombardier, resided with) was one of Jean's closest Lieutenants. We saw a lot of him at dinner. I am sure that Peter Duindon also figured prominently in the group. He owned and operated a shoe manufacturing plant, which was almost entirely devoted to making shoes for the Germans. He most likely was able to divert some shoes to the Maquis and the Resistance, as shoes were in very short supply.

I recall that my co-pilot, Bob Johnson, had lost his sheep-lined flying boots when his parachute opened and unfortunately did not wear his GI shoes with his boots. This left him in stocking feet upon landing in France.

Bob, Joe, and Ernie had found each other after landing and toward evening had knocked on a door, asking for help. Bob was given an old pair of shoes that didn't fit him well, causing blisters and sores on his toes. He suffered with them until he arrived in Aix-en-Provence

AIX-EN-PROVENCE

and was fortunately placed in the home of Peter Duindon, where he was given a proper fitting pair of shoes, much to his gratitude and relief.

Pierre brought Ernie with him when he came to have dinner at the Juvenile home one evening. It was very nice to visit with Ernie and Joe and I asked if he had seen and talked to Bob. He said that he had and that Bob was comfortable. Things moved along quite well, and Joe and I settled into the Juvenile household routine nicely.

Early one evening, Jean Juvenile had Joe and me put our shoes on and he took us outdoors to walk around the block. He felt that we both needed more exercise. At one corner, we stopped to watch a squad of Germans march by singing in cadence as they marched on the roadway. It was cold and damp, so we went back inside after only a few minutes.

At the dinner table at the Juvenile household, there was always a long and heated conversation about why the Allies didn't air-drop supplies, guns, ammunition, and other essentials to the Partisans in the south of France. As I understood it, Jean was in charge of supplies in his area, which was a rather large area east and north of Marseilles. There was always the veiled threat that if the Allies, Americans or British, didn't do more, they would turn to the Russians for help. Whether they would have gotten any more support from the Russians is questionable. This was probably just frustration showing through.

One evening at the dinner table, one of the guests said that he was Swiss and could get us into Switzerland. Joe and I knew that if we went to Switzerland, we would be interned. I had been told by group intelligence that Switzerland was not an acceptable alternative and had told this information to the others while with Marcel. We told the guest that we didn't want to go to Switzerland, and Jean assured us that we would go to Spain.

The one-armed painter was at almost every evening meal. He appeared more like a bodyguard at times, always armed with a small

Beretta. On one evening he was missing and when I asked about him, I was told that he was on an assignment. I don't know whether this was true or not, but remembering what I had been told earlier made me wonder.

The one-armed painter spoke English quite well. He said that since his mistress was an American, they spoke both French and English in their home to teach their children to be bi-lingual. I was rapidly picking up words and meanings in French. It seemed to come quite easily for me, but poor Joe just struggled along with key words and would often say to me, "Loo-tenant, what are they talking about?"

Joe and I got along extremely well. I still referred to him as Joe, while he continued addressing me as "Loo-tenant." I slowly learned a little about his boyhood in Bayonne, New Jersey, which apparently was a tough neighborhood to grow up in. When I asked him why he joined as a gunner, he said that he had enlisted in early 1942 and had chosen the Air Corps and specifically requested heavy bomber gunnery school. "Just thought it would be great," he quipped.

He had completed his gunnery training and was kept for a time as an instructor at his school. He volunteered for combat and was sent to Pyote, Texas, for a crew assignment.

Joe was of rather stocky build and could have been a truck driver or longshoreman. He possessed good humor, was a little on the quiet side, and spoke with a definite New Jersey accent. He always did his share without grumbling, and was frankly a good companion throughout this ordeal. He was at least two years older than me and probably 23 at this time. He was unmarried and never talked of a romantic relationship back in Bayonne. I often spoke to him of my high school girlfriend, Dionne, who I had corresponded with regularly while I was in service. He said the fact that I was the youngest member on the crew didn't seem to affect the demeanor or confidence of any of the crew, and I hoped that he was not just saying this to please me. They knew that I had the aircraft experience and the flying time, and Joe said that I could fly as well as any pilot in our squadron. As far as being a strict military officer, I was probably somewhat behind the curve. It certainly didn't seem to matter that much in combat, but of course when we were in the airplane; it was strictly "all business."

On another evening, Joe and I again took a walk with Jean Juvenile. This time we went several blocks away from the apartment, and once more stopped to see German soldiers marching in the street. We had our IDs just in case we were stopped by the French or German gendarmes. While it was a nervous time for Joe and me, Jean seemed to be enjoying it immensely. He said he was taking us out for exercise, but we felt certain that he also took great pleasure in defying the Germans.

One Saturday morning, Jean asked me if I could ride a bicycle. I assured him that I could and he said that he wanted to take me for a bike ride. After breakfast, we went to the basement of their apartment building, where two bikes had been left for us. He gave me my choice, and I chose the one that was a little lower to the ground than the other. My bike had a seat not much larger than a banana, and was so high that when in the seat, both of my feet did not quite touch the ground. We wheeled them out into the street and I was soon to learn that the brakes were mounted on the handlebars, instead of the rear-only brake on the bicycle of my childhood. I had never seen such skinny tires on a bike before. I was used to balloon tires with fenders. After a couple of tries, I was able to mount the bike and get started pedaling. I tried the front and rear brakes on the handlebars. This seemed awkward to me but I was able to keep up fairly well with Jean. I followed along about 50 yards behind him as instructed, and I tried to always keep him in sight.

The streets were narrow and there were no sidewalks. This being the month of February, there was some ice on the street where the sun didn't penetrate. These areas we navigated through gingerly, but smoothly and safely.

We approached a hilly section where the road was somewhat wider but still had some patches of ice in the shade. Jean would go up a hill and I would follow, temporarily losing sight of him as he went down the other side. This went on for several hills, and then as I topped a hill, I saw in front of me a line of young German soldiers completely spanning the road. They were arm-in-arm and singing as if going off to play soccer or something. I saw that Jean was ascending the hill ahead and knew that they had split to let him pass through. It was icy here at the bottom of the hill and I tried to brake to slow down, but to no avail. The bike started to skid side-to-side, as I tried to control it. My feet came off the pedals, which were still turning, hitting me in the ankles. I am sure that the German soldiers had purposely decided to wait until the last second to split and let this obviously novice "Frenchman" through, to give him a scare, if for no other reason. I was so out of control and the Germans saw this; at the last second they dodged me like a bowling ball and I got through without hitting anyone. I was still upright on my bike. I finally gained control and pedaled uphill where Jean had stopped to watch. He was laughing like it was the funniest thing he had ever seen but could detect that I was shaken and angry, so we headed straight home.

When we got back, I related what had happened to Joe, and when offered a bike ride for exercise a few minutes later, he decided to decline. We were still being told daily that we would be taken to Spain, but just couldn't believe or absorb it. It was pretty hard for us to separate fact from bravado.

On Sunday, February 20th, Joe and I were taken in the Juvenile car, along with his wife and daughter, to the home of Peter Doindon, the shoe maker. It was a very nice home and I clearly remember the highly polished wood floors. We were all given fuzzy slippers to put on over our shoes so we wouldn't mar the beautiful parquet floors. (Mrs. Juvenile was quite put out with all this and thought that Mrs.

Doindon was putting on airs, letting us know her thoughts on the ride home.)

We were introduced to Mrs. Duindon (we already knew Peter) and were taken into the sitting room to find Bob Johnson and Ernie Jenkins, along with Pierre Dudet, Ernie's host. Now I knew for sure that Bob was a guest in the Doindon home, just as was Ernie in the Dudet home. Bob said that he had been helping the Doindon son, Robert, with his English lessons and learning some French in turn. This was the first time all four of us had been together since we had left the sheepherder's camp, and it was very pleasant indeed. We parted in mid-afternoon after exchanging all that we knew about what was going on. Each had been told that we were to be smuggled to Spain soon. Bob was well pleased with his new shoes, as it was a big relief to him after the ill fitting ones he had worn during the time with the old sheepherder.

On Monday the 21^{st,} Joe and I were told to be ready for our move to Spain very soon. Mrs. Juvenile washed our clothes and we both took a bath in the afternoon. It was nice to take another bath as our clean, dry clothes would be available before evening. My old socks were pretty well worn, and I was provided a pair of knitted ones that felt very good.

That evening, the regular group was there, including Pierre and the man with one hand. They seemed to anticipate our departure, but I doubted that any knew for sure just when we would leave. Mrs. Juvenile had prepared a fine meal, as usual. This time we had ham hocks that were boiled, along with potatoes and cabbage. Of course, the preferable casserole this time was spinach. I remember this meal because I had two medium-sized ham hocks on my plate along with the potatoes and cabbage. I didn't like ham hocks when they were served at my grandmother's table. I tried one to be polite, but just couldn't finish it. Someone else took my second one and Mrs. Juvenile seemed disappointed that I didn't like her dinner choice. Joe ate his with great gusto, however.

It was a good evening, and we were now communicating quite well and could carry on a conversation of sorts on several topics. They kept trying to impress on us the needs of the Maquis to carry on their fight against the Germans. They repeatedly asked us to carry the message to the Americans and British that they needed many things, and asked the Americans and Brits to airdrop these supplies in to them. I suppose Jean Juvenile, who was in charge of equipment and supplies for the Resistance and Maquis, was more acutely aware of their needs and shortages than most at the table.

When dinner was finished, one of the guests brought out a bottle of cognac for a toast. Jean was pleased but said he was keeping his fine bottle of cognac to celebrate their liberation from the Germans. The man who had brought the cognac said that he was toasting the liberation of both Joe and me. Either way, we were pleased with the toast and with the "bite" of good liqueur.

At the noon court break of the 22nd of February, Jean came home and told us that we would be moved to Marseilles by car that afternoon. He said that Marseilles was not far from Aix-en-Provence. He told us that we would now be in the charge of the Deuxieme Bureau, the Free French Army intelligence service. We really didn't know what to expect, but Jean seemed pleased and said we were safe and surely on our way to Spain and freedom. We were so very grateful to Jean Juvenile and his family, for we knew that he had been involved in our rescue from the very first.

He had to go back to work and didn't know if he would be home before someone came for us, so we said our goodbyes and a very heartfelt "merci beaucoups." As it turned out, he did get back just before we left. It was a hurried departure, and Mrs. Juvenile kissed us and made sure we had a toothbrush and razor in our pocket, and Jean gave us both a little bottle of Schnapps.

We were taken by car a distance of what I would judge to be 25 or

AIX-EN-PROVENCE

30 km, and we seemed to be traveling south along a main road. There was quite a bit of German truck traffic, and also some civilian traffic. It was dark by now as we stopped at an apartment building on a side street. Joe was told to stay in the car and I was taken to a first floor apartment where the driver knocked on the door. A lady let us in and thanked the driver-guide as he left to deliver Joe somewhere else.

The lady, probably in her mid-thirties, spoke excellent English with a decidedly English accent. I am pretty sure that she was French but certainly had lived in England or was schooled there. She told me that she was attached to the Free French Deuxieme Bureau. Her task was to give me some intelligence information that I was to take to the British or the Americans. My first thought was "oh no," this will make me a spy and will surely get me executed if I am caught. When I related this thought to her, she said, "What difference, you will be shot immediately if you are caught anyway." Wide eyed, I totally believed her.

At this point, I decided to try to commit to memory all that she told me. She laid out French army maps marked with German troop concentrations, gun emplacements, and where the Germans had hidden fuel supplies underground for future use. She pointed to a seaplane base that was now in use, and I was told that the Germans were now using auxiliary fields instead of Salon de Provence, which was now completely unusable. She told me that at 0900 of the day of our raid on Salon de Provence, the Germans expected the bombing and completely cleared the field of all flyable aircraft. (We had formed up on this mission at about 0830 that morning.)

She told me to tell the Americans or the British that the Germans were feverishly fortifying the Mediterranean coast, and had stopped trains to make the passengers work for 48 hours before being released to continue their journey. German engineers were supposed to come to Aix in February to fortify it. I was told that in August, the headquarters of the Nineteenth German Army had been relocated to

Avignon. She tried to give me the size of the troop concentration, but said it was never a stable count as units came and went, making this information most likely worthless to the Allies.

She gave me all this information before the nine o'clock dinner hour and said we would work on it again in the morning. I ate well. The food was good and immediately after dinner she prepared for bed, coming out of the bathroom in a robe and slippers. There was a small bedroom as this was a three-room flat. The bedroom had two single beds, a dresser, and mirror, and closet, but really didn't look like a bedroom at all. There were no pictures, no men's clothing, or anything that was to indicate that she had a husband or roommate. This may have been a "safe house" used by the Free French Intelligence Bureau. I went into the bathroom, washed and brushed my teeth, and undressed down to my long underwear and went into the bedroom. She was apparently already asleep so I turned off the light and got into bed. I lay there thinking of what kind of a mess I was in. I could be caught and treated as a spy. The only evidence that I still possessed to prove that I was a U.S. Army Air Corps officer were the dog tags on the chain around my neck. If my captors snatched them off my neck, I would be "naked unto the world" as a foreign spy in an occupied country. These were definitely not happy thoughts.

To me then, it was all so simplistic. One day I was just another prisoner of war if caught, and now I was a spy and would be killed if caught. I decided that I must keep all of this information absolutely secure in my mind until I was free, not telling Joe or anyone else of my secret. I was scared but tired, and soon fell asleep.

She was up and dressed before I was awake and as soon as we had completed breakfast, she cleared the table and brought out the maps again for me to study. She grilled me on what she had told me the night before, going over this again and again.

At one time she paused and said, "How old are you?" I replied twenty, and she asked me my rank and I told her 1ˢᵗ Lieutenant. She just shook her head and went on with the lessons. I wanted to tell her that I had a lot of flying experience and had been a rated military pilot for more than two years, but there was no time for that. She just continued to hammer the information into me until she was certain that I could repeat it to the Allies verbatim.

When she was satisfied with my progress we relaxed a bit and she asked me for my French ID card, the one identifying me as Rene Costa, age 18. She gave me a Polish worker's identification card with my picture on it (a copy of the same picture that was on my French ID). She said that the new card would identify me as one Josef (I have forgotten the last name) and my age was listed as 23. I knew that I couldn't pronounce my new last name or read anything on the new card; as it was in German. It looked well worn and quite authentic. She said that if a Frenchman stopped me, I was to just show him the ID and say nothing She also gave me papers in French, stamped and signed showing that the person pictured on the ID was required to travel from Marseille to Perpignan, France. She then told me that I was to start my journey to Spain that evening and that someone would come and get me.

I asked about my crewmember Joe and she said she knew nothing of him. I told her that he was in the car when I was brought to her. She acted surprised as if this was news to her, and it may have been. We had a very early, hearty supper at just about dark. It was welcome as we were so busy at noontime, that all I had eaten was an apple.

We finished eating supper at around five or five thirty and then there was a knock at the door. She let a man in and told me to get ready to go. I went to the bathroom to collect my toothbrush and razor and she saw me to the door with the following instructions: I was to go with the man, who would turn me over to a guide who would purchase my train ticket. Follow the new guide, but not too closely. If he got on the train, I was also to get on the train but was not to sit too near him. I was to get off the train when he did. I was going to go to Perpignan. With a kiss on each cheek, a smile, and a pat, she bid me adieu. I thanked her and said goodbye. The door closed and I was again on my way. I reflected later on how professional she was. Not really friendly and not unfriendly either, just that she had a job to do. I mused that she was probably a military professional with perhaps an officer husband serving with the Free French somewhere. I will never know.

CHAPTER 10

PERPIGNON

The driver and I got into the car, and to my surprise; Joe Kinnane was waiting for me. He said that he had spent the previous time with the driver of the car and his family. I told him some of my experience of the previous night and day, but did not tell him of the intelligence briefing that I had been given. I felt that I must hide it from everyone until I could relay it to the proper authorities. Joe told me that he had tried to sleep on a short sofa, but was so cramped that he bedded down on the floor.

I related that I had experienced a good night's sleep on a real bed in the same bedroom with my hostess, and told Joe that she spoke English quite well and I had spent a pleasant day and evening with her. I'm sure that Joe assumed that I had a joyous evening with the lady, when truthfully it was just the opposite. I purposefully left it to Joe's imagination as to whether I had "made out" or "struck out." My main thought now was that I would be shot if caught, and it worried me considerably. The fun of making Joe wonder provided the only light moment out of this very tense situation for me.

It didn't seem like a very long time before we arrived at the railroad station in Marseilles. Our driver took us into the station and spotted our guide for the next leg of the trip. The guide was wearing a hat rather than a tam, and a light tan overcoat. Both Joe and I still wore the heavy coat that we had been given in Salon de Provence. Our coats were dark, military looking "pea jackets" with ordinary buttons, rather than the military buttons. This type of jacket seemed to be very common. The jacket was probably French Navy surplus. They were heavy and about "finger tip" length, and were quite warm and comfortable.

It was cold in February and I welcomed the warmth of the jacket. Both Joe and I still had our stocking caps. My pants were dark, almost black. Both Joe and I were now carrying Polish worker's identification. We had our new assumed identity as Polish workers, and were carrying French transport papers specifying that we were enroute to Perpignon from Marseilles.

The lady from the Deuxieme Bureau had tried to get me to pronounce my new name correctly, but I just couldn't. She said forget about it; if you speak, it will give you away. Probably the French guards couldn't understand it in any case. They do know how to read the papers that permitted travel on the train to Perpignon, however. I am sure that if anyone had looked at my hands, they could easily see that I was no laborer.

I still had the heavy, long sleeve, turtleneck sweater that I had been given on the night that I had exchanged my uniform for civilian clothes. With the heavy "pea jacket," it was sometimes too warm when I was inside a building, such as the train station, or on the train. Joe had a wool shirt and a scarf that he seemed to wear constantly along with his "pea jacket." Neither of us had gloves making it easy to keep our hands concealed in our pockets. Joe still had his wristwatch, which he kept in his pocket. He would wind the watch daily so we knew the time of day. We both carried our toothbrush and razor in a little bag in our pocket. We didn't have replacement blades and Joe complained about the "poor" shave he was getting. We had each been given a new blade a few days before we left Aix, but his was now quite dull.

PERPIGNON

My Polish worker ID indicated that I was 23, so I was happy that I had started to grow a mustache earlier. I wanted to look older and I was determined to see if a mustache would help. For at least three weeks, I didn't shave my upper lip. I got a little blond fuzz but that was about all I had achieved for my effort.

The lady from the French 2nd Bureau had given me a little sack with an apple, a piece of cheese, and a couple of crackers before I had been picked up for the ride to the train station. This snack was for the overnight train trip. Joe had none, so we shared it. Both of us still had the little bottle of schnapps that Jean had given us in Aix, and we occasionally "nipped."

We quickly shook hands with our new guide. He left us to get the tickets and soon returned with passageway to Avignon. We didn't know where Avignon was but we assumed, correctly, that we would change trains there. Our transit papers had stated Marseille to Perpignon. The driver left with a "bon chance" (good luck) and we were now in the care of our new guide.

Soon our train was announced, and our guide proceeded to the gate and presented his ticket for punching. We trailed along after him and got through the turnstile without incident. We followed our guide as previously instructed. The lady gave me strict rules against speaking to anyone. In a whisper, I told Joe the rules and warnings that she had given me. We knew that we shouldn't converse between ourselves where we could be overheard. We should pretend to be asleep on the train so that no one would try to speak to us. We were to never have any contact with the guide directly on the train trip or at our destination.

When the guide opened one of the compartments near the front of the railway car and entered, we chose an empty compartment in the same coach near the rear. We were separated from him, but were sure that we could see him if he was to get off the train.

245

STARDUST FALLING

We were soon joined in the compartment by a French couple with a child. Joe already appeared to be asleep. I moved over to join him on the bench seat to give the French couple an entire bench seat for themselves. I immediately put my head against the window nearest the coach aisle and feigned sleep. They stowed their belongings and settled in, and did not try to converse with us at any time. The train conductor came through the car, looked at our tickets, punched them, and moved on.

We got off the train at Avignon and followed the guide into the station. He stopped at one point and allowed us to catch up with him. He showed us his watch and pointed to one hour later. I said "merci." To anyone watching us, it would have appeared as if we had asked him when the train to Perpignon was to depart. We sat on a bench where we could watch his movements but made no contact with him. At one point he went into the station café and ordered coffee or tea. We could see him at the café counter all of this time. Joe again was asleep. I never knew if he really slept or just appeared to sleep. I have a hunch that he really did snooze; he was a very relaxed fellow.

After the guide left the café, he went to the ticket window to purchase the tickets to Perpignon. I went over to the newspaper rack and the guide joined me and slipped me our tickets. I returned to the bench where Joe was sleeping and again sat down. After a few more minutes, the train was announced and we followed the guide to the boarding gate. There was a little wait for the turnstile to finally open, and our guide was the first one through. The gate attendant was looking at each ticket before punching them. As he did this, he said a polite "merci." When it was our turn to go through the gate he punched my ticket and said clearly in English, "Thank You," he did the same for Joe. Then he continued the "merci" routine to those following.

Needless to say, this upset both of us. We hurriedly whispered as we walked on down the platform. We were wondering if our cover had been blown. We were scared that we had been spotted by the German Gestapo in the station and that they would come aboard and detain us. It was a huge relief as the train finally started to move and we were still on it. It was a mystery as to how or why the attendant changed from "merci" to "thank you" when Joe and I passed through the gate. It might have been a remarkable, but scary, coincident.

We had settled again into an empty compartment at the rear of the coach, and our guide was up near the front. We could not see him, but we knew that he would signal us if he were to get off the train. His hat gave us some advantage, as most of the men wore tams or stocking caps. Before the train started to move, three German soldiers decided to share our compartment. Joe and I sat on the seat opposite the three men. They stowed some of their gear overhead and some on the floor between us. Joe and I feigned sleep and made no contact with them.

On the train from Marseilles to Avignon, all the windows of the train had blackout curtains drawn. The lights were on in our compartment, and also in the aisle stretching the length of the car beside each compartment.

On the second part of the trip, the shades were allowed to be open, and only a blue cove light was on in the compartment and the aisle. Our compartment was connected to the aisle by a sliding glass door. I was sitting next to the wall containing the door and had a good view of the aisle forward toward the front of the car. The three Germans across from us soon went to sleep, which was a blessing. I opened my eyes occasionally as we went through hamlets and could sometimes see small pinpoints of light; perhaps the blackout curtains weren't completely closed in the homes that we were passing. There was no cloud cover, and the moon made it possible to make out the homes and even the farmhouses as we passed. Later on, either the moon was down or there was a cloud cover, as it was pitch black outside. Only the occasional pinpoint of light could be seen as we passed a station or village.

    We came into a larger town and the train stopped. I had hoped that the three Germans would be getting off here, but no such luck. It was a short stop, and after we had started again, the conductor came through checking our tickets. I woke Joe from a sound sleep, and he produced his ticket to be punched and then went back to sleep. Sometime, well after midnight, we again stopped at a larger town. All of the blackout curtains were now drawn and all of the bright lights in the coach were turned on. We wondered what was going on and were soon to find out. A German officer and a French Gendarme came into the front of the car and started to check identification papers. I nudged Joe and he understood what was happening. The Germans in our compartment were rummaging through their bags looking for their transit papers, and were making quite a bit of confusion in our compartment.

    I kept my eye as close to the sliding glass door as possible watching for our guide, who stepped out into the isle to be questioned. He then fumbled through his suit pockets and returned to his place in the compartment, apparently to check his overcoat pockets, finally producing the proper papers. He was allowed to go back to his seat in the compartment. I wondered why he had been so dumb as to bring so much attention to himself and was soon to find out the answer. The German officer and the French Gendarme came on through the car checking the papers of each occupant. Both Joe and I were nervous about whether our papers would pass inspection. When the inspectors were two or three compartments from ours, the train started to move slowly. Both of the inspectors bolted for the rear door to get off the train before they would have to take a ride to the next station. This saved us from having our papers checked at this stop. It did a lot to explain why the guide had taken up so much of the two officers' time. We later learned that both Bezier and Narbonne were regular German

PERPIGNON

checkpoints. I had seen the name Bezier on the station as we were leaving.

As we all settled down to try to go to sleep again, one of the Germans got a cigarette out of his pack and fumbled for a light. He poked me and asked me for a "strieckles." I knew that he wanted a match, and just shook my head and went back to sleep. The blackout curtains remained closed, only the cove lights were now on. Our next stop must have been Narbonne. Our rail car was not inspected this time.

Some time after we departed Narbonne, it started to get light outside. Although the blue cove lights were still on, the blackout curtains were now raised and I could see that a light rain was falling. A little later it appeared more like light, wet snow as I could see small icy droplets sliding diagonally down the outside of the windowpane.

The three German soldiers were now stirring. One after another they lit up cigarettes; apparently they had found some matches. One of the Germans unwrapped a candy bar or candy stick and began eating.

Although I was still pretending to sleep, I had one hand over my face and eyes and could see through the slits my fingers made. I was able to see that we were passing through small villages, and soon the villages were more numerous and perhaps larger. I hoped that we were getting near our destination, as I was stiff and sore from leaning against the wall pretending to sleep. I don't think that I actually slept any of the way. I really believe that Joe was able to sleep, at least for much of the trip.

Soon our destination of Perpignon was announced. Nearly everyone in our car began to stir. I imagine that this was the end of the line for anyone who was not intending to proceed on into Spain. The three German soldiers were preparing to get off the train, and had to retrieve their duffel bags from overhead and pull the bags from under our feet. I stepped out into the corridor and Joe did the same to

249

make room for them. In the better light, we could see that a light, wet snow was falling. The visibility outside of our rail car was poor because of the fog and snowfall.

The train was going very slow and stopped a couple of times as we approached the station. Several people opened their coach doors and got off at cross streets as we were stopped or were just barely moving. Our guide was standing up in the corridor near the front of the car. We could see his hat. He looked at us and knew that we were watching him. He got off the train at the next cross street. The train was now barely moving and we also got off the train.

We could see our guide trudging up the street with his head down to ward off the snow. He never looked back, but I'm sure he knew that we had seen his signal and had gotten off. We trailed along after him, a little closer than I had planned because the visibility was so poor. We had left the train before it had gone all of the way into the railway station.

We followed our guide as he led us into the downtown area of the city. He then turned off the main street and we followed him onto a side street where we continued our walk for some time. We began to wonder if we were on our way to the border now, or if we would get a little time to rest before going over the Pyrenees. We were both hungry and hoped to eat and rest before the walk over the mountains began.

The guide entered a bakery shop, which was warm and smelled good inside. He spoke to the baker and then led us out the back door of the bakery. We crossed the courtyard behind the bakery, and went into the back door of a building that turned out to be a small hotel, or pension. The shop and the hotel seemed to both use the courtyard, as it had covered metal tables and chairs on both sides. This was probably quite beautiful in the summer, and was convenient for the bakery customers as well as the hotel patrons.

PERPIGNON

We entered the hotel just off the kitchen area, and were met in the hallway by a man that seemed to be expecting us. He took Joe and me and our guide into the empty kitchen where coffee was brewing and gave us some croissants and preserves. The coffee was better than the "ersatz," and we assumed that better coffee was to be had here in the south of France. Possibly he had brewed it especially for us or was getting ready to feed his pensioners. The guide left after shaking our hand, and our host put us in a little alcove off the kitchen. It looked like it was the place where the help ate or had coffee breaks.

Soon a young lady came in to greet us. She spoke excellent English, saying that she taught English language in a local school. She introduced herself as Simone, and said that we would be staying with her for a day or two until our companions (Bob and Ernie) caught up with us. We would be given a room in the back part of the hotel for the day, and we were to stay in the room until she came for us after school. After she left, we were shown to a small room on the first floor where Joe and I shared the one regular bed and it was most welcome.

I took off my coat and shoes and fell into the bed, rolled over, and slept until she came for us around 4PM. It was just about dark when we left the hotel with her. We went out the back into the courtyard and around the hotel, through a gate and out into the street. She walked between us with her arms looped into ours. This reminded me of the casualness of the girl who led me through the city of Aix-en-Provence to her grandfather's home.

We didn't have far to go, as her apartment was on the same street a few blocks from the hotel. We could see in the dimming light that we had entered a courtyard with apartments facing into the center. The apartments were all one story high. Hers was the second apartment from the entrance on our right as we entered. The entrance to the courtyard was gated, but I'm not sure that the gates were ever closed. The back of her apartment contained the kitchen cubicle, toilet, and

251

bath area. There was a small window over the bath covered with a heavy blackout curtain at all times. Another curtained window faced onto the courtyard.

Her apartment was quite typical of the size that a young, single, schoolteacher would occupy. It was basically just one room. It had a fireplace for heat and a small alcove for cooking and a small bathroom. One single bed also served as a couch in the daytime, along with an upholstered chair and a lamp. A table with two chairs served as a place to dine and also as a desk for her school chores. On one side of the fireplace there were the usual fireplace tools, and on the other side stood a tall vase resembling a fat baseball bat. It was thin and slender at the top where she had placed some dry fall or winter pussy willows.

The plan was for her to stay on her normal schedule. She would come home from school and cook dinner for us. We would build up a nice fire in the fireplace for warmth, and at about nine she would go to her girlfriend's apartment for the night.

We slept with one of us on the mattress on the floor and the other on the box springs. Sleeping on the box springs left something to be desired, but we certainly had slept on worse. We alternated on the good and the bad. Simone came in before daylight to prepare our breakfast, and then would leave for work.

She had been told that Bob and Ernie were scheduled to arrive in Perpignon a day after we had arrived, which would have been Friday. There was no word of them as yet by Friday night. On Saturday, she thought that surely they would come soon, and she spent most of the day in the apartment talking to us. She wanted to know about our life in the United States and all about our actions in the war. All day she was relaxed with us and it was pleasant to talk to her. She told us of her family who lived a distance north of Perpignon.

Our other two crewmembers had actually left Marseilles a day after we did, and had arrived in Perpignon on the morning of Friday the 25th. We later learned that they had been captured by the Gestapo that morning as they left the train station. News of their capture was slow in getting to the Resistance people involved in our escape attempt.

When they didn't arrive when scheduled on Friday, the concern was that for some reason they had not gotten on the train when they were scheduled to depart. When again they didn't arrive on Saturday morning, the Perpignon Resistance people sent someone to Marseilles to find out what had happened. Had they boarded the train in Marseilles, or had they somehow been delayed? The messenger that was sent to Marseilles was to telephone or wire a coded message to the Resistance people in Perpignon to let them know the status of the other two Americans.

We had been warned by our hostess, Simone that almost every night, one of the women in another apartment was visited by a member of the Gestapo. We had heard a car stopping on the street on Friday night and heard the tap-tap of the officer's heels as he went to her apartment.

On Saturday night, we again heard the car stop out front and instead of the normal tap-tap of heels, there were the sounds of two people walking into the courtyard. I grabbed the large poker from the fireplace and Joe up-ended the tall vase to use it as a baseball bat in case the Gestapo had come for us. Fortunately, they passed by, and from the sound of the voices, it appeared to be a man and a woman, probably the Gestapo agent bringing his French girlfriend home from dinner.

We gathered the pussy willows from the floor and put the vase and poker back in their place. Joe and I were both quite shaken by this incident and it took some time to get over the fright and settle down for the night.

On Sunday, Simone Pasquet (we had learned her last name from her mail and magazines in the apartment by this time) received the news from her contact that our companions had indeed left Marseillle on the evening of the 24th. A few hours later she heard from her contact that they had been captured on the 25th by the Gestapo and that their guides, a man and his wife, had also been caught by the Gestapo. It had been confirmed by the contact that the poor guides had been executed by the Germans that same afternoon.

This was indeed a bad Sunday for all three of us. She wondered what would happen to us - would we continue on our journey, or would we be attached to another group - what would be our fate? She wanted us out of there, but she knew that if we were turned out on the street, we would probably be captured and she would be in mortal danger.

On Sunday afternoon, "Black Sunday" as I remember it, the attitude was all gloom and doom - what should we do? I have never seen anyone suffer as much as she did after she heard that Bob and Ernie were captured. The thought that she might be stuck with us for a long time was overwhelming. I felt so sorry for her, knowing that we were causing her to be distraught and in such agony. I couldn't help but think of the carefree girl that had brought us into her apartment arm-in-arm a few afternoons before. Little did she know then how much trouble it would be to harbor us?

After the war, I learned the story of the capture of Ernie and Bob near the train station in Perpignon on that fateful Friday morning. They had left the train station in trail of their two guides, a young man and his wife. They kept a good distance behind the guides so as to not appear to be following them. As they crossed the square in front of the railroad station, two men in plain clothes grabbed and tried to hold them. They shook the two off and continued on across the square and onto a path across a vacant lot. The two plain-clothes men followed them across the lot, and then put a gun to the back of their neck and told them that they were under arrest. The men identified themselves as the Gestapo. They took them to a military headquarters a block

PERPIGNON

away and turned them over to the German army. The Gestapo men then left and hurried out to catch the two French guides who they must have spotted.

The German military questioned both Bob and Ernie non-stop for the remainder of the day. They wouldn't let them sleep, making them sit on stools in a small room. They were cuffed around a bit, and when one of them fell off his stool in sleep, they shook him awake and continued the interrogation. To all questions they would only give name, rank and serial number. This seemed to infuriate the Germans. In mid-afternoon, they were told that their guides had been captured and were going to be shot.

A short time later they heard, through a high barred window, the orders being given to the firing squad. They heard the shots ring out, and then one of their guards came in and said that the two guides had been executed. Neither Bob nor Ernie believed this at the time. They thought that all of this had been staged to frighten them into talking. They still would give only name, rank and serial number. Finally, after dark, they were taken to a jail cell in the regular city jail in Perpignon and pushed into a cell with only straw on the floor - no bed or blankets.

The next day they were put on a train to Paris where they were jailed for a few days, and then taken to the German interrogation center at Dulag Luft. They were interrogated constantly for several weeks, and then were sent to Stalag Luft #1 at Barth, Germany, for the remainder of the war. They were liberated by the Americans in April of 1945. The former POW's were flown in a B-17 to camp Lucky Strike in France, and eventually returned to the United States by ship to Norfolk, Virginia in early July.

Both Bob and Ernie thought that the Gestapo had been tipped off as to our transit to Perpignon. Possibly the only reason that Joe and I weren't also caught was that we had gotten off the train short of the station in the wet snow and fog. If we had waited to get off the train in the station, the Gestapo also would probably have picked us up.

On Monday, Simone went out to find her contact. When she met the person, she was given the assurance that we would be moved as soon as possible and that a new group was being formed. She had bought a Monday morning newspaper containing pictures of Joe and me on the second page. It stated that we were enemy agents and were known to be in the Perpignon area. There was a heavily outlined warning that anyone helping or harboring us would be shot on sight. It told the readers that if they saw either of us, they should turn us in immediately. This warning was just devastating to Simone, as well as to us.

We couldn't figure out how they had gotten our pictures. The photos were copies of the same ones that had been on our French ID and were now on our Polish identification card. We recalled that none of us was given an extra copy of the pictures when they were taken for our original fake ID's.

The mystery was solved when Simone received word that the pictures were found in the heel of the shoe of the man who had been guiding Bob and Ernie. I don't know why the pictures were in his shoe. He may have had all of our pictures hidden there because he was to hand all of us over to the guide who was to take us over the mountains into Spain. This is just one of several possible explanations, but it will always remain a mystery.

For the three of us in the little apartment to say that Sunday was bad, Monday was HELL. Simone had decided on Sunday that she would call the school to inform them that she was ill and wouldn't be in for her classes on Monday. She left the apartment to see a doctor friend who gave her papers to the effect that she was overworked and nervous and needed some time off to recuperate. She told us, on her return, that she would go Tuesday morning to get the papers she needed to be able to travel to her parents' home in a rural area east of

PERPIGNON

Bordeaux. She would also check Tuesday morning to see if another group would be forming. She didn't come back at suppertime Monday night, so Joe and I found some food in the apartment and fixed our own meal.

She came in early on Tuesday morning and fixed our breakfast. This, being a leap year, was Tuesday, February 29th, 1944. She left the apartment that morning saying that she was going to get her travel papers to go to her parents' home, and also to check with her contact. She said she would be back as soon as possible.

She came back to the apartment at one o'clock all smiles, telling us that the contact had said that we would leave that evening for sure. Both Joe and I had our misgivings; we had both seen how unpredictable these things could be. I prayed that this poor young lady wouldn't be let down this time.

She said that in celebration, Tuesday afternoon would be a treat for us. She would flip pancakes to honor "Shrove's Tuesday." I didn't know what "Shrove's Tuesday" was about, so I asked Joe. He, being catholic, said it was something having to do with "Mardi Gras." She laughed and said that "Mardi Gras" was French slang for "Shrove's Tuesday."

She proceeded to make some pancakes for us. She made thin pancakes that she would expertly flip over in the air and catch in the frying pan, turning them over to cook the other side. She wanted us to try this, so we both had a hand at it. We would get the majority of the batter in the pan, but some of the uncooked pancake would run down the side as well, providing a great laugh at how clumsy we were at this maneuver. All ended well when we had our fill of the thin pancakes, dusted with powdered sugar and some sweet dried fruit that she had brought home.

She said that she was to make up food for us for the two-day trip over the Pyrenees Mountains and into Spain. She had gotten two pairs of knit gloves and a warm scarf for us. The scarf was for me

257

because I didn't have one and neither of us had gloves until now. We thought that the gloves would be welcome, and they were.

She packed each of our food parcels with two halves of the long French bread, a nice piece of cheese, a piece of hard salami, and a tin of sardines. She carefully tied the packages with string. She then gave us each a water bottle that was probably two-thirds of a liter in size, and re-filled our two small medicine bottles from a bottle of Schnapps. She was so warm and cheerful that I couldn't help but feel, "Please God, don't let her down," send someone for us tonight.

At about 5:30PM there was a coded knock at the door, and she let a young man into the apartment. He told her in French that he had come for us. She translated this to us, and we put on our coats with the Schnapps safely in one coat pocket, and the gloves and scarf in the other. Neither of us thought to bring our safety razor or toothbrush. We picked up our food bundles, and with a big hug and a kiss on both cheeks, she said au revoir, and in English, "God go with you." It was in this manner that we left this heroic young lady for our hike over the Pyrenees Mountains into Spain.

CHAPTER 11

CROSSING THE PYRENEES

Early that evening, we left the apartment, hoping that Simone Pasquet would make good her private escape to her parents' sanctuary, and would be able to survive the war. We had spent six tense days and five nights in Perpignon, and were ready for the next leg of our trip to freedom.

Our guide led us south out of the city. We stayed fairly close behind him, as he was wearing dark clothing and it was hard to see him in the moonless night. Soon the sidewalk ended and we started down an asphalt road. We could see the dim lights of a car coming toward us, so the three of us hid in the tall grass along the side of the road until it passed. Our guide led us across a field, and then by a pathway where we came to an area of high grass and spongy ground. After walking some distance into the tall grass, he told us to crouch down to wait.

We quietly squatted there with him, waiting until we could hear a rustling in the grass near us. There was a low whistle, as another group was led to us composed of American and British air crewmen. We were being attached to this new group. Our leader quickly disappeared and we followed along with this group as the new leader took us farther into the grassy area.

This guide was in charge of handing us over to the people that would actually take us into Spain. He gave each of us a token, a

French franc bank note torn in half. We were told to keep it safe, and only give it to the guides when we were safely in Spain. Further along, we met up with two mountain guides who had a group of French civilians and a Russian Jew with them.

I learned later that all of these civilian people had to pay the guides in advance or maybe half-down and the remainder on delivery into Spain for their crossing; apparently making their own deal with the guides. This now made up the entire group to make the border crossing.

The new guides appeared to be more Spanish than French, or may have been Basque. They both were short, slight and wiry. They could easily have been father and son, and most likely were professional smugglers. They spoke to the group in French. One of the French civilians spoke excellent English, as well as several other languages, and became our communications link with the smugglers.

We were told to walk in a single file close to the one just ahead and to remain completely silent as there were German sentries posted all through this area that might hear us. We then filed forward at a very fast pace. It wasn't exactly a run but it was certainly a very fast walk.

We followed a path for a distance and then came to a road. The lead guide sent the younger one to scout out the road and then with another low whistle, we were hurried across. In this fashion, we crossed several more roads, and skirted some farms.

We walked through some fields that made for pretty easy going. Sometimes, however, we were led through a vineyard where the vines would bind around our legs, making the going pretty tough in the dark. One of the Americans fell in one of the vineyards and let out an oath that could be heard for a mile. A dog close by barked, and we all froze. The lead guide hesitated and then went on.

When we were clear of the vineyard, the guide stopped. He passed the word through our French interpreter, that if anyone let out a sound like that again, he would be left behind and the offender could not continue with us. We felt that we had been properly warned.

After the first two hours of walking, we were given a 15-minute break, where I had a breathless chance to get acquainted with some of our GI companions.

When the rest time was up, we heard the familiar "Allez vite" (go, hurry up, move). We were to hear this from the two guides continuously for the entire trip. It was always "allez, allez, vite, vite." The allez sounded like "allay" and the vite like "veet." We soon called the two guides, "Allez #1" and "Allez #2." "Allez #1" always led and "Allez #2" brought up the rear of the line, and prodded the stragglers.

We still did not seem to be in the mountains but were traveling in the foothills more or less, perpendicular to the coast. This course led us a few miles inland and into the lower foothills of the mountains. Sometimes we would hear a dog bark and the guide would halt for a moment. I think that it was possible that he could discern the barking of the local farm dogs from the dogs of the German patrols.

The next rest stop was near midnight and Joe and I felt that we just had to open one of the food bundles, as it had been a long time since the flipping of pancakes. We borrowed a knife from one of the Frenchmen and cut a nice slice of bread and cheese and washed it down with water and a nip of the Schnapps.

Some of the others had fruit and wine and all sorts of food. Many of the French carried suitcases packed with food and clothes. It was my decision that since Simone had done such a good job of tying our bundles, we would only open mine for this snack. Before we had barely gotten through eating, we heard the familiar "Allez vite."

I tried to re-tie my bundle as I walked, but I couldn't get it to stay together properly. I took the scarf out of my jacket pocket and put it around the food bundle, put my water bottle alongside the food in the scarf and tied the four corners together and thought that I had a neat

261

way to carry my provisions.

In our group was a Russian Jew, who had walked away from a German work camp in Poland, to try to escape into Spain. Our interpreter spoke Polish and could communicate with him. He was quite tall and thin and had very large hands and feet with a sallow face and appeared half-starved. We were to marvel at his stamina. Both Joe and I commented on how much his face reminded us of Marcel, having the same "bedraggled" look that Marcel wore most of the time.

We had finally started a gradual climb upward. Once we heard dogs baying in the distance. The dogs must have been accompanying a German patrol, as we quickly changed directions to take us away from the peril. The rear guide spread pepper along our trail from a sack attached to his belt. This was ordinary ground table pepper that apparently was carried for this purpose.

The Frenchman who spoke several languages, stayed up front with the lead guide so he could relay instructions to all of us in a whisper. This was then passed on down the line. We soon approached a rushing mountain stream that had to be crossed. It was fairly wide but did not look to be very deep. The water was extremely cold, as it was runoff from the melting snow above.

We stopped at the stream bank and watched as both guides took off their shoes and socks and rolled up their pant legs as high as possible. The first guide walked across with no problem at all. We all had taken our shoes and socks off and rolled up our pant legs and long underwear. We tied our shoestrings together and put the shoes, with the socks inside, around our neck, just as the guides had done. I noticed that the first few going across were getting the bottom of their long coats wet so I decided to take my jacket off and also tie it around my neck as well.

Now it came my turn. I waded into the icy water and found that the stones on the bottom were quite rough and slippery. The larger submerged stones were just barely visible, so I tried to use these as

CROSSING THE PYRENEES

stepping-stones to get to the other side. I slipped off one of these rocks and went down in the cold water. I regained my footing and was wet to the waist but made it to the other side with a couple more long steps. My shoes, socks, and jacket were just splashed with water.

When I went down, I had the scarf with the bundle of food and water bottle in one hand and lost hold of it. I saw it swiftly disappear downstream. After gaining the other side, I sat down on the bank and put on my dry socks, shoes, and jacket.

While I was putting my shoes on, I saw one of the Frenchmen begin to cross the stream. He was in trouble almost immediately. He was carrying a suitcase in one hand. He almost went down twice and finally nearly made it to shore. When he jumped for a rock just under the surface, he slipped off and went completely under. He may have hit his head on one of the submerged rocks. I didn't see him try to get up or struggle, or swim to shore. He disappeared in the dark just as my scarf and bundle of food had.

The lead guide went down the stream bank for a few minutes looking for him but soon came back and said "Allez vite," and off we trudged again. We all hoped that the unfortunate man had reached the shore somewhere and perhaps made it back to Perpignon, but it would have been very difficult, being totally soaked with the icy water.

My pants and sweater back below the waist were very wet; I found that my socks and shoes were soon saturated by the runoff from my wet pants. I felt that the exertion of the hike would soon dry my clothes, but that was not to be the case. I was now quite cold and started shivering a lot.

We came to another stream, which had to be crossed. I decided to take my socks off but to put my shoes back on since they were already wet. I rolled up my pants and long-johns and got across with the shoes on just fine. I took off my wet shoes, poured the water out, put my damp socks on and sloshed along with the group.

I just couldn't seem to keep from shivering. Even though I had the warm sweater and heavy jacket on, I was still very wet and cold. I was exhausted and thoroughly miserable when we made our third rest stop. I was apparently fortunate that my upper body was relatively dry or I would probably have been in serious trouble.

Joe didn't seem too upset that I had lost my food. He said that he would share his with me. He was more concerned that our remaining one water bottle would sustain both of us. I worried about the food as well as the water. I was afraid that we wouldn't make it across in two days if we were pinned down by a German patrol or a change in the weather, like a blizzard.

Water had not been a problem so far as we filled our one bottle at every stream although we knew that when we got up to the snow level, running water would be hard to find. I still had my little bottle of Schnapps and my gloves, although I had lost my scarf.

We went through one area where the guide passed the word that there was a German sentry post nearby and had us all crouch down and walk in total silence for quite a while.

We were now obviously climbing more and it was harder to keep up. There were stragglers and several gave up. They sat or lay down and wouldn't get up despite the prodding of the rear guide. The guides were upset by this and finally said that if anyone couldn't keep up they would be left behind. Our American Sgt. Harrison was one that sat down and was about to be left behind - He finally did get up and was miraculously able to make it to the next rest stop.

After the midnight rest stop it was getting harder and harder for Joe and me to keep up. Joe was having a lot of trouble and I urged and coaxed him along. He said several times, "You just leave me here Loo-tenant." I couldn't leave him any more than he could have left me of course, but we did get somewhat behind. We were never last, but we could hear the rear guard saying to the stragglers "Allez, allez, vite, vite," almost constantly. "If," I ever enjoyed another night's sleep again, I was certain I'd still hear those hideous words in my dreams…nightmares!

This put us at a disadvantage at each succeeding rest stop, making each stop shorter. It was with a lot of relief that we saw the eastern sky begin to lighten up. We hoped that we would be bedded down during the daylight hours soon. At about this time, we heard dogs baying and barking in the distance ahead of us. The guides seemed to be quite alarmed and we again, started to backtrack for quite some distance. The rear guide spread the pepper again, as we went back along the trail from where we had come. We stopped and waited until the guides were satisfied that the dogs were not on our scent.

The mountains looked closer and more formidable as we viewed them in the daylight. The guides led us to an area of thick brush near some large boulders and told us that we were to stay hidden in the thick brush for the day. It was perhaps 7:30 or 8AM. Joe and I counted 18 or 19 still in the group when we bedded down on this morning of March 1st. This was the end of our first night of travel and we were all absolutely exhausted.

The guides did not stay with us during the day. They were apparently hiding nearby where they could observe us but not be seen. We could see snow covered peaks ahead. We had obviously gained some altitude but we knew that we were nowhere near the top as yet.

Fortunately the morning sun was fairly warm as we tried to sleep. We stayed in the sun as much as possible. There was a trickle of melt water coursing down the rocks near us and we wet our faces and drank our fill. After resting for a couple of hours, Joe and I ate some of our shared ration.

We now had a chance to get acquainted with our GI traveling companions. There were 7 Americans, 3 officers and 4 sergeants. The seven in our escaping group were the 2 other officers, 1st Lts. Roland Marean, and James Shilliday. The Sgts. names were Spellman, Harrison, Hasson, and my sergeant, Joe Kinnane. There were also three RAF airmen with us. One was Sgt. Banner and I can't remember the names of the other two. I think that there was one RCAF man with us during the first night, but was not with us in the morning.

The English speaking Frenchman crawled over to us and joined our conversation. We asked him a lot of questions and he told us that we may have to spend some time in a Spanish prison, but he thought that eventually we would be given over to the Americans or the British.

He told us about the Russian Jew that was with us. Our interpreter said that he was told by the man that he had been a forced laborer for the Germans in Poland and had escaped. He had crossed Poland, Germany and France and now had hopes of reaching freedom in Spain. He hoped that the Spanish would not turn him over to the Germans to be returned and executed.

The Frenchmen in our group were very sympathetic to the Russian, and vowed to see that he would not be sent back to Germany. They helped him whenever they could and provided cloth strips to bind his bleeding feet before he put on his oversized shoes. He crawled to the little stream of icy water every so often during the day, and bathed his feet until they were numb to kill the pain. We could see his bloody feet with the large bleeding blisters. We all were "rooting" for him and hoped that he would make it across the mountains and finally be free.

The courage and stamina of some people who are seeking freedom is truly amazing. He certainly was an inspiration to me to keep going.

The Frenchman also told us the stories that some of the other Frenchmen had told him. One was trying to escape being sent to a German forced labor camp. Another was a "maquis" trying to escape. He told us the stories of his countrymen dodging the Gestapo, hiding in the countryside and of their effort to get to North Africa to join the Free French Army. We had a very good feeling about the French. They all seemed to be patriots; at least all that we were in contact with. The ones that Joe and I knew personally were our heroes.

The French interpreter was eager to talk to us about the war. He had been subjected to German propaganda and thought that perhaps the war was not going well for the Allies.

He spoke several languages, having taught languages in school prior to the war. He had been a French Army officer who had been captured by the Germans when France fell early in the war. He was in a POW camp for some time, and finally repatriated to his home to teach school. He told us that he was active in his local resistance movement and had taken part in several clandestine actions with the underground. He was now trying to go to the Free French Army in North Africa, where he hoped to be an officer in the artillery.

When we left Perpignon, we knew that there were more in our party than the number that were in the day camp with us. Some had lagged behind and probably went back the way that they had come. Then there was the fellow who was swept away in the stream, and also the RCAF man.

It may be hard to imagine that young men would be so overcome with exhaustion that they could not continue. Many had been cooped up in attics or hidden in barns for many months and had no chance to exercise. All of the exercise that Joe and I had experienced was the walk each day for water or firewood when we lived with the sheepherder. My never to be forgotten trek across Aix-en-Provence with the young French girl and oh! I will never forget the bike ride, either.

As the conversation continued, everyone in camp was talking rather loudly. Soon the younger guide came into camp and warned us through the interpreter, that we were too noisy. He said that we could be heard a kilometer away. He told us to be quiet and rest. We spoke in whispers there after.

One of our fellows started to light a cigarette, the Frenchman, who had been a "Maquis," stopped him, saying that the Germans could smell the cigarette smoke for quite a distance and it might give us away.

After eating, we spent a couple of more hours resting and sleeping on the hard ground. We were trying to stay out of the shade and in the sun. My clothes were nearly dry but my shoes were still wet. Just below the thicket, there was a small grove of spindly young trees. I saw several of the Frenchmen go down there and cut saplings for a walking stick. Joe was asleep, so I borrowed a knife and went down and cut a stick. I found a nice sapling that had a "Y" in it about five feet above where I cut it. I trimmed the two branches that made the "Y" to make the top end somewhat like a crutch. I had the notion that if I sprained an ankle; I could hobble along with the stick as a crutch.

I crouched down and went back up to the camp. As I lay there, I was thinking of the situation that we were in. I didn't know what kind of a reception we would get from the Spanish officials. I knew that Spain was sympathetic to the Axis powers although they were officially neutral. I also thought of the horrible predicament that we had created for poor Simone in Perpignon. I hoped that she had made good her escape and was now safely on a train going to her parents' home.

I fanaticized, like any 20 year old male would, about the girl in Aix that had led me across town to her grandparents' home. I again wished that I had written my name and home address on a slip of paper for her and hidden it under one of pictures in the old man's picture album. If she survived the war, I hoped that she would have written to me. In an after-thought, however, I concluded that it probably wouldn't have been such a good plan, as the Germans might have raided his home and found the note. I didn't want to cause her or her grandparents any trouble like we had for Simone. My thoughts then drifted to Dionne back home. I thought about the many pleasurable times we had spent together. I was trying to think about anything except the predicament that we were now in.

CROSSING THE PYRENEES

Finally, late in the afternoon, we decided to eat a little bit more of our shared food. We had a couple of slices of the bread and opened the only tin of sardines that Joe had in his food bundle. We each put some sardines on the bread and poured the oil left in the tin on the bread. We felt that we needed all of the fuel that we could get. We cut a little more of the cheese and nearly finished off the salami that was left.

We watched as the rest of the group ate their food. We both were still hungry, but we didn't think that we could afford to completely finish off our entire food ration at this time.

One of the fellows pulled a large apple out of his pack and started eating it. Just the sound of him biting into the crisp apple made a big impression on me. I wished that we had some fruit to eat. After he finished eating the apple, he threw the core on the ground near where he was sitting. I watched until his attention was elsewhere and moved over to where the core was laying and covered it with dirt and sand. When the man and his companions crawled away, I scooped up the core, dirt and all, in my fist and crawled to where the water was running down the rocks. When I felt that I was alone, I washed the sand and dirt off the apple core and ate it all. I was a bit ashamed of myself, but my stomach growled its approval.

Many in the party had poor shoes. Shoes were scarce in France and often the evaders had very ill fitting foot-ware. Some had shoes too small, causing a lot of foot trouble. Sgt. Spellman had shoes with wooden soles. Some had shoes too large for their feet and they stuffed rags and even straw in them for comfort. It was very hard going, constantly up and down hills, even for those wearing shoes that fit well.

At every rest stop, some would remove their shoes and socks and rub their feet and show others the blisters that they were sporting. Joe and I were lucky that we still had our original GI shoes, the ones that we had on when we landed in France. Our shoes were well worn but were quite serviceable for the hike over the mountains.

At about 6PM, we gathered up our belongings, formed a single file behind Allez #1, and began our second night of walking to Spain. We were all relieved to be on our way on what we thought would be our last night in France.

Joe and I were still hungry, but we had a full water bottle and each had taken a nip of our Schnapps before we trudged off with the group. We talked about emptying our little Schnapps bottles and using them for water. We decided that since they were small medicine bottles that they wouldn't carry enough water to make it worth the effort. Besides we thought that the Schnapps might come in handy later.

We tried to stay up near the front of the line as best we could. This night was one of climbing over one hill after another. The ground was mostly rock and shale and the uphill side of the hills was often covered with ice and snow. The walking stick came in very handy and I was sorry that I hadn't cut one for Joe also. The stick kept me from falling many times.

We had to be as quiet as possible as the Germans were heavily patrolling the border over which we were trying to cross. It was almost impossible to be completely quiet, as we were often walking on shale and it created some noise of its own.

The progress going up the hills was usually taking two steps up and sliding one step back. The short down sides of the hills were sliding and slipping and sometimes falling. After a couple of hours of this, we were thoroughly exhausted and Allez#1 gave us a rest stop.

It was most welcome as Joe and I needed the rest. We had run out of water but now we were in snow and we continually scooped up snow to keep our mouth moist. It just seemed like we could never get enough water to appease our thirst. There were some trickles of snow melt water on the down (south) sides of the hills, but the guides would not slow down long enough for us to completely fill our one, small neck, water bottle.

CROSSING THE PYRENEES

At each rest stop, some of our companions would remove their shoes and socks and try to rub the feeling back into their cold feet. One of the British airmen had only canvas sneakers on his feet and he thought that his toes were possibly frostbitten.

Scooping up snow for water just wasn't as satisfying as a good 6 or 8 ounces of cool water. We surely missed the water bottle that I had lost in the stream the first night.

As we pressed on, I became very weak and it was hard for us to keep up. Joe seemed to have gotten a "second wind" and was the strong one now. He kept saying "Come on Loo-tenant, you can do it." I was just putting one foot ahead of the other, weaving back and forth as I struggled up the hills.

Our French translator kept saying that Allez #1 said that, "Spain was over the next hill." By this time, we had heard this message from Allez #1 at least a half dozen times. Meanwhile several of the men just sat down and wouldn't get up. One of the RAF airman sat down in the snow and couldn't get up. Several tried to help him but gave up as they were getting too far behind. Those that couldn't get up were left where they fell. The Russian Jew was still with us, but was being supported at times.

I was thinking that I just wasn't going to make it. Joe would push ahead in the snow and tow me with the walking stick. I thought that the stick might come in handy but I surely didn't anticipate using it in this way.

At the next rest stop, we all just flopped down to get some rest and tried to pump up some reserve to be able to keep on. I hoped and prayed that we would make it into Spain this night, for I felt that I couldn't go through another night like this without food.

We seemed to be out of the heavy snow area now. When we again stopped for rest, Joe and I talked about our situation and made the decision to finish off our rations. We would eat the bread and cheese and the little bit of salami and "go for it," After we had finished all of

271

our food, we knew that we had to make it over the mountains that night or we wouldn't be able to make it into Spain.

All too soon, we heard the "Allez vite," got up and begrudgingly trudged off into the dark. It was very rocky now, and as we were going around a hill on a narrow path, one of the Frenchmen slipped and fell into the gully below. We could hear him falling and tumbling in the dark. We all stopped and waited for Allez #1 to come back to see what the fuss was all about. He took a look at the steep hillside, shrugged and went back up to the front and it was "allay veet" per usual, leaving the poor man to his fate. So much for human compassion of one's fellow man.

After we had negotiated the narrow ledge one of the Frenchmen turned around and went back. I suppose he intended to try to find his friend and to see if he could help him. Quite sadly, we never saw either of them again.

As we got nearer the border, a searchlight was turned on. This light was on a peak above us and was probing the area. We all dropped down and lay there perfectly still, curled up like rocks, hoping that if the light did find us, we would look like the landscape and blend into the hillside. After 10 or 15 minutes of probing the hills all around us, the light went out and we began again. This was a warning to us that the Germans were indeed guarding the border and that we had better be extra careful. Although I was scared at this point, this hesitation afforded me a chance to regain some energy.

Our guide slowed down a bit now because we had so many stragglers that it was often hard to see the person ahead to keep in line. This was absolutely becoming a life or death struggle for me. I couldn't keep up and pleaded with Joe to go on. I said that I would find my way into Spain after I had rested but he kept coaxing me along. I didn't know the term then but I had literally "hit the wall." My mind said, "go on" but my feet would not obey. Joe would grab me by the arm, push and shove, and make me move along. We heard over and over again that "Spain was over the next hill."

Sometime after midnight, we had a rest stop in an area where there was some melt water. We broke the thin ice and had a good drink, filling the bottle to the brim, and I felt a lot better. I may have been dehydrated, causing me to feel so weak and unsteady. Joe was now in trouble as he was stumbling and falling often. I tried to help him as much as I could. I would tow him by the arm and dig in with the walking stick to get some leverage.

With our "pea jackets" and stocking caps, I am sure that we were staggering like two drunken sailors after a big night of drinking. In the movies this might have been comical, for us however, it was sheer survival.

Digital reproduced photograph of "Stardust" with Mt. Vesuvius, Italy in the background. Created by Graphic artist Alex Reyna

2nd Lt. W. Amundsen
Navigator - Left Front Gun

2nd Lt. E. Jenkins
Bombardier - Right Front Gun

S/Sgt. E. Madigan
Flight engineer - Top Turret Gun

1st Lt. W. Coss
Pilot

2nd Lt. R. Johnson
Copilot

Sgt. A. Najarian
Radioman - Upper Rear Gun

Sgt. H. Rice
Ball Turret Gun

Sgt. C. Henderson
Left Waist Gun

Sgt. J.M. Kinnane
Right Waist Gun

Sgt. J. Hoskins
Tail Gun

The B - 17 was truly a "flying fortress"

Back row, L to R: Sgt. H. Parks, **Sgt. H. Rice**, ball turret gun, **Sgt. J. Hoskins**, tail gun, **Sgt. C. Henderson**, left waist gun, and S/Sgt. F. Rogers

Note: Parks and Rogers were replaced by Sgt. A. Najarian, and S/Sgt. E. Madigan. They are pictured at the bottom of the page and Sgt. J Kinnane, pictured at the bottom of the page, was part of original crew but unavailable for this photo.

Front row, L to R: **2nd Lt. E. Jenkins**, Bombardier - right front gun, **2nd Lt. R. Johnson**, Copilot, **2nd Lt. W. Amundsen**, Navigator - Left front gun, and **1st Lt. W. Coss**, Pilot

S/Sgt. E. Madigan
Flight Engineer - top turret gunner
Killed in action aboard Stardust

Sgt. A. Najarian
Radioman - upper rear gun

Sgt. J. M. Kinnane
Right waist gunner

These three men completed the ten man crew on January 27, 1944

Typical unimproved tent in Tortorella, Italy "Dec & January, 1943 - 44" Courtesy of 99th BG Historical Society

The four officers below, first occupied a tent like this in Tortorella, Italy. Note the doorway that often was improved with scavenged parts. Also, the stovepipe emerging out the peek with the metal flange.

Stardust Officer Crewmembers

L to R: **1st Lt. Wes Coss** - Pilot, **2nd Lt. Walter Amundsen** - Navigator, **2nd Lt. Bob Johnson** - Copilot, and **2nd Lt. Ernest Jenkins** - Bombardier

P38 like the one (with the left engine shut down) that tucked under our formation for protection on the way home.

Airplane pictures provided by Jeff Ethell collection www.ww2.com

We were shot down on January 27, 1944, by a mixed squadron of ME-109's and FW-190's

Above: German Messchersmit ME - 109

Right: German Folkerwolf FW - 190

German Junker JU - 88
This is the sight we saw of the JU-88 passing low over our heads, when we were hiding out with the sheepherder.

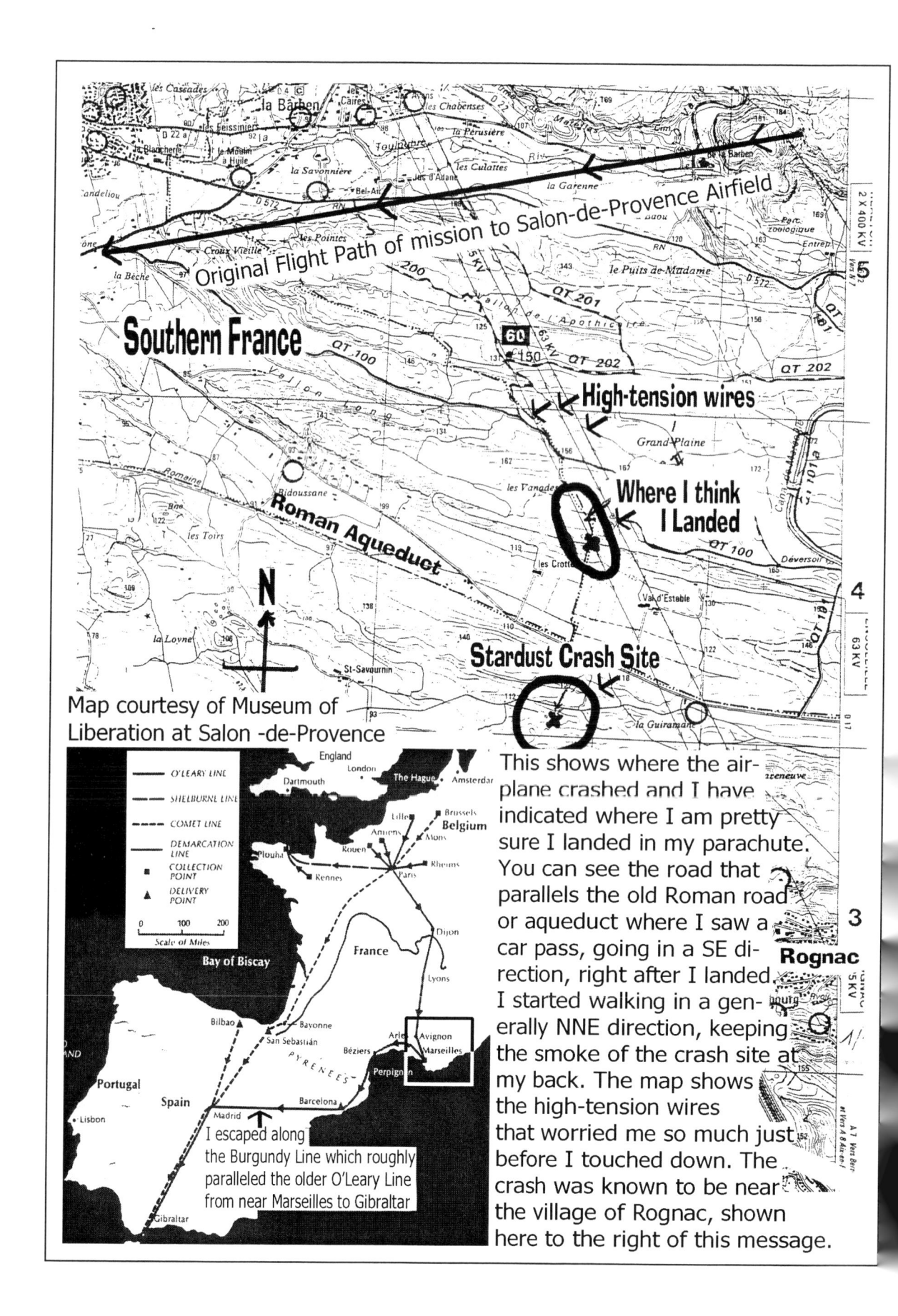

Original Flight Path of mission to Salon-de-Provence Airfield

Southern France

High-tension wires

Roman Aqueduct

Where I think I Landed

Stardust Crash Site

Map courtesy of Museum of Liberation at Salon-de-Provence

This shows where the airplane crashed and I have indicated where I am pretty sure I landed in my parachute. You can see the road that parallels the old Roman road or aqueduct where I saw a car pass, going in a SE direction, right after I landed. I started walking in a generally NNE direction, keeping the smoke of the crash site at my back. The map shows the high-tension wires that worried me so much just before I touched down. The crash was known to be near the village of Rognac, shown here to the right of this message.

I escaped along the Burgundy Line which roughly paralleled the older O'Leary Line from near Marseilles to Gibraltar

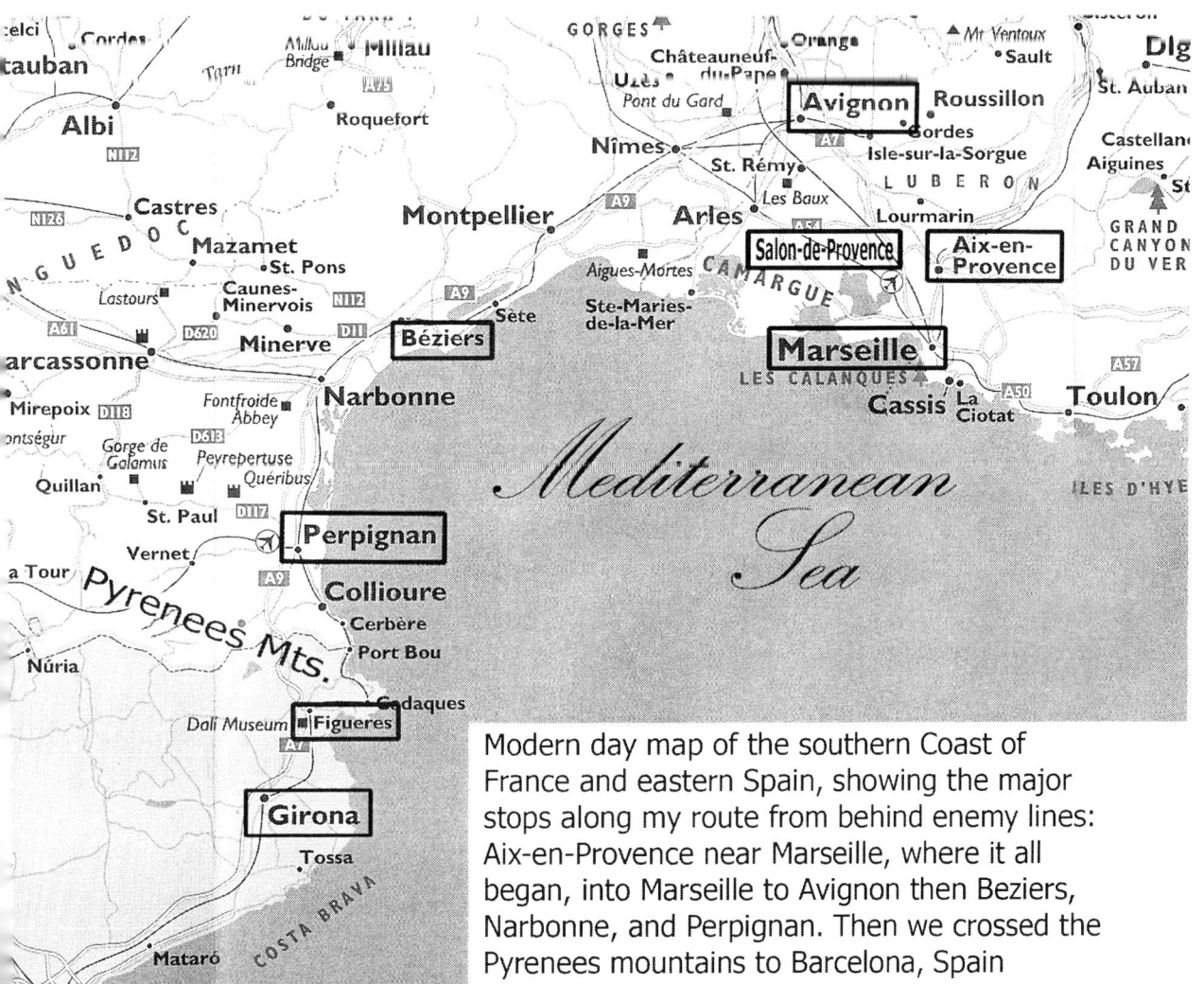

Modern day map of the southern Coast of France and eastern Spain, showing the major stops along my route from behind enemy lines: Aix-en-Provence near Marseille, where it all began, into Marseille to Avignon then Beziers, Narbonne, and Perpignan. Then we crossed the Pyrenees mountains to Barcelona, Spain where I then received my British ID papers and British assistance.

A picture of our benefactor, Jean Juvenile. He was the leader of the group of Resistance workers that engineered our escape from the start until we were taken to Marseilles to join the Burgundy escape line for our transport to Perpignon and eventual freedom. Both S/Sgt. Joe Kinnane (known to the Kinnane family as "Mike") and I lived with the Juvenile family in Aix-en-Provence for some time, until we could continue our trip to Perpignon and the very difficult walk across the Pyrenees Mts. into Spain. I continued to correspond with the Juvenile family after the war and was able to thank them for their courage and help. I was also grateful to receive this photograph of him.

AVIS

Toute personne du sexe masculin qui aiderait, directement ou indirectement, les équipages d'avions ennemis descendus en parachute, ou ayant fait un atterrissage forcé, favoriserait leur fuite, les cacherait ou leur viendrait en aide de quelque façon que ce soit, sera fusillée sur le champ.

Les femmes qui se rendraient coupables du même délit seront envoyées dans des camps de concentration situés en Allemagne.

Les personnes qui s'empareront d'équipages contraints à atterrir, ou de parachutistes, ou qui auront contribué, par leur attitude, à leur capture, recevront une prime pouvant aller jusqu'à **10.000 francs**. Dans certains cas particuliers, cette récompense sera encore augmentée.

Paris, le 22 Septembre 1941.

Le Militärbefehlshaber en France.
Signé: von **STÜLPNAGEL**
Général d'Infanterie.

-- Poster presented to AFEES by the Museum of the Resistance and Deportation in Angouleme, France

WARNING

All men who aid directly or indirectly the crews of enemy aircraft coming down by parachute or having made a forced landing, will be shot in the field.

Women who render the same type aid will be sent to concentration camps in Germany.

People who capture crews who are forced to land or parachutists, or who contribute, by their actions, to their capture will receive up to 10,000 francs. In certain particular cases this compensation will be increased.

Digital Artwork depicting how J.M. Kinnane & Wes Coss looked before crossing the Pyrenees.

French warning sign courtesy of Air Force Escape and Evasion Society

Musée de la Libération de la Provence

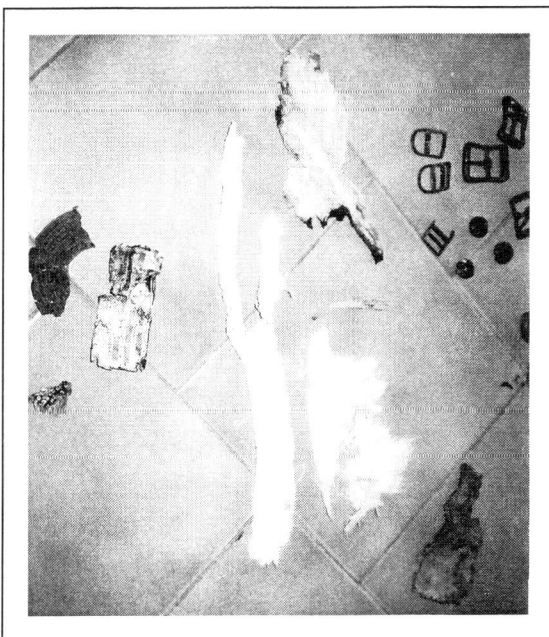

Some of the remains of Stardust are on display in the museum, including S/Sgt. Madigan's torn & burned parachute. Also unexploded 50 cal. ammunition and machine gun parts from the Stardust crashsite.

Association Loi 1901

"Le Grenier du Soldat"

Salon-de-Provence

Musee de la Liberation de la Provence
Chateau du Pigeonnier
5m Quartier du Pont a'Avignon
13300 Salon-de-Provence, France

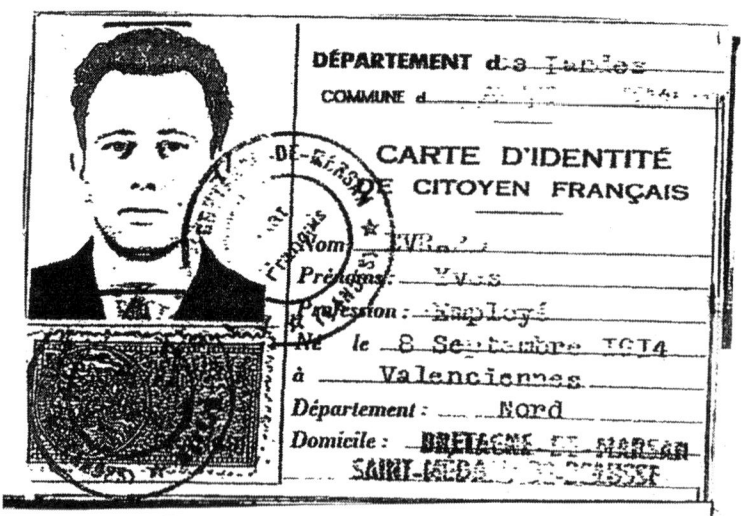

Major "Wayne" Eveland's French ID Card

Major "Wayne" Eveland's picture taken at the same time as mine (below) for our British citizenship papers. Note the difference between his two photos. The walking trip across the Pyrenees took a heavy toll!

History of the "Winged Boot" or "Winged Foot"

The exploits of aircrews who walked back to their bases after bailing out or crash landing in the desert of N. Africa were responsible for this highly respected wartime award. This boot was awarded to each British crewman who was fortunate enough to "walk out" and was proudly worn on the British uniform. The U.S. Government did not recognize this awarded insignia; however, the American evaders who walked out, wore it covertly beneath their left lapel. I had mine sewn on at Hobson's Clothiers, London, 1944.

The "winged boot" emblem that I wore under the left lapel of my uniform that identified me as one of the evaders who had walked out of enemy territory and had returned to fly and fight again.

My picture (above) taken in the "Penny Arcade" in Barcelona, for my British Citizenship and passport. My French ID card was similar to Waynes, but was left behind.

CHAPTER 12

SPAIN

It was the usual "Spain over the next hill" when at 0130 in the morning, we actually saw the lights of Spain spread out ahead. We checked with the interpreter to find out if we were actually over the border and out of France and he said, "Yes, we are now in Spanish territory." This was March 2^{nd,} 1944. The interpreter passed the word to be extra quiet as the Spanish patrols were to be feared. We stopped here on the rolling hillside to let everyone catch up.

When the lights of Spain could be seen, the Russian Jew finally gave up and sat down, shaking with exhaustion and overcome with emotion. We left him there with one of the Frenchmen, who volunteered to remain with him. He had been lagging behind all night, and I was surprised to see that he had actually made it into Spanish territory. The two were left with water and food aplenty and with rest; they should have made it down the mountain to freedom. I have often wondered as to the fortune of that Russian; did he really gain freedom in Spain? I certainly hoped so.

Then it was the familiar "allez vite," as we got up and started off downhill. A couple of the American sergeants, Harrison and Hasson, with a sudden burst of energy, ran on ahead; passing "Allez #1," pell-mell down the hill toward the lights. The guide didn't stop them, but they soon stopped on their own and let us catch up.

We continued single file on the descent, with the lights that could

287

be seen on the horizon being a great lift. There were still patches of snow in places, but also the beginning of some sparse vegetation along the path. It was wet and we slid along, often falling in our haste to keep up. Walking on the sides of our shoes was the common method of descent, as it had been in our climbing and descending earlier.

We had a rest stop at about 3AM, near a deserted stone hut that probably was used as a shelter for sheepherders in the summer who pastured their sheep up this high. The guides let us go inside for warmth, except that there was no such amenity available. Some wanted to light a fire, but the guides told them they couldn't. They did allow all who wanted to smoke to do so inside the shelter. It was soon smoky inside, and Joe and I sat on the ground outside with our backs against the stone hut, looking at the lights below. I am sure that both of us wondered what would be ahead when we again approached civilization.

I took this occasion to talk to the English speaking Frenchman, and I asked if the people of Spain would welcome us. He said that in northern Spain, the nationalities were so much like that of southern France that it wasn't uncommon for some of the Spanish to be French sympathizers. He was counting on this to help him on his way to the Free French Army in Africa. He said that some of the Spanish in northern Spain were blue-eyed blonds, which was encouraging to me, also being blue-eyed and having light brown hair. Hopefully, I wouldn't create any extra attention.

It wasn't long before we were again heading downhill single-file. It was easier now that we were descending, but still exhausting. We all seemed to stumble quite a bit and were somewhat giddy at finally being in Spain. After another short rest stop, when they again begged the guides to let them build a fire, "Allez #1" stood up in disgust and growled his; "Allez veit," and we were off again. A little before daybreak, we could see the dark outline of farm buildings, and one or two had what appeared to be lantern-lights showing. We walked along a path by a stone wall and then circled a small village. The dogs in the village barked, but the guides paid no attention to them at all.

The guides finally led us into an area of tall reeds, and told us to crouch down and hide there. Both guides went off to get food and drink for us, or so they said. For a short while, I wasn't sure if they had not abandoned us. Then I remembered that we had the tokens that were to be given to them so that they could get their pay. Although they were gone for quite a while, if they wished to get paid, we were pretty certain they would come back.

It was very uncomfortable in the marshy canebrake, as it was too wet and soggy to sit and our shoes were soaked. We stood and squatted alternately to try to pass the time. It would have been very nice to have taken a nap.

I counted the number of people that were left in our party, which included the 7 original Americans, two RAF and 2 French, including the one that interpreted for us. We had been fortunate to have him along on the journey over the mountains. I know that some of the Frenchmen had split off from the group, perhaps finding their own way, now that they were in Spain. They had probably paid off the guides at our rest stop at the stone hut.

The guides returned so silently that they were upon us before we knew it. Being exhausted, our senses were none too sharp. It made us aware how easily an enemy patrol could sneak up on us. They had a large bundle wrapped in newspapers and three or four bottles of wine, as well as another man who was to be our new guide. He appeared to be a local Spaniard. They opened the package that was wrapped in the newspapers and we saw that it was fish and chips, a most beautiful sight.

We were all so hungry that we crowded around and scooped the food with our hands and ate with abandon. I took a big mouthful of fish, removed the bones, and swallowed it. My empty stomach revolted and I knew that I was about to vomit. I turned away from the hungry group and did just that. I went back as soon as I could, and took a drink of the red wine to get the sour taste out of my mouth and to bring my stomach back to reality. I started over, taking it a little easier. I tried the chips and they went down very well.

The chips were not long like our "French fries," but were chunks of potatoes fried in oil. I continued to eat now, thinking that this food was delicious. I knew that the fish was not only cold, it was greasy, as were the chips, but it didn't matter. This was the first time that I had really eaten all that I wanted in a couple of days, and I had burned all of the fuel in the tank and was now starved. It was no wonder that our stomachs revolted of course, but at the time we gladly accepted whatever was offered.

After we had eaten everything and had finished off the wine, the interpreter told us to produce the "souvenir" that we had been given. At first we didn't understand what he meant by the word *souvenir*. Then we remembered the tokens that we had been given when we started the journey. We gave them to "Allez #1" so that they could be paid. The guides then huddled with the two Frenchmen, who apparently paid the money that was still owed for their passage. I heard later that the amount the guides were paid for each Allied serviceman they delivered into Spain was the equivalent of $1,000.

The local man would now be in charge of us and our guides, "Allez #1 and Allez #2", left without another word to us. No goodbye, good luck, or adieu. They simply disappeared to lead another group of evaders to freedom and spread a few more nightmares. The interpreter said that they were probably going into Madrid or Barcelona to be paid, and then to stock up on silk stockings and other things to trade to the Germans back in France.

Our interpreter friend and the other Frenchman bid us "adieu" and said that they were going into the town of Figueros, Spain, which was nearby. The French interpreter told us, before he left, that he had been told that we would go to Barcelona. Our new guide spoke broken English and we were instructed to follow him. We thought that we were being taken to a rail or bus station for that purpose.

We Americans and the two British followed the new guide out of the marshy area and up a two-lane paved road, continuing for a hundred yards or so and then turning off onto a dirt road bordering the local farms. As we walked along, the guide didn't seem to mind if we walked behind him, two-abreast.

Judging direction from the sun, we seemed to be circling around the town, which we had been told was Figueros. We followed the new guide for more than an hour without stopping, and seemed to now be west of the town. We all helped the Brit, with the tennis shoes, who thought that he had frostbitten feet. He was in severe pain by now and it was hard for him to keep up.

We were told to lie down in a field of tall weeds that we were walking through, and to be silent. The guide was concerned about something he had either seen or heard. He left us lying in the grasses to investigate. He came back about an hour later to say that the Spanish police had been alerted that a group was seen east of Figueros, and they were looking for us. We were to stay down and sleep until dark, and he would return for us.

We were anxious that we might have been abandoned, but what could we do? We had been concerned before, and the guides always seemed to show up, so we again trusted in them. As soon as it was dark the Spanish guide reappeared and we again fell in line behind him.

At about 9PM, we arrived at a farm with a stone fence surrounding it. We entered the farmyard and the guide signaled a knock on the door of the house. This was a modest but sturdy house built of stone, with a huge fireplace covering one entire end of the dwelling. It was on a bit of a slope and had two levels; the animals were housed below, and the people lived above. This was similar to the arrangement that Joe and I had seen everywhere in Italy, and to the structure housing Marcel in the mountains near Aix about a month earlier.

The guide did not eat with us, but before he left, he said he would send a doctor for our British buddy with the frostbite, but it would probably be morning before the doctor would arrive. The young man was in constant pain and we hoped that he could get help as quickly as possible. The guide also told us that we would rest here in this house for a couple of days while arrangements were worked out for our transport to Barcelona.

The couple, probably in their 40's, living in the farmhouse, appeared pleased to see us. They had obviously been expecting us earlier in the evening, as dinner was being kept warm inside the huge fireplace. We quickly washed outside at the pump, and came in and sat at the large wooden table in the middle of the main room. The meal the lady had prepared for us was a big pot of food that had cooked down to where it was now almost something like a chicken stew. By now the vegetables were overcooked and the chicken had fallen off the bone. She pantomimed an apology but it smelled wonderful and we were too hungry to care.

We dug into the bowl of stew with gusto. There was plenty of bread and we used chunks of that to dip in the stew gravy and made a hearty meal of it all. Of course, this was washed down with red wine. We were seated around the table on benches, a stool, and one hard chair.

When we had finished, and seemed to all be "nodding off," the man of the house, using a lantern, led us up a short stairway to the loft over the area where the animals were kept. There was plenty of straw for bedding, and four blankets for cover. We were all so exhausted that we flopped down and literally "hit the hay" for some much needed rest. The man carefully held a lantern for us until we were bedded down and covered with the blankets. We tried to share the covers as best we could, but it seemed that someone was always cold and complaining.

After our first night's sleep, we had coffee, real coffee, and some hard bread and cheese for breakfast. After we had finished breakfast, the doctor and another man came and asked to look at the feet of the fellow with the frostbite. The doctor examined the airman's feet and insisted that he be taken to the hospital.

The doctor's companion spoke some English and he asked us if anyone else had frostbite or other injuries. A couple of the fellows had the doctor examine their toes to see if they might also have frostbite, but none of the others seemed to have serious enough problems to keep them from proceeding on. We asked the doctor, through the interpreter, if he knew what would happen to the fellow, and he said that he would be cared for, and that the British would be advised of his whereabouts.

With that, the doctor left with his companion and the injured man. The young man seemed reluctant to go, but was sure that he needed help. He gave his RAF friend his home address so that he could notify his parents that he was safe in Spain and no longer MIA.

The lady told me to take off my torn pants and she would sew them. She made me understand by pointing to my pants and pantomiming a sewing motion. I went to the loft and took off my pants and had Joe take them to her. Joe said, "What are you going to do all day, Lootenant?" I replied, "Stay in bed, I guess." The others roamed around the stone fence of the farm, smoking and talking. I took to the bed, with plenty of blankets for the entire day. When I did have to go down to the pen for short visits, I wrapped a blanket around myself.

Early that afternoon, the lady brought each of us a welcomed apple, which we enjoyed both the sound of as well as the tart taste.

At dusk, the lady came up to the loft with my pants. She had stitched the pants expertly as well as laundered and dried them in the fireplace. It was nice to put on warm, clean, whole pants, and I think that everyone else was jealous, as all wore filthy clothing by now.

I will never forget our first full meal with the couple. The fare was lamb chops, beans, and potatoes; all cooked liberally in olive oil with lots of garlic flavoring everything. The man of the house sat and ate with us, and the lady ate at a sideboard and kept the food coming. Besides the lamb chops and bean dish, we had a couple of loaves of warm, hard bread and two large bottles of red table wine with our dinner.

After we had eaten, our host brought out the familiar Schnapps, or anisette or some other after-dinner drink. He mixed the liqueur with water so that it looked like weak milk. Actually, it was a very pleasant after-dinner drink. We then raised our glasses to the lady who had prepared us this delicious dinner. She looked a bit embarrassed, but smiled broadly as she understood the compliment. We sat, for a while, around the fireplace before going to our loft bed.

The beans and garlic produced a lot of gas, and we had a real chorus going for a while, followed by the usual GI remarks with each outburst. Although the loft was still a bit airy, the smell was ever-evident. This was somewhat different than when we had lived with Marcel in the mountains near Aix. There, we had no roof overhead and no garlic, just beans, and only four of us contributing to the offensive odor and rank comments that followed. But here, we all became eight obnoxious teenage boys once again.

If we had to go down to the animal pen at night, we had to find our way in the dark to the stairway, and then run our hand along the wall as we descended the steps to the door and the pen below as well as reverse the process to find our way back up to the loft.

One of the officers, either Marean or Shilliday, thought that he knew enough Spanish to communicate with the couple that were sheltering us. It didn't seem to work well as they spoke some dialect, much different from his textbook Spanish. He made a mighty effort but they would just shake their head, unable to understand. We shortly turned to hand-signs or pantomime to communicate with one or the other.

At dinner that next night someone asked for vinegar to put on the beans. We tried every word that we could think of to ask for vinegar. Finally, I said in a loud voice, "Forget the vinegar," and the lady responded, "Ah, vinegar," and she brought it out for us. She shook her head again though when she saw him pour it over his plate of beans.

From out of the main room, there was a landing, and steps up to the loft as well as steps down to the animal pen. The house consisted of one large room and two small rooms. Probably one of the small rooms was their bedroom and the other was used for storage. It had no indoor plumbing, and only the large stone fireplace for heat and cooking. There was no kitchen - only the sideboard for the lady to prepare the meals.

A large pot of water hung at the back of the huge fireplace and was always warm. A cooking ring, elevated on four legs, surrounded the fire pit and was used for the large frying pan in which the main dish was prepared. A couple of smaller pots hung alongside the frying pan. The fireplace was so huge that there was a chair and a stool placed inside of it, so that the couple could enjoy the heat in the evening by sitting in the fireplace as the coals died down. The lady also used the stool when she was preparing and stirring the food for the meal.

I have a mind's eye picture of the two - one sitting on the hard chair smoking, and the other sitting across from him sewing. A lantern hung on a peg near the front of the fireplace for her to see to cook and sew. She was surrounded by her cooking utensils, which were hanging on their hooks.

Our daytime was spent walking around the farmhouse yard and pen. The only animals that used the shelter were sheep and they were put in an adjacent pasture during the day. Some of our time was spent sitting in the loft with our backs to the warm stone wall that was common to the rear of the fireplace. We had offered to cut firewood for the fireplace but it was declined, as was the help at clearing the table when we finished eating. At night, we slept with our feet against the fireplace wall for warmth. We talked endlessly of our experiences of being shot down and of our time in France. Some reminisced about their hometowns in the USA. We talked about girls or the war or flying, but did avoid some controversial subjects.

We had spent two nights with the farm couple and were starting to get anxious about moving on. There was no one to ask about when we would be moved. The man walked into a nearby village each day to bring home warm bread and other staples. On the morning of the third day, the man produced a safety razor and two new blades. The blades were double-edged, and I guess he thought that two blades would be enough. The old statement "they don't make them like they used to anymore" certainly does not apply to safety razor blades.

The man put one blade in the razor that he had brought and handed us the other blade. He indicated that he wanted us to shave and to look a little more presentable. Joe and I had been through this shaving episode before and we knew what to expect. I pointed out that my sergeant, Joe, had a very heavy beard and looked like the typical GI Joe in the "Stars and Stripes." I suggested that he should go first and I should go second. There was some grumbling and disagreement about this arrangement, so I suggested that the two lieutenants and two sergeants should go first with one blade, and that Joe and I and the two others would finish with the second blade. They agreed that this would be fine and I asked for two volunteers, who had a light beard like mine, to wait and shave with Joe and me.

Someone brought a pan of warm water from the reservoir in the back of the fireplace. There was only hand soap for lather and the first lieutenant proceeded to shave. We didn't have a mirror so we helped each other with the chore, trying to point out where each had missed with the blade. The four finished with the one blade, and there were complaints from the last man that the blade was very dull. We put the second blade in the razor and I think that everyone expected that I would shave first with the new blade.

I surprised them when I handed the razor to Joe and told him to begin. I suggested that he be careful to only use one side of the razor blade and leave one sharp side for us. I knew that we three had light beards and would be able to manage after Joe had finished. I had a very good shave, and somehow spared the little mustache that I had been cultivating. I handed it to the next man and he too got a decent shave. The last man complained but what else could he do?

After we had finished, we brought out another large pan of warm water and tried to wash and clean up, as best we could. We hoped that shaving and washing was a sign that we were to be moved soon. This was our first shave since the morning before leaving Perpignon. Both Joe and I wished that we had brought our razor with us.

Another sign came in mid-afternoon, when the lady of the house announced that we were to have an early dinner, giving us hope that we were going to be moved that night. The farm couple may have been told when to get us ready for our departure. We weren't disappointed when a man came for us at dark and told us, in halting English, that we were to get ready to move on. Accordingly, we gathered up our meager belongings and were ready to "hit the road." We said goodbye to the farm couple, who had been very kind to us, and departed the farm single file following the new guide.

We followed paths alongside farms and cut across fields on our journey. We thought that we were being taken to a station to board a train to Barcelona. We finally reached the outskirts of a town at about 9PM, and went into the rail yards and waited. After a few minutes, a freight train with coal cars came to a halt near us.

The guide led us to the coal cars and told us, in passable English, that we were to ride in the gondolas of the coal cars for a short distance. The gondola was a compartment at one end of each coal car. The space was rather small with a narrow sliding door on each side. There was a large brake wheel inside the compartment for the use of the brakeman in an emergency. The guide had five of the guys get in one compartment, and he and the three others, which included me, were to ride in the gondola of the coal car just ahead of them. He had instructed the other guys to watch closely to see when he got off the train, and for them to do the same.

The ride was bumpy and we weaved from side to side as the train rolled along. A couple of us sat down and tried to rest as best we could. There was a film of coal dust constantly sifting through the compartment. We couldn't help but inhale it, and we covered our nose and mouth with whatever was available from our clothing to help filter out the worst of it. The fellows in the car behind us had to post a guard to watch our car just in case the guide decided to get off the train. We had thought that we were to be on the coal train only a short while, but mile after mile went by, and it was nearly daybreak when the train slowed to near a full stop. The guide opened the side door of our gondola and got off. We followed the guide and the guys from the car to our rear fell into line behind us.

We trailed him across the rail yard, through a fence and into a wooded pasture adjacent to the railroad yard. A small stream ran through the pasture, and he stopped us there and told us to wash up in the stream to get as presentable as possible. He left us to go into the nearby passenger station to purchase our tickets. We did the best that we could, but without washcloths and soap, it was nearly impossible to get the coal dust off our faces and hands.

Thank goodness that Joe and I had our stocking caps on the whole trip and our hair was pretty coal dust-free. Neither of us had a comb so we put our caps back on after we had dusted them off. The man finally came back with the tickets and gave one to each of us, saying he wouldn't be going with us; we would be on our own into

Barcelona.

It was daylight now, and the man was unhappy with our clean-up job and had us wash again and dust off our clothing, especially our shoes. He had a small pocket mirror and had us look at ourselves in the light of day. We pulled up tufts of long grass and dusted off again. When he was satisfied, he led us to a clear space near the stream and proceeded to show us a picture of a building in Barcelona that we were to memorize and look for. He said that it was the British Consulate and there would be a British flag flying from the upper front of the building. He then drew a map in the dirt with a stick, showing the train station in Barcelona and the route to the building shown in the photo. He carefully traced out the route several times so we could all memorize it.

He told us that we were to wander into the nearby station, and when the train to Barcelona was called, to get aboard. He also advised us to ride in separate compartments on the train. We filed silently into the train station; arriving in two's and not connecting with each other or speaking to anyone.

The guide explained that the Spanish Police were on the lookout for evaders like us, and that they might be in the train station looking around. He warned that if any were caught, to not endanger any of the others. He also cautioned us that when we arrived in Barcelona, we were to wander out of the station in the same manner as we boarded and take the route to the building with extreme caution. He added that in addition to the Spanish police, the German Gestapo was around the Barcelona station and watching the British Consulate trying to prevent the escape of any Allied airmen. He informed us that the German Gestapo was active in their hunt for evaders in all of northern Spain.

We already understood that Spain was neutral in the war but sympathetic to the Germans, however we didn't know that the German Gestapo hunted down evaders in Spain. He told us that any they found were taken back to France, and eventually to a German

POW camp. He also said that some of the Spanish Police would turn evaders over to the German Gestapo for a price.

This news shook us up and we again went into the same mode and state of mind that we had used to evade capture in France. Joe and I paired up and took the short walk into the train station at Gerona, Spain, about 50 or 60 miles north of Barcelona. The train to Barcelona was called, and our tickets were checked before we went through the turnstile. We then had to pass a Spanish Gendarme in full uniform; he wore one of the patent leather, cockade-style hats, and scrutinized all who boarded the train.

We got into a compartment with a family couple, whereupon Joe and I immediately faked sleep and did not speak to each other or to those in the compartment with us. The conductor came to our seats when we were underway, punched our tickets, and we went back to *sleep*. Joe, being really comfortable at sleeping on these train journeys.

On one portion of the trip to Barcelona, I opened the sliding glass door and moved from the compartment to the train aisle. Joe joined me and we shared the one Spanish cigarette that we had. We went back into our compartment and Joe fell asleep again almost instantly. I certainly envied him as I was tired from the dusty coal car ride overnight, but could only fake sleep. We made quite a few stops as the train made its way to Barcelona.

We finally arrived at the Barcelona station around 10:30 in the morning. Joe and I wandered out of the station and up the street per our instructions. We stopped to look into the window of a confectionery store and also a furniture store. We wandered along, trying to be as inconspicuous and casual as possible. We tried to look like tourists who had come to the city for a visit.

We followed the mental map and finally entered the street that would take us to the building that was pictured. It was recognizable in the next block as it had a British flag on a staff flying from the second story balcony.

We were now on the right street but across from the entrance. We were both very eager to get into the haven awaiting us. We walked up the street opposite the entrance expecting the Gestapo to step out of every doorway we passed. When we were directly opposite the entrance to the building I said to Joe in a whisper, "Let's go for it," and we both dashed across the street toward the door. The guard at the entrance opened the door for us and we went directly in.

There was a long stairway straight ahead and the guard indicated that we were to go up to the second floor. Once our eyes were adjusted to the dim light, we moved up the stairway. At the top of the landing, a lady was sitting behind a desk with a large book in front of her. She asked one question, "Are you from the frontier?" We replied, "Yes," and she asked us to sign our name and rank in the book. I noticed that, as I signed in, my signature was on line 390-something. She pushed a buzzer and a man came out from a room behind her and invited us in. He asked if there were any others in our party. We told him there were six more, and he said that two had already come in, and now he knew that there were still four out there.

We waited only a few minutes before the last of the four made it into the building. We were all taken to a room where we were asked to wait until the doctor could come and check us over. He was apparently already checking on the first to arrive.

The doctor soon came in and asked us to follow him down the hallway into a clinic-type office and dispensary. First he asked if we had any injuries, frostbite, scrapes, or other wounds. Two of the sergeants wanted their toes checked for frostbite. The doctor told all six of us to remove our shoes and socks so he could check our feet.

After a cursory review he advised the two Sergeants, Harrison and Hasson, that their toes needed better scrutiny after they had showered. He told all six of us to go into the adjoining room to strip, get a shower, and wash our hair. We assured him that we were quite happy to comply.

This was the first hot shower that I had taken in 6 weeks, and it was totally wonderful to strip off the old "long johns" and get the grime and coal dust off my entire body.

There was a safety razor and a real bar of shaving soap waiting for us to use when we came out of the shower. I was really enjoying all of this when a man came in with a robe and slippers for each of us. The doctor came in and checked our hair for mites or lice. Even though we had slept on straw and hay, this was the first time that I had thought about the creatures. I certainly should have, since I had some experience with the nasty little critters on our week-long trip across North Africa.

After the shower the doctor again checked the two with frostbitten toes and they were taken to a nearby hospital for observation and treatment. We didn't see them again. Of the group that had crossed the mountains together, only the three officers and three enlisted men, Sgts. Joe Kinnane, Spellman and RAF Sgt. Banning remained.

Our group was taken into a room with a table filled with shorts, undershirts, and socks, and were told to take two pair of each. Then in the next room there were rows of clothes hanging from the rods and we were to pick out a suit, shirt, and necktie. All of the outer gear appeared to be used, but we were encouraged to be sure that the clothes "fit us properly." We all picked out what we wanted and went into the dressing room to dress in our used finery.

As soon as we were dressed, a man came in with boxes of shoes for us to try on. I protested that I wanted my GI shoes back, but he said that they had already been thrown out. I doubted that, but I went ahead and found a pair of shoes that felt good and put them on. Next, we were told to select an overcoat that would blend with our new ensemble. I had a dark brown suit and brown shoes, so I selected a lighter colored overcoat.

I had worn so much black or dark blue for the last six weeks that I

SPAIN

thought brown would be a good change. When I picked the light brown overcoat, I was thinking of the light tan coat that I had bequeathed to Capt. (Doc) Neuman at our base at Tortortella, Italy. I really hoped that he'd gotten it, rather than someone else.

After we had dressed, we were escorted into another room where it was explained that we were the guests of the British and were in the British Consulate in Barcelona.

The lady who was addressing us went on to say that we would be housed and fed at a small hotel that catered to foreigners. The owner and personnel at the hotel could speak English and many other foreign languages. We were told that we could expect German people to be there, as well as other foreigners.

We would be provided with an English-speaking guide who would be with us whenever we were outside of the hotel. We were told to stay close to him at all times and never wander off on our own. We were to never leave the hotel without our guide, and to keep our conversation down, especially in the hotel lobby and in the dining room.

She further cautioned that the Germans might be seated near us at mealtime, and if we were overheard they might surmise that we were evaders and alert the Gestapo to try to seize us on the street.

We were told to not speak in loud tones on the street to each other, as our American style of English would surely give us away. The Gestapo might be following us. She informed us that we were to report to the consulate each day, in the company of the escort.

The consulate headquarters was on the 3rd and 4th floor of this building and we were to use the elevator and come directly up to the consulate. We were to check each day, to see if we were scheduled for transport to Gibraltar. She said that we were to receive spending money in the equivalent of $5.00 U.S. per day. The per-diem was in Spanish Pesos and Pesetas.

Another group of evaders had come in right behind us and they were going through the same routine as we did. By this time, including the new group, we were about nine or ten in number. It took some time to mobilize the Spanish guides, but finally they came in and introduced themselves, and each chose three of us to escort. I was chosen along with Air Corps Major Ivan (Wayne) Eveland. I requested that Joe Kinnane be in the group with me and it was granted. Lts. Shilliday and Marean and one of the sergeants made up another trio.

We asked if someone from the American Embassy or Consulate would come to see us. We were told that the American authorities were aware of the fact that we were in the care of the British. They told us that there was a U.S. Army Air Corps attaché there in Barcelona, and that he would be notified of our arrival. We were told that he would come to see us, perhaps that very day. He didn't show up before we left that day or the day after, and that annoyed Major Eveland.

The guide of our little group took us out to the front desk on the 2nd floor, where he told the person at the desk that he was taking us to a place where we could each get a photograph. Apparently, we needed a photo to facilitate the making of the identification papers that we would carry while in the country. We then would be taken directly to our hotel. Before we left the 2nd floor, we were asked to write our signature three times, on three lines, just the way we would sign our own papers or one of our own checks. I wondered if they were going to use my own name on the identification papers.

By this time, it was mid-afternoon and we were really hungry. The guide received some money from the lady at the front desk, and we went trooping out into the public for the first time, supposedly free. After all, weren't we guests of the British?

The escort took us to a place that looked like a "penny arcade," and we each took our turn sitting in the little photo booth to have our picture taken. The escort handed us a peseta for the coin slot. We closed the curtain and put the peseta into the slot, and instantly our picture was snapped. We looked at the first picture, and since our eyes were down looking for the coin slot, the picture wasn't what he wanted. The guide gave us another peseta and had each of us take a second picture. This time our eyes were at least somewhat open, even though we were, "dead tired." He took the best picture and gave each of us the poorest one.

From the penny arcade, we went directly to our hotel. On the way, we were so hungry that we asked the guide to stop at a corner fruit vendor and get us a Valencia orange. He did and we started to peel and eat the orange right away, but the guide stopped us and said to put it in our overcoat pocket to eat in our room. We were told that the dining room would open at 6:30, and we had at least an hour to wait. Just as soon as I got to my room, I peeled the orange and found it absolutely delicious. It tasted like candy as it was so sweet, and I could have eaten a couple more before dinner.

I am sure that we were an emaciated lot when we walked into the hotel lobby. I think that I had lost at least 20 lbs. throughout the ordeal of crossing the Pyrenees. Major Eveland, who became a good friend, looked far thinner and more haggard than I. He had been through a horrible time crossing the Pyrenees Mountains about 40 miles west of where we had crossed. He told me the story of his crossing, and about the frostbite and frozen limbs that they had suffered when they were caught in a blizzard.

Major Eveland had been a squadron commander in one of the groups based in England, flying the B-17 heavy bomber. On his last flight, he chose to fly co-pilot with a new crew and new pilot flying in the #10 position, "tail-end Charlie." In this way, he could observe his squadron and evaluate the squadron leader and each element leader.

They were heavily hit by enemy fighters and flak, and the airplane, being badly damaged, went out of control. They parachuted out, and although he was hurt, he wandered south foraging for food and shelter for many days. He finally made his way to the French/Spanish frontier, and was taken across the Pyrenees in a snowstorm by the Basque, crossing the border near Andora.

They were mistreated badly by the Basque. He said that some of his companions lost limbs from frostbite. The Basque held them for several extra days, while they bargained with him to sign a paper which would allow them to receive more money for delivering them. They finally made it to Barcelona at about the same time as our group. While his group probably crossed the border a day or two earlier than we did, they encountered weather quite different from what we experienced.

When they arrived at the British Consulate, several of this group required immediate medical attention. Major Eveland had slightly frostbitten toes, but was declared fit and didn't have to go to the hospital.

Our guide showed us the dining room and told us goodbye, reminding us before he left, to eat like Europeans and not Americans. We were told to keep our fork in the left hand and the knife in the right. Forewarned, we were shown to our rooms. My room was next to Wayne Eveland's, and we rested until 6:30 and then went to the dining room.

Some of our guys and one or two of Wayne's party were already seated at a large rectangular table that would seat ten or twelve. We took our seats and were greeted by a short, jolly waiter who spoke excellent English. We asked for water to which he frowned, and brought the familiar bottle of table wine instead.

It is hard to realize how much your body craves cold water when you have been deprived of it and are now expected to drink warm wine at the dinner table. Finally, after some urging, he did bring glasses and a pitcher of water with lemon floating in it. We were afraid that this desire for water with our meal made us somewhat conspicuous so thereafter we determined to drink the customary wine with each meal. This decision wasn't unanimous but anyone wanting water with the meal tried to be discreet about it.

The menu, which was presented with a flourish, had two or three items on the entrée - fish, chicken, and lamb. I had eaten enough lamb or mutton for a lifetime, and was ready for anything else but. I chose fish or chicken every night that we were there. We started with a very small shellfish or crab cocktail, and then vegetables and finally a separate plate with the fish or chicken. This was very delicious and was followed by a green salad. I ate everything on my plates and was now ready for the gelatin dessert.

Sometime during our first meal, the owner came by our table visiting with all of the diners in his establishment. He was cordial, but didn't seem overly friendly. He visited a table that hosted Germans and several other foreigners. There was another small table, in an alcove, which was occupied by British guests; at least we could hear them speak English at that table. Since we had RAF Sgt. Banner with us, we tried to copy his way of handling the silverware.

When we finished our meal, we had to walk past the table where there were two full-dress uniformed German officers and their two ladies, who appeared to be their guests for the evening. They were absorbed in their companions and fortunately paid no attention to us, but you could clearly hear the German language spoken. As we were leaving, the waiter said that breakfast would be from 7:30 to 9AM. We thanked him for the splendid service and meal, and he said that he would see us in the morning.

I went down for breakfast at around 8AM and found Joe and several others already at the table eating. I sat down and soon Wayne Eveland joined us at our table. The waiter brought a pot of coffee and poured each of us a real cup of coffee. We were then offered a fruit cup and one soft-boiled egg in an egg-cup. The egg was served with some type of soft bread, like a croissant, and soft cheese. When the waiter brought my egg-cup, I noticed that the egg had a cartoon figure drawn on it. The waiter picked up the egg and very discreetly presented the egg to me with a view of a caricature of Franco drawn in pencil on the eggshell. He then smashed the face of Franco on the edge of the egg-cup and poured the half-cooked, soft-boiled egg into the cup, putting the eggshell in the napkin that he carried over his arm. I was pleased with breakfast, although I could certainly have eaten more. The waiter went through the same ritual with the egg for Wayne and several others in our group, showing us his defiance of the Franco dictatorship.

Just before we finished breakfast, our guide came in and was ready to escort us to the consulate. We walked out of the hotel with our escort walking in two's, Wayne with the guide practicing his Spanish, and Joe and me trailing behind. I had thought I might get another orange on our way to the consulate; however we didn't see any fruit vendors on the street corners that early in the day, so I went without the coveted orange for the time being.

When we took the elevator up to the consulate on the 4th floor, we were told to go down to the second floor as they were expecting us. Our guide led us to a room on the 2nd floor with small cubicles, each with two chairs facing each other with a desk in between. We were each put into a different cubicle. I was put in one of the spaces with a young, pink-cheeked, Brit who proceeded to show me my new identity documents.

In addition to a British passport, with yesterday's "penny arcade" picture on it, there was a birth certificate showing that I had been born in England. The birth certificate named my mother and father, and had a doctor's signature attesting to the facts of my birth. I was born in January 1927, so I was now 17 years of age, and as a matter of fact, had just barely turned 17 according to the fake documents.

The story that I was to memorize was that I had been sent to France to attend a boy's school when I was 13. This was sometime before the occupation of southern France. The boy's school was in

Narbonne and I had to memorize the name of the school as well as the city. My passport didn't look new and had stamps attesting to my entry into France. My new name was William Clay Wells; a name I remember well. I had wondered why the forger had used that name. Later on I finally figured out that he used as many letters from my real signature, of the day before, to copy my method of making these letters. It was quite easy for me to write the name William Clay Wells, as all of the letters in that signature except the letters I, A, and M were in my real signature.

I was drilled for about an hour and a half on my story. I could name the city and county in England where I was born, and the name of my father and mother and only sister. My tutor went through it until he was satisfied that I could recall it for my interview with the Spanish police. If I were convincing enough the Spanish official would then issue a temporary Spanish ID card identifying me as a British citizen. This would allow me to get a food ration book and it would make me officially welcomed into Spain as a foreign guest.

Going to the police was quite upsetting; we all knew that we had to do it, but it wasn't going to be pleasant. Our guide kept telling us not to be afraid, that he had taken many more, like us, through the procedure and it hadn't been a problem.

Before we left the office of the British Consulate, we were given a small envelope and asked to put our dog tags, if we still had them, in the envelope prior to going to the police station. This really unnerved me, as I had thought of my tags as being my only connection to the American military. We were assured that when we returned from the Police Station that our tags would be promptly returned. To remove our dog tags was a precaution that a search might have revealed that we were American rather than British citizens.

We left the building and walked with our escort the few blocks to the police headquarters. I don't know about Joe and Major Eveland, but I was just plain scared. I thought about all that we had been through, and to now end up in a Spanish jail cell was inconceivable. This was very depressing. As we walked, I started to really concentrate on my story so that I wouldn't be tripped up when reciting it to the Spanish authorities. The other two were also deep in thought, perhaps trying to recall all the details of their individual story to back up the fake British documents.

Our papers were in the large envelope that each of us carried. It seems that the three of us; the Major, Joe, and I; were the first of our group to be scheduled to go before the Police Commandant. At that time, I wished that a couple of our buddies had tested the water before we had to go in. Joe did look older, and I think that his story was that he was a British coal-mining engineer that had also been trapped in France. I have forgotten Wayne Eveland's story, but I do remember that he was said to be 21 or 22 years old, and Joe was listed as 25, which was two years more than his actual age.

As we entered the police station, our escort spoke to every Spanish officer that he met; they seemed to be well acquainted. They appeared to know why he was there, leading three British citizens. He took us down the hallway and knocked at a door and we were let in. A young man, who spoke broken English, greeted us and asked what he could do for us. The guide said that we were British citizens, guests in his country, and wished to apply for a Spanish ID and receive ration stamps for food and clothing. The young Spaniard took our papers and scrutinized them carefully, and then started to question each one as to the reason that we were in Spain. We all said that we were headed home to England.

We told our stories, starting with the Major, and after the interpreter had heard the narratives, he took Major Eveland into the Police Commandant's office, through a connecting doorway, to meet the official.

The interviewer had left the door between his office and the commandant's office slightly ajar, so we were able to overhear what was going on. Evidently the interpreter told his Commandant the story, as it was told to him by Wayne Eveland. By the tone of voice, we surmised that the Commandant was raging at Wayne with "You don't expect me to believe a story like that do you?" Wayne, who spoke some Spanish, began to answer him in Spanish, which only further enraged him. He went on and on with his tirade, until Joe and I thought that we would all end up in his jail for sure. Finally, Wayne was returned to the outer room and it was now my turn.

The Commandant was resplendent in a full uniform, leaning back in his chair smoking a cigar and looking like the cat that was about to eat the canary. The interpreter told him my story and he looked at me intently. He just shook his head and commented something in Spanish, (which was later translated to me by the interpreter as, "I had a pretty good mustache for a 17 year old.)" How was I to know that my age would regress to 17? It wasn't much of a mustache but it still showed. With a nod of his head and a puff on the cigar I was dismissed and taken out of the room. Joe was ushered in next. I joined Wayne in the outer office where his ID card was being typed up and he was issued food ration stamps for a two-week stay in Spain. Joe came in about the time that I had received my ID card and I had just signed it William C. Wells. We waited in the room for Joe to finish the paper work and receive his ration coupons.

The door to the Commandant's office was still partly open, and we could hear our escort talking with the official and both were having a hearty laugh. Our escort came into the room and ushered us outside with our new ID cards and ration stamps. In our packet that we had brought from the consulate, in addition to our birth certificate, there had been a valid British passport. The Spanish kept the passport and said that it would be returned upon our departing Barcelona.

As soon as we were out on the street, Major Eveland questioned the guide about what was so funny back there in the office. He told us that the Police Commandant thought that we were evaders and that we

311

were from the same bomber crew. He thought that Joe was the "chief," the pilot, and he thought that I must have been a gunner, perhaps a tail gunner, and Major Eveland was probably the navigator or the bomb aimer. We were all sure that the guide gave the Commandant a fat envelope of money before leaving, and according to Wayne's memoirs, "He certainly earned it with that first act of bluster."

We made our way back to the consulate and immediately went to retrieve our dog tags. It felt so good to feel them around my neck and inside of my shirt again. Then we left the second floor and went up to the fourth floor, where we signed for and received our first spending money. We never went to the second floor again, as it was apparently devoted to clandestine operations, doing all further business with the people on the fourth floor. We checked each day for orders and received our spending money.

We three went out on the street with our guide and he suggested that we have some coffee. He guided us to a small café that had outdoor tables and ordered for us. We sipped our coffee and watched the world go by. The coffee was strong and bitter, and I ordered milk and sugar to see if I could make it more palatable. He kidded me about being a sissy and I told him that, after all, I was "only 17" as I stroked my dinky mustache, and we all laughed.

We were expected to pick up his tab for the coffee as well as our own. This same procedure prevailed everywhere, whether it was in a café or bar or wherever we went. I must say that, as a rule, he took us to nice places. When we bought cigarettes on the street we had to get a pack for him as well. We had to give ration stamps for everything but the oranges that were sold by the street corner vendors. We often bought oranges on the street, but the guide would only allow us to eat them in the park where there were receptacles for the peels. He said that you just didn't eat on the street while you were walking. Thus, we passed the second day in Barcelona, and at about four o'clock

SPAIN

went back to our hotel to get some rest before dinner.

We went to the dining room, and in whispers were trying to find out what had happened to all who went through the police ordeal of getting their papers. It seemed like each one went smoother. Some forgot their story and were prompted by the interpreter as he read from the documents. I think that the Commandant put on his supreme act for the first applicant, Major Eveland. He had apparently run out of dramatics as he went through each group. I have no way of knowing if the Police Commandant had been paid all of the bribe money up front by our guide, or if each guide, in turn, had a fat envelope for him.

Before we had gone down to dinner that early evening, I was in Wayne's room and we were discussing the events of the day. I expressed some small outrage that a fat bribe had to be paid to the Spanish to get our papers and ration stamps. He rationalized it as follows: Why should the Spanish do anything out of patriotism? They were on the Axis side in sympathy and were neutral. They didn't owe the Allies any support, other than the fact that they could see now how the war was going against the Axis, and wanted to play it down the middle. It didn't really matter to them, which side won. I then wondered if the Spanish farm couple, near Figueros, had been paid board and room for us while we were there. He said, of course they were. Everything that is done for this effort in Spain is bought and paid for. I asked him who is paying the bill. He said that he thought that the entire business in Spain was a British operation, but that the U.S. was probably backing it with the cash. I still believe this to be the case.

When we went to dinner this evening, we gave our waiter our ration stamp book and he extracted the amount of stamps that we owed the hotel for our meals up to that time. That evening after dinner, we wandered back to our rooms and prepared to visit with each other.

313

I was visiting with Wayne when I told him the story of wishing that I had saved my condoms for water pouches after I had bailed out. He told me his own condom story. He said that his group commander called the group bombardier, and told him, in the middle of the night, to get 2000 condoms for the flight crews by takeoff time the next morning. The group commander had been troubled by the problem of crew urination and had the bright idea that condoms could be used as pee pouches. This solved the urination problem, but Wayne was worried that some of the unused condoms in his footlocker would be sent home to his wife with his belongings and might need to be explained upon his return home.

I was still in Major Eveland's room with a couple of the others when there was a knock on the door. It was the owner of the hotel, who invited us to come down to the bar and have a drink with him. The bar and dining room were closed and we were able to converse with him freely in English. We were also invited to join him in the bar a couple of nights later, but had been warned by the consulate to not frequent the area during the hours that it was open to the public. We respected that, with the one exception when Wayne and I bought an after dinner-drink in the bar when it was nearly deserted.

The hotel owner told us more of life under the dictator Franco and how he hated living under this rule. He said that he had thoughts of moving to some other country after the war was over and the Allies had won, and how he believed the Americans would help the Spanish people overthrow Franco.

When we went to the British Consulate the morning of the third day to get spending money, the American Air Corps Attaché was finally there to greet us. He had brought a couple of cartons of American cigarettes for us. He told us that this entire operation was under the control of the British. He was just there to see if we had any questions or requests. Someone asked if he could send a telegram to our parents and/or wives advising them that we were no longer MIA.

He said that he could, but told us to keep it short.

We each wrote a note with our home address and he put them in his pocket. We inquired about our future and he said that we would eventually go to Madrid, then to Gibraltar, and would be returned to our units in England.

I told him that Joe and I were from a unit in Italy, and I asked if we would go back to Italy. He said that he didn't know, as he hadn't run into that situation before. He did say that none of us would be allowed to fly combat again in the European theater of war. He said that the "Geneva Convention" rules forbid us from engaging in any more combat in Europe. With that, he left and said that he would see us again soon.

We divided up the packs of cigarettes and were thankful to get American smokes again. They weren't my favorite "Camels," but they would do. It seemed that almost everyone in the military smoked and no one had, as yet, heard that it was bad for the lungs and could cause cancer.

I had been convinced that I would go back to my unit and would fly my remaining missions. The comment that we could no longer fly in combat in Europe was more of a relief than a disappointment to me at the time.

We were told that another group had arrived, and that the hotel was full and we would need to double up. I told the man at the front desk that I had only a single bed in my room, and that the room was not large enough to put an extra bed in there. He said that the hotel owner would figure out something.

Major Eveland asked if he could be put in a local home, as he spoke some Spanish, and that his moving would free up the two singles in his room. He was told that he would be advised about this before the afternoon was over.

Our escort took us to a nice place for lunch, and we sat out in the sun in the afternoon and drank rum and coke on the plaza. Paying for the escort's lunch and drinks, in addition to our own, kept us nearly broke most of the time. There was no money to buy souvenirs, and perhaps we would not have been able to keep them if we had. Still, we had enough money to get back to the hotel with an orange in our pocket. They were cheap and so delicious.

We all felt better that the telegrams had been sent to our families, and now we were starting to enjoy our surroundings a bit more. We were still careful and stayed close to the guide at all times. We didn't want to be picked up by the Gestapo, but we felt a little safer now that we had British citizenship papers and Spanish ID's

It was arranged that afternoon for Major Eveland to be placed in a local home. I don't know if it was a relative of the hotel owner or the home of someone from the consulate. At least it was someone who could be trusted. He said goodbye before dinner and left in the company of his new host. Two new officers moved into his room and I met them at the dinner table that night. I didn't see Wayne again until we were boarding the train to Madrid.

On that same evening, our favorite waiter was serving our table and also another one containing some German officers. There were two German officers there that night and one civilian. Our waiter overheard the Germans discussing the fact that they were quite sure that the ones at our table were probably an American bomber crew evading capture. He continued to listen when he could, and he heard them say that they should poison us and do away with us. One of the Germans said that he would take care of it. Our waiter related what he had heard, and said to us in a whisper that we shouldn't be afraid; that since we ate in "his" dining room, no one would be poisoned - he would see to that.

We were apprehensive about this and considered phoning the consulate with the rumor that we had received. We thought better of it, and decided to tell the consulate people the next day and to see if they could move us to a safer place.

When we picked up our spending money on the next morning we told our story of the German threat to the consulate officials, but they didn't seem to be that concerned. We were told that some of us would leave by train early the next morning for Madrid.

We had a nice day with our escort eating and drinking, and that evening the owner again invited several of us to the bar for a nightcap. He knew that some of us were leaving the next morning, and we said goodbye and many thanks for the wonderful hospitality. He had invited us to his bar to show his defiance of Franco and his appreciation of our effort in this war. He was really the only Spanish civilian that we met that was able to speak freely of his opinion of the Franco dictatorship.

CHAPTER 13

MADRID AND GIBRALTOR

Early On the morning of Saturday, March 11^{th,} our group of evaders departed the hotel by bus, en-route to the Barcelona railway station. Major Eveland again joined our group at the station. Our British passports were returned by a consular official. We were escorted to a special Pullman-type railway car that was owned or leased to the British Embassy. As such, it was considered British property and the Spanish could not board without their permission.

The railway car was attached to a train and soon we were on our way to Madrid. There were several passengers aboard, along with our evader party. They were couriers and also some British Consulate personnel who were going to Madrid or elsewhere for vacation. The railway car was stocked with food and drink for our trip, so there was no need to buy from the vendors that rapped on our windows at every stop. Being a sealed car, we could not get off the train at any of its stops.

We were told by one of the Brits traveling with us that the railway car made a round-trip from Gibraltar through Madrid to Barcelona about every 5 or 6 days. The trip to Madrid took the entire day, even though we were attached to an express train that made very few stops. I was quite interested in the countryside as we passed. At first it was quite green, even though it was early March, with farms of cattle and sheep. Before too long, the pastureland turned into rolling hills and we saw acres and acres of vineyards. It seemed to be more arid as we drew farther away from the coast, and eventually was almost barren. The rail car was only partly occupied, so we all had two seats to ourselves. We arrived in the Madrid station after dark and were met by a bus from the British Embassy.

Being early evening, we were bussed directly to an International hotel where we were met by the doorman. He directed us to the hotel desk, where we signed in with our guest ID's, and surrendered our British passports. Before going to our rooms, we were escorted to the dining room, which had just closed to the hotel guests but had a table prepared for the late arrivals. There were at least 15 or 16 now, as some of the English travelers joined us for a late dinner. Dining with the English guests gave us a good chance to brush up on our European eating etiquette again. We were fed and then shown to our rooms.

This was a much grander hotel with a larger, less intimate, dining room than the one in Barcelona. The food was good and the menu was expanded, so that we were able to experiment a bit with some of the Spanish delicacies. Major Eveland, being able to read from the menu, let us know generally what was offered. The waiters also were fluent in English and would help anyone make a choice from the menu. Still, we longed for hamburgers and meat and potatoes again. It was amazing to me how the rest of the world eats, and it was an unforgettable experience for this American mid-westerner.

The person from the British Embassy, who met us when we arrived at the train station, rode with us in the bus to the hotel. He told us that a bus would pick us up after breakfast in the morning and we would be taken to the Embassy. He said that arrangements had been made for us to see a bullfight the next day, a Sunday afternoon, and all who wished to go would be welcome. Our guys and a couple of the Englishmen quickly took him up on the offer to see a real bullfight. We had seen posters for bullfights in Barcelona but were not there when one was scheduled. If we had been, I'm certain that our

MADRID AND GIBRALTOR

Barcelona guides would have wanted to spend our money for tickets for them as well as for ourselves.

Breakfast was over at 9AM, and we waited in the lobby of the hotel for the bus to take us to the Embassy. When we arrived, we were greeted by the British Embassy people, as well as an American Lt. Col. Air Attaché. He welcomed us and informed us that we would be in Madrid for a few days, and that we should conduct ourselves as guests of the British and the Spanish. He cautioned us to stay out of bars and to remain in the hotel at night. We were not to wander off on our own, and he also advised us that the Gestapo danger very much existed here, as in Barcelona. We would receive five dollars a day per-diem in Spanish currency, just as we had in Barcelona, but we must report to the Embassy each day to receive it. He gave each of us a couple of packs of American cigarettes along with his farewell.

There was one escort assigned to the four officers, and two to accompany the Sergeants (I believe that there were now six or seven sergeants in our group, including RAF Sgt. Banner). We caught a city bus back to the hotel and were told to be ready to leave for the bullring at noon. We had time before we were to leave to go out on the street with our new escort to look around and sample the oranges on sale in Madrid, knowing that we were going to miss the noontime meal at the hotel. We went to a nice park where we sat and ate our oranges, enjoying the beautiful scenery and anticipating a day at the bullring.

At the appointed time, our escort led us to a city bus that took us to the arena. It was crowded, but we didn't mind as we continued to people-watch. Our escort had the tickets, and we were directed to the proper entrance to the arena where we had good seats on the sunny (more expensive in the winter) side of the stadium. It was a very festive crowd. The Spanish brass band was playing, and all were anxiously awaiting the bullfights to commence.

Earlier that morning, during our walk outside of the hotel, we had seen large posters advertising that afternoon's bullfight. There was to be one headliner bullfighter and two novices on the card. The third and sixth bulls were to be challenged by this famous matador, whom we were told was one of the most expert bullfighters in all of Spain.

Our escort explained that the Spanish national anthem would be played before the bullfights began, and that we must stand and raise our arm in the fascist salute for the entire playing of the anthem. He said that there would be guards in the bullring, facing the crowd, to spot any who would not give the salute. Before the start, the Spanish anthem was played, just as predicted. The Spanish police, in their little patent leather hats, were stationed every few feet in the bullring, looking into the crowd for any person unwilling to salute the dictator Franco. We all stood and gave the fascist salute in all of its *disgusting* glory.

The trumpets blared, signaling the start of the first bullfight, and out strolled the Matador, strutting into the ring along with his attendants at a respectful distance behind him. He pompously stepped along the perimeter of the ring, stopping every so often to bow and doff his hat to the crowd and to the applause and cheering of the waiting throng.

The trumpets blared again and the gate was opened as the bull was let into the ring. The bull paused for a few seconds to assess his surroundings and then, after spotting the bullfighter, made a charge directly toward him. The bullfighter nimbly sidestepped and turned around to face the bull coming at him again. He worked the bull for a few passes and then two men came into the ring on padded horses. Each used a long pike spear to pierce the bull in each shoulder to further enrage him.

The bullfighter continued to work the bull with his cape and sword for another pass, when suddenly the poor man was hooked by one of the horns of the bull and thrown high and away from the bull. The attendants rushed in with large capes to distract the bull until the bullfighter could regain his feet. He indicated that he was all right, except for a tear in his costume in the groin area, and he again faced the bull.

He made several more passes with the cape before two very nimble men on foot came into the ring and stuck flagged darts into the shoulders of the bull. By now the bull was tiring and stood facing the bullfighter with his head down in defeat. The bullfighter then thrust his sword into the bull, right between the shoulder blades to the hilt. The animal weaved back and forth a couple of times before collapsing in a heap. Someone rushed in with a short dagger and plunged it into the base of the neck of the downed bull to be certain that he was dead. The crowd roared their approval and the dead bull was dragged from the ring by a team of horses.

One of our officers and a couple of the sergeants told the escort that they would like to leave and go back to the hotel, but were told that they must stay, as it would not only be rude to leave, but would likely alert the police and possibly the Gestapo of their presence in the area. Most of us thought that the poor bull didn't have a chance, and it was cruel to torture the poor animal in this way. I doubt that anyone in our group, with the exception of the escorts, thoroughly enjoyed this spectacle, but we knew that we had to sit and watch five more bulls be slaughtered before the day was over.

We tried to amuse ourselves with observing the crowd, and were able to buy a glass of wine when the vendor came along, this being an experience in itself. The vendor had a small wine cask and a leather water bucket, one over each shoulder. He carried several small wine glasses attached to his belt between the cask and the bucket.

When we ordered our wine, he filled one of the wine glasses to the brim and passed it, hand-to-hand, to the patron placing the order. After collecting his money, he would continue on to the next customer until he ran out of glasses. When we finished our wine, the empty glass was passed back to the vendor. He would slosh it in the water bucket, shake it vigorously, and put it back in the holder on his belt; ready for the next patron. The wine glasses were small, about two good gulps of vino. This was definitely not the time or place for leisurely imbibing. In turn, we each ordered wine and he used his four or five glasses over at least twice to accommodate all, lingering at our row for quite a while. He seemed to appreciate the business that we provided him.

The second bullfight was just like the first, except that the bullfighter kept his feet and lightly danced around the bull until it was time for the kill. I was frankly a bit tired of this, but had to stay for the rest of the program. The next bullfight was certainly worth the wait.

This veteran showman was obviously different as to style and bravery. He was flashy but crisp in his performance, and had a magnificent bull to fight that he completely dominated from start to finish. He even walked proudly away from the bull, with his back turned, to show his domination of the animal. He then faced the bull, took off his cap, and made a bow to every corner of the ring, again having his back to the bull for an instant. After the usual goading by the men with the picks and the darts, he finished off his performance with a masterfully instant kill of the poor animal.

Everyone stood and applauded and cheered as the judges gave him both ears and the tail as a reward for the perfect performance. Although I still would have cheered for the bull, I could see the artistry and bravery of the matador, and now had a slight appreciation of the spectacle, still doubting that I would ever again see a bullfight, however.

The fourth and fifth fights were not nearly as colorful as the third, and one could easily see the difference between the novices and the accomplished bullfighter. In the last bullfight, the veteran again came out to a mighty cheer. The bull was released into the ring and it

MADRID AND GIBRALTOR

circled the ring as if looking for a way out. The audience "booed and hooted," as the bullfighter did his best to get the bulls attention, and begin the face off. The bull tried to jump over the bullring wall into the walkway dividing the actual ring from the crowd, and succeeded in getting into the walkway and scattering the attendants in his path. A door to the ring was opened and he had no choice but to again go into the ring and face his destiny. The bullfighter did his best, but the performance was lackluster compared to his first bull. Our escort hissed to us, "bad bull," and with this the bullfight officially ended.

We filed out with the crowd and onto one of the waiting city busses to deliver us back into the vicinity of our hotel. Almost everyone was silent on the ride back to the hotel, each, I suppose, thinking of the scenes we had witnessed and assessing if he wanted to see another bullfight or not.

We kept checking for our transfer to Gibraltar each day, hoping that we could soon continue our journey. We were content in the assumption that our parents and wives knew that we were safe in Spain and that we were on our way back to our units. Little did we know that the American attaché in Barcelona either did not send our messages home, or was not permitted to do so. We were still MIA as far as our loved ones knew. This knowledge would certainly have changed the tenor of our visit in Madrid.

The days were pleasant as our congenial escort showed us around the city as we visited the various bars and coffee shops, where we managed to spend almost all of our per-diem money each day. This touring was strictly in daylight and I don't believe that anyone went outside the hotel after dark. We were still asked to not visit the hotel bar, but Major Eveland and I, along with another officer, went to the bar one evening for an after-dinner drink. It was nearly deserted, as in Barcelona, and the Major felt that we could safely disobey the rule.

We spent another three or four days in Madrid seeing the sights and drinking rum and coke at the various bars. We would be served at outdoor tables when the weather permitted, as it was pleasantly warm, although somewhat windy for most of our visit and quite cool at night. Some of the fellows bought leather wallets, although they really didn't have much to put in them. I bought a leather cardholder for my Spanish ID and the one photo that I had kept when my photo was taken in the photo booth in Barcelona. I still have that first picture, the one with my eyes searching for the coin slot.

When we reported to the British Embassy on Thursday the 16th, we were told that we would be leaving for Gibraltar that afternoon. We were to be ready to leave the hotel and board the bus to be taken to the train station.

When we arrived at the station, we were escorted to a railway car similar to the one in which we had arrived in Madrid, (which may actually have been the same Pullman car), experiencing the same procedure as we had upon leaving Barcelona. The American attaché had come to see us off and wish us "good luck." The more important thing was that he brought us a carton of Chesterfields to see us through to Gibraltar. There were a few more people aboard this coach than we had on our trip from Barcelona with the normal couriers, Embassy employees, and one British General, with his personal "batman."

The British Brigadier took up one end of the coach for himself, his batman, and his numerous belongings. We evaders took up a position at the opposite end of the car to be as far away from the obnoxious General as possible. Our departure from Madrid gave us a good chance to see much of the local landscape before dark. After we had left the metropolitan area, the suburbs stretched for some miles south of the city, and then it was semi-arid farmland with grape or fruit orchards on both sides. We were soon tired of the same scenery, and relaxed to enjoy the ride and eat some of the food that the British had boarded. The fig bars and the all-too-familiar tea were satisfying and we all settled down for the ride in the coach. We had the feeling that

MADRID AND GIBRALTOR

there was no "love lost" between the Brigadier and our group of Yanks. We kept well separated accordingly, trying to not let this pompous character disturb us in the least.

We had left Madrid in mid-afternoon and traveled the distance to Gibraltar overnight. We awoke in the early morning to freshly brewed tea. It didn't take the place of coffee, but it was still hot and most welcome. Tea for breakfast, with milk and sugar, reminded me of my earlier days in the RCAF.

Our train actually arrived in the Spanish city of San Roquet, which adjoined the British zone of Gibraltar. This was the morning of Friday, March 17th. All in the British railway car were taken by bus through the neutral zone and into British Gibraltar, with the exception of the Brigadier and his batman. There was a special automobile awaiting him and his belongings.

We Americans were then bussed to a large Quonset type building manned by Brits, where we were greeted by the British and one lone American sergeant. We hadn't eaten, so they bussed us to a small mess hall where we were fed breakfast, again typical British style. When we went back to the building of our arrival, we were told that we would be stripped of the clothes that we had been given in Barcelona and relieved of our British identity papers as well as everything else that we had -- except for our dog tags.

The American sergeant told us that we would be issued GI clothing and that he would take us to the American Headquarters on the other side of the rock, as Gibraltar was known. We had signed in with name, rank, and serial number when we had first entered the building and they surely knew at a glance, who was an officer and who was an enlisted man, or so we thought.

We were all treated the same, however, and had to go into the next room to completely disrobe. Everything was taken from us - our clothes, our underwear, shoes and socks, everything. Even the little kit bag that the British had provided in Barcelona with our razor and

327

toothbrush were taken. Some of the fellows tried to keep the leather wallets that they had purchased in Spain, but they too were taken. I had the little cardholder that I had purchased in Madrid and was ready to surrender it when I thought of the picture of myself that I had put in the card-holder. I decided to try to hide the photo, so I slid it between the boards of the bench seat next to where I sat. We were told to go into the showers and would be issued new GI clothing when we came out.

We returned from the hot shower and saw that the American sergeant had lined a long table with new GI-issue clothing. All of the clothes were GI summer wear - khaki pants and shirt. We were to each take two pairs of underwear and socks and even an olive green handkerchief. There was another table loaded with GI shoes. We each selected the appropriate attire and shoes that would fit and proceeded to dress. My sergeant, Joe, was sitting right over the place where I had hidden my picture, and I said, "Move over Joe, I want to sit there." He looked at me quizzically and moved without saying a word. I retrieved the picture and put it in the pocket of my new shirt. When we were safely out of the building, I told Joe why I had asked him to move. He smiled his quiet smile and said that he wondered what it was all about. We were now all alike. Officers and enlisted men were dressed in the exact same uniform. This didn't bother me, as we had pretty much acted rank-less for much of the foregoing time.

We were bussed around the base of the rock to the American compound, and were greeted by the adjutant and his assistant. We again signed in as to name, rank, and serial number and were escorted, one by one, into an interview with an American intelligence officer.

He asked the normal questions of me, such as my group and squadron and location thereof. He wanted to know if I had any intelligence information that I was supposed to deliver to him. I told him the same things that I had told the British intelligence officer at our briefing in Barcelona. His questioning was quite penetrating, and he said for the first time that we were all considered possible imposters, agents of the Germans, and until we had been positively identified, we would be treated as such.

This was a bit of a shock, as I had thought that when I showed the Americans my dog tags, I would be accepted as a 1st Lt. in the Army Air Corps. Now I knew that until we had been officially identified, we would remain *rank-less*. Joe and I imagined that we would be flown back to Italy, where our squadron commander could identify us and we would be back in our normal status.

We were told that orders would be cut giving us the equivalent of $5 per day, to be paid in British Gibraltar currency. We asked how long we could expect to be in Gibraltar and were told that they didn't know. I explained that Joe and I were from the 15th AF in Italy, and that we would need to go in a different direction than the other evaders. The adjutant said that we were the first evaders from Italy, to his knowledge, to come through Gibraltar, and that he would have to see what could be done for us. I thought; why not send us directly home if we were not going to fly any more combat missions in Europe?

We were taken to an area of Quonset hut billets next door to the American Liaison Headquarters, and told to check in. We were fed our evening meal at a small GI mess hall just down the street, and were given the breakfast schedule.

The next morning, being Saturday the 18th of March, we received orders stating our per-diem and were given the equivalent of two days subsistence. I noted on the orders (which I still have) that Major Ivan W. "Wayne" Eveland was from the 401st bomb group, and 1st Lts. Shilliday and Marean were both from the 388th bomb group; all from the 8th Air Force, stationed in England. We were temporarily attached to the American Air Corps Liaison Office in Gibraltar for further orders. As we left the headquarters, Major Eveland reminded us that we had to salute all officers, as we were now "buck" privates in this man's army.

We were told that we were free to leave the American compound and go on a sightseeing tour of the rock. We were advised that a small American PX was open that morning where we could buy cigarettes if we wished. We wished, of course, and I had visions of my first "Camel" in a long time. We hurried to the PX before they ran out of our two-pack limit, and while they weren't "Camels," we welcomed them anyway. We were told to be back on the base no later than 1600 hours (4PM) that afternoon. We were anxious to get to see as much as possible of Gibraltar, and we four officers left by the front gate and caught a taxi into the town. The driver was eager to show us around and off we went.

The taxi driver looked Spanish or Moorish but spoke English with a clipped accent. He was a little difficult to understand, but I was catching most of his words while he gave us a tour around the rock. From our drive we could see the rock looming above us. As we climbed a bit, we had a view of the airport, which seemed to be in a flat area north of the rock. It looked to be a rather short runway, oriented generally east and west.

After some time of driving and noon was approaching, we asked the driver to recommend a good restaurant where we could get fresh seafood.

We descended a bit as he took us to an area two or three blocks above the harbor, and said that he was taking us to the best place for fresh crawfish that could be had in Gibraltar. We asked what a crawfish was and he said, "I guess you Yanks call it shrimp." Sounded fine to us, and we asked to be picked up at 1330. He said he would be back, but would like to be paid the fee that we already owed him. We reached deep into our pockets and came up with 3 pounds, Gibraltar money (about six U.S. dollars, I think).

MADRID AND GIBRALTOR

He stopped in front of a gaily-colored restaurant with outside tables and let us out. He cautioned us about getting out of the taxi, as we had been driving on the left side of the roadway, instead of the right as we were normally used to. We reminded him to come back and pick us up at the appointed time, and he assured us that he would.

The four of us sat at an outside table under an awning and requested a beer and the menu. The café manager came out, welcomed us, and said that fresh crawfish, had just come in, and if we would like to try some he would bring a bucket with the beer. The waiter came out with the four beers, cool but not cold, and soon the owner delivered the shrimp. The waiter wiped the table with a dirty bar rag and the café owner dumped the bucket of shrimp in the middle of the table.

I had never seen shrimp with their heads on or little black eyes staring out at me, and was fascinated by the feast in front of us. We began to shuck and eat them, even before the waiter brought out a tray of salt, pepper, and wedges of limes and lemons. He said to enjoy them and let him know when we would like to order from the menu.

The shrimp were still warm from the boiling pot and so very good. We went through the first bucket in just a few minutes. We ordered a second beer and thought that another spread of shrimp would be in order. We all slowed down a bit as we got into this second round. Someone wondered if we still intended to order from the menu. We all decided that the shrimp was enough lunch for one day.

We sat there in the shade of the awning to smoke and finish our beers as we took in the sights of the harbor below us. It was a pleasant time and we felt secure for the first time in many weeks. We didn't know it then, but we had one more scare from the enemy ahead of us. For now it was a serene time, secure at last, we were able to relax and enjoy the surroundings and the togetherness.

We paid our tab and waited about half an hour for our taxi. We still had a couple of hours to kill and some money left in our pockets, so we asked the taxi driver to continue with the tour. He said that the best way to see the other side of the rock was from Queen's Road, but didn't think that the taxi could climb that high with such a heavy load. We settled for a beautiful drive past the governor's mansion and back down the steep and winding hill in grinding low gear. We were all hoping that the old taxi didn't slip out of gear and that the brakes didn't fail as we made the descent.

We finally arrived at our front gate, where we paid the driver and re-entered the base. As we walking back to the headquarters building, we met a couple of our sergeants and stopped to ask if there was any news. A couple of local junior officers passed us and we dutifully saluted them, giving the sergeants in our group a reason to chuckle.

We walked into the office of the adjutant at about 1530 and were greeted with the news that we would be taking off for England that evening. I asked the adjutant if Joe and I would be on the orders, and he said, "Affirmative." I asked if we would eventually be going back to Italy and he said that they could sort that out in the U.K. Joe said that in England we would be closer to home and I certainly agreed. I hoped that if we did get sent home directly from England, our clothes and other belongings would be sent to our home, or at least to our new assignment. I especially wanted my camera, and definitely my RCAF logbook, as all of my military flying time was meticulously logged therein.

I fully expected to get everything back except my "great coat" which I had bequeathed to our squadron doctor, Capt. Neuman. He had admired the coat and I certainly hoped that he got it as promised. I knew that if I got back to my unit, he would happily give it back to me if I asked. We had been issued GI jackets along with our summer uniform and were sure that the jacket would come in handy on our arrival in the U.K.

We washed up and went to the mess hall as early as it opened for supper. We weren't particularly hungry after the shrimp lunch, but

MADRID AND GIBRALTOR

knew we needed something before boarding the bus to take us to the airport and the flight to England. Sgt. Banner was not with us now; apparently the RAF was taking care of his transport.

It was a short trip by bus to the airport Quonset hut air terminal. We got in line and waited to be processed for the flight. Soon there were several behind us, perhaps couriers or civilians that were to be on the military flight with us.

When they were ready to check us in, we were checked off by name and told to go out on the apron and wait for our call to board. Our GI jackets felt good, as it was getting chilly. We saw a big four-engine B-24 being loaded with mailbags right in front of us and thought that this was to be our "horse" to England.

It had been another case of hurry up and wait, as we shifted from one foot to the other while waiting to board. Sometime before midnight, we finally climbed the steps with our little cloth sack containing our extra underwear, socks, shaving kit, and our transportation orders.

This B-24 had been converted to carry cargo and passengers. All of the armament had been removed and plywood covered the floor where the two bomb bays had been. The mail sacks had been loaded in that area and were secured with cargo nets from the ceiling to the floor. There was a narrow passageway between the mail sacks to allow passage to and from the cockpit.

Plywood flooring extended into the cabin for 15 or 20 feet, this appeared to allow for more cargo to be carried in the cabin, if necessary. Only where the armament had been removed were there windows, and a small latrine was located in the cabin just to the right rear of the passageway into the cockpit. There were fold-down bench seats lining both sides of the cabin where we sat side by side, with our backs to the wall facing each other. Seat belts were fastened on the benches to be used by the passengers for takeoff and landing.

The bench seats had been folded down and bolted in place for our flight. The airplane was not crowded, so we thought that we would be able to stretch out on the plywood floor or the seat benches and sleep. There were backpack-type parachutes for all on board stacked and secured across from the main cabin door. Along side the parachutes was a stack of blankets and pillows, so we were looking forward to a pleasant and comfortable flight.

There were probably 15 passengers aboard when the passenger door was closed and the engines were started. After a couple of minutes, the engines were stopped and the passenger door opened to admit another passenger.

Two additional travelers came up the steps, and unfortunately turned out to be none other than our Brigadier and his batman from the Madrid to Gibraltar train trip. After all of his baggage was shoved aboard, the pilot re-started the engines again and we taxied out for our takeoff. The Brigadier didn't have time to do much more than fasten himself in before we were airborne. As soon as we were in the air, we all grabbed a blanket and a couple of pillows and staked out a place on the cargo flooring in the cabin or on the benches and prepared for sleep.

The Brigadier declared this was not to be allowed, and claimed a large section of the cabin near the entrance to the passageway to the cockpit. With his walking stick, he thrust his way through and told the men starting to bed down to move aft, as he was going to have the whole forward cabin section. He signaled for his batman to follow, and took up the center aisle and both sides in the very front of the passenger cabin with all of his baggage and sleeping mattress.

The batman had just unrolled his mattress in the middle of the aisle and the Brigadier prepared to settle down when Major Eveland got up and walked up to the General, mad as hell and about to "blow his cork." I had never seen Wayne this angry before as he berated the General, in no uncertain terms, stating that these men, meaning the

MADRID AND GIBRALTOR

evaders, had been shot down defending HIS country and were now on their way back to their unit and should not be treated in this manner. He was crisp and firm, but had his say and when finished, the Brigadier said "and who might you be?" He replied, "Major Ivan W. Eveland, United States Army Air Corps, sir." The General said "You can go to hell, Major whoever you are," and then we heard him say, "Insolent Yanks." With that, he settled down on his mattress, pulled a blanket over his head, and appeared to go to sleep.

His batman, who was a Lance Corporal, stretched out on the bench beside him and smoked a cigarette. I think that he might have been embarrassed by the whole incident. The Corporal finally put the baskets and gear on the bench seat opposite himself so we could squeeze past the General without actually stepping on him. A tempting thought, actually.

We all tried to settle down on either the benches or the remaining floor space, wherever there was room. The Brigadier and his batman and baggage had taken up nearly half of the available sleeping space. Every time anyone had to go to the latrine, he had to step carefully past the Brigadier and his baggage, which cluttered the entire front of the cabin.

The pilot of the B-24 came back to our part of the cabin, stepping over the General. When he heard that we were evaders, he wanted to talk to us. The pilot was a U.S. Air Corps Captain and he invited us up to the cockpit anytime "if you can get past that old bastard, that is."

The American crew of our airplane consisted of a pilot, co-pilot, navigator, flight engineer, and radioman. Members of the crew, from time to time, came back to stretch and smoke a cigarette as an excuse to talk to us. I tried to sleep, but it was hard getting into a comfortable position. There was enough room for some to stretch out on the bench seats, but they had to contend with the seat belt attachments and it was uncomfortable. The best place for a nap was on the floor, but when anyone got up to go to the latrine; his spot was immediately claimed by someone else. We droned along through the night with the thought that in the morning we would be in England. I had often wondered what England would be like and now I was going to find out.

We were cold in the airplane as we were in summer "khakis," but that couldn't be helped. On one of his visits to the cabin, the flight engineer said that we were flying at an altitude of 5000 feet and were beyond half way to Britain. I dozed for quite a while and then went forward to the latrine. With the coming of the new day, the cabin started to lighten up. After I left the latrine, I squeezed between the mail sacks and made my way to the cockpit. I was curious to see what the B-24 cockpit looked like. I spoke to the crew and introduced myself as a B-17 pilot. They asked me what group in England that I was from and I told them that I had been with the 99th in Italy before I was shot down. Someone asked me, "How did you escape?" and I replied that while I couldn't say, "It wasn't easy."

Standing between the pilot and co-pilot's seat, I had a good view outside and it was generally overcast below. Suddenly, with a little break in the clouds, I saw land below. The co-pilot saw it at about the same time that I did. I pointed to it and said one word "ENGLAND?"

The whole cockpit sprang into action. The pilot shouted to the navigator "Where the hell are we, that's France below us." The Captain told the co-pilot to turn 90 degrees left as he got out of his seat to go to the navigator's table. They were trying to figure out where the coastline of France and the safety of the sea would be to protect us from being shot down.

I left the cockpit, as I was in the way there, and went back to the cabin and our group. Most had been awakened by the steep left turn and asked me what was going on. I told them that we were lost and that I thought that we were again over France. This caused a lot of excitement and all tried to crowd to the few windows to look down and see if we were actually over land. Someone confirmed the land sighting, which put a chill over us all. We were collectively thinking

MADRID AND GIBRALTOR

that we could again be shot down over France. Deja' vu cloaked all too tightly around us.

Those of the passengers who were not glued to the windows headed for the back and the parachutes. Joe handed one to me and I put it on and tightened the straps. I was standing in the middle of the aisle when the Brigadier's "batman" shoved past me clutching two parachutes. He had had the presence of mind to grab a chute for himself *and* his General.

Despite the fierce sense of fear that pervaded the cabin, I have the memory of the batman trying his best to get the old "gent" into the parachute. The memory is comical today, but it was anything but, in the situation we found ourselves in that morning. I sat on the bench seat and put my head in my hands and prayed that we would be delivered once again safely. There was nothing more that I could do and I knew that my fate was in the hands of the Lord.

We had no way of knowing if we were flying over a large defended coastal city or a defended coastline. There was the threat from enemy fighter aircraft and also from anti-aircraft guns. It seemed like an eternity, but it probably wasn't very long before someone said he could see the coastline and then another, from the other side, said he saw water below. We hoped and prayed that we were again out over the ocean. We knew that we wouldn't be safe until we were well out to sea, and we were "sweating it out." After 20 or 30 minutes, the pilot made a correction in the heading to the right, and then we felt that the navigator had figured out where we were and we were again "on course." Most of us lit up a cigarette and let some of the fear and excitement, subside, with smiles all around. It was indeed a helpless feeling to be in an unarmed airplane over enemy territory.

The flight engineer came back and we asked him, "What happened?" He said that the navigator had allowed us to get off course, and that we had been over France for a while. He confirmed that we were back on course now and the weather in London was below landing minimums so we might have to hold over London for a time.

We again settled down and time droned on for another hour and a half. Wayne Eveland went forward and talked to the crew, and came back to our group and said that the weather in London was still below landing minimums, and we were going to our alternate and refuel.

It wasn't too long before we started our instrument approach for our landing at the alternate airport. We became clear of the clouds at about a thousand feet above the ground, and came in for a landing at a large airbase somewhere in England.

We had to stay on the airplane while a car was brought up for the General, and he and his batman deplaned, taking all of their baggage with them. We dreaded to have to re-board with the old Brigadier, but thought that we could put up with him and his indignities for the last leg into London when the weather cleared.

CHAPTER 14

ENGLAND

Finally, someone came for the evaders and we were put in a covered, open-backed truck and taken to a mess hall nearby. We were now under guard, very much like prisoners, and were escorted to a long table at the rear of the mess hall. None of us were allowed to go through the "chow line," so our food was brought to the table and we began to eat. Someone asked about coffee, and one of our two armed MP Officer guards went to the counter and got two large pitchers for us. Now we were able to top off our breakfast with official GI coffee.

There weren't many GI's in the large mess hall as it was fairly early Sunday morning, March 19th 1944. More than 7 weeks had passed since Joe and I had been shot down. We finished our breakfast and coffee and were escorted back to the truck by the two, armed officers. Both were U.S. Army Air Corps 1st Lts. who wore black MP armbands. I wondered why so much attention was being shown to us, as I would have thought that a sergeant guard would have been sufficient. I knew that until we were definitely identified we were suspect, but two officers to guard us seemed "overkill."

We all piled back into the truck, with me last to get in and sitting on a bench-type seat opposite one of the officer guards at the very rear. The truck driver raised and bolted the tailgate in place, and off we drove to return to the airplane.

As we started to leave the parking lot of the mess hall, a bicycling sergeant pedaled up behind and followed us to the street. The sergeant on the bike yelled out to me, "Hey! Wes, do your folks know you are O.K.?" I said "Well hi Amby, I'm sure that they do." "Don't think so," he replied, "I heard from home yesterday and they said that you were still missing in action." With that the MP Lieutenant told me to "Knock it off," and to Amby, "Sergeant, get away from this truck and shut up." The man on the bicycle was Sergeant Ambrose Moore from my hometown. When the MP Lieutenant yelled at him, he promptly turned around and pedaled off in the opposite direction.

We arrived back at the airplane just as the refueling was complete, and we were ushered aboard. There was no sign of the Brigadier and we hoped that if he did come back, we would takeoff and leave him on the tarmac. After we had boarded, Joe asked me who was talking to me when we left the mess hall. I told him that he was a friend from my hometown, and that he said that he didn't think my parents had been notified that I was no longer MIA. This was disconcerting, as we had been sure that the American attaché in Barcelona had sent our telegrams to our parents, saying that we were now out of France and in Spain. I was upset by this turn of events to say the least, and thought about this all the way on the flight to London. I wondered how long a letter took to get to Amby from our hometown, and if my parents even received a telegram from Barcelona telling them that I was OK.

It seemed to be a fairly short flight on to London. The weather had cleared up considerably, and we now were flying over scattered to broken clouds, allowing us to get a glimpse of the ground. We landed near London before noon. Our excitement and fear generated by our incursion over France earlier that morning was nearly forgotten with our jubilation at being in London.

We went through the usual check-in as to name and rank by a corporal holding a clipboard. We were put on a bus, and taken into

ENGLAND

the City of London, to a place where the U.S. Air Corps Intelligence did the de-briefing and reassignment of all evaders entering the U.K. This time only one, armed sergeant MP guarded our bus.

This narrow but long brownstone building, split level and three or four stories high, was located at 63 Brook St., somewhere near Hyde Park in the City of London. There were five or six steps leading up to the entryway of the building, where we were greeted by several staff members and were asked if we were hungry. We indicated that we were always hungry, and were escorted downstairs to a mess hall, located partly below the street level but with windows allowing plenty of light for a very pleasant dining room. The food there was truly amazing with roast beef and mashed potatoes, canned sweet corn, and even pudding for dessert. This was all served to our table family style. When one bowl was emptied, another quickly replaced it. We all ate more than our fill.

After the big lunch, we were taken to a room and were matched off with a person who took our particulars. He wanted to know our group and squadron numbers. When I said that my sergeant, Joe Kinnane, and I were from the 15th Air Force in Italy, he said that it might take some time to get someone up from Italy to identify us.

Joe and I were sent back to the waiting room and waited there until everyone else in our group of evaders had been interviewed. It was mid-afternoon or later when a lady, Air Corps Captain Dorothy Smith, came into the room and beckoned for us to follow her into her office. She introduced herself and said that since we were from Italy, it would be some time before we could be identified. She stressed that we would be asked only the information we had brought to them, if any, and only information as to our trip out of France that couldn't wait until tomorrow.

I told her all of the data that I had divulged in my briefings in Barcelona and Gibraltar, and said that I thought that I could pinpoint some of the airports and fuel storage areas and other information if I

341

just had a map. She produced a detailed map of southern France, and I studied it but couldn't seem to make sense of the information that had been drilled into me by the French Intelligence lady. I commented that I had been drilled on a French military map, and she assured me that she would have one available the next day.

We asked if we would be billeted and confined to the building. She said affirmative to both, and added as we were about to leave her office, "Do either of you know anyone who is now stationed in England who could identify you?" Joe nodded "no," and I said I didn't know anyone either. Joe then spoke up and said "Loo-tenant, how about that guy who hollered to you when we were in the truck this morning?" I said, oh yeah, Amby Moore, but I don't know the name of the airfield where we landed for fuel. Captain Smith said that she knew where we had landed and asked the question, "Could this fellow positively identify you?" I said yes, he's from my hometown and I went through high school with his brother. She had me write his name and rank, and said that she would have him sent here to identify me. She added that they knew the whereabouts of every American GI in the U.K. With that, I was shown to a room on the floor above and told what time to be down to the mess hall that evening.

Dinner was plenty of everything again, all we could eat and more. With dinner over, we were shown to the basement of the building, one level below the dining room, which was used as the air raid shelter. We were told that if the air raid siren goes off, day or night, we should quickly dress, be sure to wear our shoes, and to hurry to the shelter. The sergeant added that they hadn't had an air raid warning for a couple of nights, but one was likely soon. With that we went up the stairs to the second floor and to our rooms. I enjoyed a good uninterrupted sleep and was ready for my detailed briefing the next morning.

My room was small but more than adequate. Each officer's room had a single bed, a chest of drawers, and a small desk and chair. After

ENGLAND

breakfast, I went to the briefing room and waited for my turn to be fully de-briefed.

Most of the other guys had a reunion with someone from their unit that morning, and after they were de-briefed, had gone through the identification procedure. Some stayed over at 63 Brooks for a few days, but most left for their units when orders were cut and their business at 63 was completed. Some returned periodically to get TDY orders to go to other units and lecture on escape and evasion techniques. I had a chance to say goodbye to most of my evader friends before they left.

Major Wayne Eveland left on Tuesday or early Wednesday and I said goodbye to him, but unfortunately never had a chance to get together with him again. (He had been like an older brother to me and I appreciated our short association).

Sgts. Hasson and Harrison were returned to the UK in May after their recuperation from frostbite but I was never able to connect with either of them.

Lts. Shilladay and Marean also left as soon as they could leave. If they came back to 63 Brook St. to get lecture orders, our paths did not cross.

When it was my turn to be interviewed on Monday the 20th, I was interrogated by 1st Lt. Don Emerson. It was mid to late afternoon when both Joe Kinnane and I were called in by Lt. Emerson. We were to be interrogated simultaneously, as we had been together with the exception of the first two days we spent in France. We went over the same ground as I had the afternoon before with Capt. Smith, diverting only in utilizing the now available French maps (Michelin). The following information came from the actual briefing summary, which was de-classified, and I received a copy through the Freedom of Information Act, as did many evaders in 1996. It is copied verbatim.

343

a. I had been told that the airfield southeast of Berre (intersected by 3G 20, sheet 84, Michelin, France, 1:200,000) is still used as a seaplane base. (I had pointed out the base to the interrogator on the French map and he had supplied the map information).

b. Both Joe and I supplied the information that we had been told - that the bombing on Salon de Provence airdrome on the 27th of January was very effective.

c. I told him that the Germans are now using auxiliary fields, one of them near Les Mille, a former staging base.

a. We were both told by the French that at 0900 on the day of the raid on Salon de Provence airfield, the Germans expected the heavy bomber attack. They cleared the field of all flyable aircraft. (My comment: Our group formed up and became enroute at about 0830.)

b. I was told that the Germans are feverishly fortifying the Mediterranean coast. They will stop trains and make passengers work for 48 hours.

c. We told him that German engineers were supposed to have come to Aix-en-Provence in February to fortify it.

d. I was told that in the past August, the headquarters of the XIX (19th) German Army had been relocated to Avignon.

I was able to locate, on the French map, the location of the fuel supply area and the position of the anti-aircraft guns, as shown to me by the lady in Marseilles, which he noted but said that they already had that information. (I am surprised that they didn't already know that the German 19th Army was located in Avignon. They surely had known it, although he listed it in the report anyway.)

After he had taken the information that was to be transmitted to the proper channels, he then asked us to relate our experiences as to the flight on the day in question, and the circumstances of our being shot down.

ENGLAND

He wrote all of this down in long hand and I found it difficult to read his writing. Often he wouldn't finish a sentence before he would start the next. It followed the story of our bailout and landing, and of our evasion in France. He omitted, or we didn't relate, our experiences in Spain. He stopped at our entry into Spain at 0130 on March 2nd, 1944.

The information that I gave him then differs slightly from my recollections now of that day in several details; the following is quoted from the written testimony that I gave him on the day of the interrogation. This is from the interrogation material that I received in 1996. "I went out at about 19000 feet and held the jump to about 3000 feet. (He had originally written 1900 feet then crossed it out and put in 2000 feet and then crossed that out and put in 3000 feet)"... Still quoting from the written interrogation material, I stated that, "I had looked at my wristwatch during the free fall and saw that it was 1226. When I landed it was 1229. I fell most of the way on my back with my feet slightly higher than my head. It was a comfortable feeling, and I could not tell that I was going fast. When I opened my chute it seemed as if I started to go up as fast as I had been going down. I saw my ship go around me, making a dreadful noise, roll over on its back and descend into the hillside, rolling down the hill like a ball of fire." I went on to say that "I drifted badly in a 35 mile wind." "I was afraid that I was going to hit a high tension wire and tried to slip my chute to avoid it. I had never received instructions in guiding the chute but missed the wire anyway, although I landed in a bramble of thorn bushes. I sat about 30 seconds and could see eight other chutes in the air."

Lt. Emerson's only comment after I related the circumstances of the bailout was that "some of the 8th Air Force airplanes had returned to England on two engines, safely." I said that I did not have 2 good engines. We only had #4 engine putting out full power, #3 was producing about 1/3 of its rated capacity, and on the left wing, #1 engine was on fire and useless, with #2 engine completely stopped and the propeller feathered. It certainly did not look like a win-win situation, as I would have had to fly over 250 miles of cold water to get to the safety of Corsica.

(I received Joe Kinnane's testimony attached to mine as we were interrogated together. I am quoting from his written testimony.) He stated, "The ball turret gunner was the first man out the waist" (exit). Joe said, "When I tried to get out, I got hung up in the door. The other waist gunner pushed me out. I had my hand on the ripcord, counted five, and pulled, receiving no jerk. I saw seven parachutes, two of them close to me. A German plane circled me. I saw that I was drifting toward a lake and was afraid that I was going to come down in it. I came down in some low trees and landed easily. A Frenchman came up through the bushes and kissed me and I told him that I was American". Joe went on to say, "He helped me off with my harness and gathered up my parachute; he pointed out where another had landed, and ran off to the woods with my equipment. I ran over to the parachute and found a crewmember. While people were telling us to hide, another crewmember came up. The three of us were taken to some brush. The Frenchmen went off for food. We saw seven Germans coming up the road and thought that they had seen us. We walked away slowly, and saw a German heading toward the others. We hid and were not troubled."

I am still quoting from Joe Kinnane's interrogation papers. "We decided to head northeast toward Switzerland. I had never been warned not to head for Switzerland. I had never been briefed in the theater of operations on evasion and escape at all. Enlisted men were not admitted to briefings; consequently, it wasn't until much later that I was warned not to head for Switzerland. We walked all day; about evening we stopped at a house where we saw a light. We heard talking. A man passed us and one of my crew-members touched him on the arm. The man was scared to death. My crewmember told him that we were Americans. The man took us in immediately and wanted to know all about us. After we explained who we were, we were fed and our journey was arranged. After some days, I met Lt. Coss and traveled with him."

This completed the testimony of Sergeant Joe Kinnane, and was compiled and signed by D. E. Emerson, 1st Lt., AUS.

I had only a hazy memory of Joe's story but having it before me, as I wrote this, was a big help. The other two crewmembers that traveled with Joe were 2nd Lt. Bob Johnson and 2nd Lt. Ernest Jenkins, my co-pilot and bombardier respectively. I also had a chance to talk with my bombardier Ernie Jenkins and his recollection was very similar to Joe's testimony.

Monday's de-briefing was over in late afternoon and I was told that my friend Ambrose Moore would be coming soon to identify me and I could then identify Sgt. Joe Kinnane. I went to my room to rest before dinner. I had lost at least 25 pounds in the last couple of months, and eating at 63 Brook St. certainly helped to gain some of it back. Some of the guys were anxious to get back to their units to see if they could reclaim any of their belongings. I asked several times if we would go back to Italy, but was always told that they didn't know. I would have been happy to get orders back to the USA, but this was not to happen for a while at least.

The next morning after breakfast, I was summoned to Lt. Emerson's office and given a list of questions to which I was to write an answer, if I knew the answer. They were questions about my family, my hometown, my high school principal and teachers, etc. Also, there were questions about the Ambrose Moore family, from which I deduced that they were getting ready to question Amby Moore when he arrived to identify me. I had no idea that he was already in the building and in an adjoining office, providing answers to the same set of questions that I had been given.

When I finished with my written questions, Lt. Emerson told me to wait in his office and he would be back shortly. In a few minutes he came in with Sgt. Ambrose Moore in tow to officially identify me. Amby and I met and embraced, and of course were all smiles at seeing each other. The paperwork was made out and signed by both Ambrose and me, and my right thumbprint was put on the document. The paper was taken to W. F. Maranda, Special Agent C.I.C., for his initials, and the document was stamped CONFIDENTIAL. This was March 21st, 1944. At the top of the document was penciled in the number 485, which became my official escape and evasion number.

I was now officially a 1st Lt. USAAC again. Joe Kinnane was brought in and I identified him and a like document was made out for him. I testified in his document that I had known him prior to his being reported missing in action over enemy territory. I signed his document, and he also signed and was thumb printed to make it official. We were both now in status and grade, the moment that we had been hoping and waiting for. I introduced Joe to Ambrose Moore, and Joe spoke of the stroke of luck that we had when Ambrose had recognized me in that mess hall on Sunday morning.

We were told that we were free to go outside the building now, and that I could invite Amby to our lunch that noon. I had been issued an Army Air Corps GI jacket in Gibraltar, and I put it on and went outside to sit on a bench in front of the building to smoke and talk with Amby. Under the jacket I still had on the same clothes that I had been issued in Gibraltar, which were definitely not winter issue, and I knew that I had to get some proper clothes soon.

Ambrose told me that after he recognized me in the mess hall he tried to get within speaking distance of me. He got his chance when I sat nearest the tailgate of the truck. He was curious as to what kind of trouble I was in because I was in a group of prisoners being guarded by two MP Officers.

ENGLAND

He said that early on Monday morning he was called to the base adjutant's office. He was afraid that he was somehow in deep trouble. When he arrived, the sergeant at the desk outside the adjutant's office said that orders were being cut for him to report to Intelligence Interrogation Headquarters at 63 Brook Street, London. He was told to leave by train that afternoon and to report at 0900 the next morning. He also learned that an officer from his base would be accompanying him. Ambrose asked to be escorted by Capt. Keith Harris. Keith was an officer that he knew from Earlville, Illinois, a town near our own hometown. He picked up his travel orders and per-diem, and he and Capt. Harris were on their way by train to London by late afternoon.

He still didn't know what this was all about and why he was to report to the Air Corps Intelligence. He had come to London overnight and had reported as ordered. I didn't know the location of the base where he was stationed even though I'm sure that he told me, but I don't remember. In papers that I now have it is only referred to by the code word "Valley." I have since learned that both he and Capt. Harris were stationed at Warton Air Depot near Burtonwood, England. This is where we had re-fueled and Amby had made contact with me.

The subject changed to my questioning him as to when the letter from his parents saying that I was still MIA had been sent. I wanted to find out if it was before or after the telegram from the Air Attaché in Barcelona was sent. He gave me the approximate date of his parents' letter that he had received at mail call on the Friday morning before he saw me.

I felt that my parents should have gotten the telegram from Barcelona before his parents had written that I was still MIA, and blurted out, "That damned attaché in Barcelona didn't send the telegram as he promised." I realized right away that I had said something that I shouldn't have. I knew that Amby had been given a statement to read and sign that said that he couldn't reveal anything of his mission to Intelligence Interrogations Headquarter in London, except to his Commanding Officer. I hoped that he didn't add my Barcelona remark to his report, if one was necessary.

I knew that I had to send word home telling my folks that I was OK, so I told Amby that I didn't have any money to send a telegram home and asked if he would do it for me. He got up from the bench and said that he would be back as soon as he could locate a telegraph office and have the telegram sent.

I anxiously waited and smoked in front of the building for about an hour, and finally Amby came back in a taxi. He said that he had walked some distance and asked directions of several people before he found a telegraph office.

He sent the following telegram to my parents in Paw Paw, Illinois that morning. "Dear Folks. In good health - hope to see you soon - Love Wesley Coss." Although this was sent at about 1100 Tuesday morning the 21st, because of the time difference, it arrived in my hometown at about noon on the same day. The local train station agent who copied the telegram from Western Union took it to my father at work. My dad closed the barbershop and hurried the two blocks to our home to show it to my mother.

Amby had arrived back at 63 Brook Street at about lunchtime and I invited him to have lunch with me. He was surprised to see how we were treated in our mess hall. We sat at a large table with several sergeants and officers together, and were again served family style. They kept bringing food until we could eat no more. Amby said several times, "I can't believe this." After we had eaten, I asked Amby to stay for a while so that I could receive some money and pay him for the cost of the telegram he had sent for me. He said that he didn't want me to pay him for the telegram, but that he intended to stay another day in London and was to meet Capt. Harris later on that afternoon.

ENGLAND

After lunch, papers identifying me as a 1st Lt. in the U.S. Army Air Corps were cut, and I headed for the paymaster's office in the 63 Brook St. building to get some of my back pay. I took a 300-dollar advance (in British pounds) of the pay owed me and I was ready to hit the street.

I put on my GI jacket and left with Amby Moore in a taxi. Before I went to the tailor shop, I asked the taxi driver to take me to the telegraph office so that I could send a back-up telegram to my parents. I sent the second telegram of the day, saying, "Am visiting with Ambrose in London, Wes." (I was allowed to pick a phrase from a list and I filled in the blanks with Ambrose and London and my name and it went out on Western Union that way.) I used my shortened first name, so that they would know that it was authentic.

We then went by taxi to the tailor shop. Amby remarked that it was good that we hadn't encountered an officer in our time out of the building, as I didn't have a hat or cap to go with the summer pants and the GI jacket. I was happy when we arrived at the tailor shop and was outfitted with a proper uniform. This tailor, recommended by Lt. Emerson, seemed to have an "insight" into what was going on at 63 Brooks and knew how to handle my situation.

After the tailor had fitted me with a blouse, shirt, pants, and all else that was needed, I was measured for an "Eisenhower" battle jacket. The tailor casually asked me if I wanted a "winged boot" sewn on the inside of the lapel of the new blouse jacket. I asked what the "winged boot" was all about, but he just smiled and said for me to ask them at 63 Brook St.

(The "Boot" was a British tradition begun when British Airmen were shot down over the African desert. These boot insignias were worn proudly by the Brits to show that they had "walked out." The American evaders adopted this custom, but not being an official Air Corps emblem, had to have the "boot" sewn under the left lapel of their blouse. The small cloth boot was in black with silver thread.)

STARDUST FALLING

Ambrose and I said goodbye at the tailor shop and he went off for his sightseeing trip in London. I thanked him for all of his help as he left in a cab, while I caught another back to 63 Brook St. I contacted my sergeant, Joe Kinnane, as soon as I could find him and suggested that he also go to the telegraph office and send a telegram to his parents to let them know that he was safe. He still didn't know that the Air Attaché in Barcelona might not have notified his parents. He hurried out to hail a taxi and send a telegram "on the double." (We were to learn later that the telegram from Barcelona was never sent to our parents.)

I was allowed to spend another night in the building at 63 Brook St. and was to be billeted at a nearby VOQ (visiting officer's quarters) the next day, where there was an officer's club and dining room close by. I was also told to report to 63 Brook Street every day, as I was officially assigned to them until some decision could be made as to my next assignment.

The next night we experienced our first air raid. The sirens went off just after midnight, and I got up and put on my pants and shoes, without socks, and no shirt, just my undershirt and my jacket, and headed for the basement air raid shelter in the VOQ building. It was cold in the shelter and I wished that I had dressed a bit warmer. I heard the noise of what I thought were bombs falling somewhere nearby. One of the people permanently stationed in the building said that the noise that I was hearing was not from bombs, but from the big guns in nearby Hyde Park firing at the Germans. It wasn't too long before the all clear sounded and I went up the three or four stairways to bed again.

This building that was for visiting officers was located within walking distance of Brook St. and had been a hotel before being taken over by the Americans. The first floor was for the offices of the permanent personnel, as it was often necessary to extend "temporary duty" of those who were housed there. The paper work and such was completed there also.

The second floor and on up were for the officers who had checked into the VOQ. The lower-ranked officers were confined to the second and third floor. Field grade officers were assigned the upper floors and some had balcony rooms, depending on their rank.

On the second or third day after we were identified, Joe and I were told that we were to go on TDY to an airbase of the 8th AF. We were to report to the intelligence officer there and were to lecture on evasion and escape. We left that same afternoon and reported the next morning as ordered.

The intelligence officer took us in to meet the group CO, and we were told that we were to meet with two of his squadrons that afternoon. We tried to hurriedly put together what we could, and could not say. We had received a briefing paper before we left on the trip, and it pretty well spelled out what was and was not to be talked about.

We were to keep our talk to a general nature, and to not disclose how we in particular, were able to escape. We were not allowed to refer to our other crewmembers in any way, especially the two who were captured by the Gestapo in Perpignon. I went first, and talked about what to do and not to do when one first landed in occupied territory. I emphasized that it was most important to have your own shoes. I knew that, since the 8th AF crews were equipped with electrically heated flying boots, the boots would be too conspicuous if they were to be worn in an evasion and escape attempt. I recommended that they wire their regular shoes to their parachute harness.

I told them of a story that I had heard of a crewman who had bailed out with only his fur-lined flying boots on, no shoes, and that both boots had come off when his parachute opened. He had landed in his stocking feet and had to try to escape without his shoes. In no way did I indicate that it was my co-pilot that I was talking about. I said that it was extremely difficult to escape without good, well fitting shoes. I told them to expect to do a lot of walking, and also emphasized that shoes were in very short supply in most of the occupied countries. They could not expect to be given something close to proper fitting footwear for an escape attempt. Good shoes were probably their "best friend," I stressed.

I then touched briefly on making an extended free-fall in the bailout if that was possible. I was allowed to say that I had made an extended free fall and apparently was not seen by the German ground forces, as I had no pursuit at all. I also stressed that the German fighter pilots liked to shoot at Allied airmen floating down, and this free fall would eliminate that. I was told to stress the fact that if they did attempt a long "free fall," they should not delay opening their parachute below 4000 feet above the ground. This was written into my briefing speech and was underlined. I was to emphasize that when you are in your parachute, drifting down, this is the very best time to survey your surroundings and form a plan of evasion and escape.

Joe got up to speak next and told about his difficulty in getting out of the airplane, and of the scare he had when a German fighter plane circled him as he was in the parachute, and how he thought that he was going to be killed by the German pilot. We then opened the meeting up to questions.

There were so many that I thought that it would never end. Most, we could not answer. We asked to please not be asked where we had landed, who had helped us, and how we had managed to escape. I don't think, at this stage of the war, that any of the people that we were speaking to had ever met anyone who had actually escaped. We were numbers 485 and 486 to be processed in the U.K., and most of the ones preceding us had returned to the States before those to whom we were lecturing had started their tour. I am not sure if the evaders that preceded us were sent to any group other than their own to lecture before they were sent home or re-assigned to non-combat duty.

When Joe and I returned from this trip, we were called into the office at 63 to see how we had been received, and if we felt that this effort was productive and necessary. We told them that from the questions asked of us and from our general reception, the effort was indeed positive.

We were then told to report the next morning for a briefing session. We arrived on time and were taken to a room and seated around a large table with at least half a dozen or more recently arrived evaders. Capt. Dorothy Smith told us what the session was all about. We should all try to formulate a list of do's and don'ts and ideas that would help in briefing the flight crews to escape.

There were to be several teams that would go out as Joe and I did, to brief the flight crews of the various heavy bomb groups located in England. We were to stress the fact that if any of our airmen landed in occupied territory, if they did the right things and had some luck, they had every chance to evade and escape capture by the enemy. We were to tell them that many airmen that were now listed as MIA were really in hiding, helped by the locals, and would probably escape capture and may even be returned to England. This was certainly a true statement. When the Allies liberated the occupied countries, more than a thousand airmen were found to be in hiding and were returned to safety. We worked on this concept for the full day and into the next morning until we had it like we thought it should be. We had it typed up and it was reviewed by either Lt. Don Emerson or Lt. John White and this was the guide to be used on our lecture tours.

As I remember, it went pretty much as follows:
1. Never approach two people on the street for help; one might not trust the other and so they would have to turn you over to the authorities.

2. It was much better to knock on a door than to approach anyone on the street. Preferably do not be seen by neighbors. At night the streets and homes were blacked out so that was the best time to knock on a door and ask for help.

3. A priest or minister could probably be trusted to help you if they could, and were to be approached with discretion.

4. If you ask someone for help they may say "no," leave their presence immediately; they will probably not turn you in, but could, if they thought they were being observed talking to you, by a bystander.

5. When you find help they will be wary of you; they will expect a German plant, so be careful with words that sound German like "yah" and do not say "nein" or "nix" or any other word that might sound German. Be very cautious of this as once you are in the hands of the Resistance, if they even suspect that you are a German plant, you will be executed.

6. Do exactly what your benefactors tell you to do. Trust them even if you are unsure of their intent. If they say "hide," do so; if they say "follow me," comply. You do not have much choice but to trust them. They are sticking their necks out for you if they are genuine. If they are not, they will lead you directly to the Germans and you will become a POW.

7. If you are being helped by the Resistance, give them any information that they request. You are not restricted to name, rank, and serial number. They will probably compare your information with others of your crew to see if you are genuine. They probably will ask about your mission, group and squadron, even squadron commander's name, and most surely the names of your crewmembers and where you were based.

8. Don't complain about your food or living conditions; they are probably doing the best that they can to accommodate you and keep you from being captured, as well as to keep themselves from being caught helping you.

ENGLAND

9. If you are out in the public, do nothing to call attention to yourselves or your escort or guide. If there are two or more traveling together, do not speak in English; remain silent if possible. English is a very recognizable language and will be a tip-off that you do not belong there.

10. Keep your dog tags, if possible. You will probably be asked by the Resistance to give them up, but strongly resist. They will probably be the only part of your belongings that you will retain in hiding. They will be indispensable if you are captured. Keep them if at all possible.

11. Be very aware that your benefactors face certain death if they are caught helping you; being a prisoner of war will be your fate. Always keep this in mind. Be very mindful of your helper's position.

12. If you do make a delayed free-fall before opening your parachute, open it at least 4000 feet above the ground so that you can survey the surrounding territory to make a plan as to which would be the safest and best way to go once you have landed.

There were probably several more items on this paper that we were to stress, but these are all that I can recall now. These rules or suggestions were "confidential" at the time, and we were not allowed to pass out the written text, only to read them to the audience. They probably became regular escape and evasion reading soon thereafter. (Probably they had to be approved by higher-ups).

At this session, I now had met several new officer evaders like myself, and traveled with them on our trips to the various 8th AF units. I became well acquainted with two lieutenants from northern Illinois. One was Lt. Paul Packer, from Chicago, and the other was Lt. Earl Wolf from Princeton, Illinois. Princeton is about 30 miles from my home. We either traveled alone or in pairs. At about this time, Joe and I had been notified that we would be retained to lecture for a while, but when that was over, we would be rotated back to the U.S. rather than be returned to Italy.

STARDUST FALLING

I was out on one of those trips on March 31st visiting one of the 8th Air Force bases, so I requested to stay over an extra day to try to get some flying time so I could get my flight pay for the month of April. I had no trouble in getting the flying time, as I flew on a test flight and on an aircraft acceptance flight in a new B-17G. I was then flown back to London on the 2nd of April in a B-17 with a general as a passenger, and I logged co-pilot time on this flight. I had more than enough flight time by the 2nd of April for my flight time pay requirement for that month.

When I was able to spend the night on the various 8th AF airbases that I visited, I was struck by how different it was in England than in Italy or North Africa. There were always local girls that had been invited to the Officer's Club each night. Those crewmen who didn't have to fly early the next morning partied like I had never seen before.

I was always very welcome and it seemed that everyone knew that I was an evader. I tried to quiet the talk, being aware that the ladies were taking it in, but to no avail. I attempted to watch from a corner and stay away from the loudest groups, but invariably someone would come over to me, along with his date, introduce her and say, "This is the guy that was shot down and escaped." When I mentioned this to the people at 63 Brook, their only advice was to stay out of the Officer's Club at night. This was tough, although I tried to be discreet.

I had a date with a girl in London that sang in a piano bar not far from our quarters. I stayed at the bar until it closed, and then was walking the young lady home when the air raid sirens sounded. I asked her where the nearest air raid shelter was, but she shrugged it off with a, "Never mind, if it's going to get us, there isn't much we can do about it." I argued with her, and she took my hand and we ducked into a covered doorway where we stood with our backs tight against the closed door while the air raid was in progress.

ENGLAND

I was plainly scared, but she took it all in as if it was an everyday occurrence. To her perhaps! The searchlights were on everywhere and I think that every gun in London was firing at the intruders. The noise and concussion from the guns were very impressive, and then there was a bright flash and a solid concussion from a bomb that had fallen near us. She said it was probably over on Baker Street, wherever that was. I had been hearing what sounded like falling pebbles or metal on the cobble stone street in front of us, and I asked her what it was that I was hearing. She said that it was small pieces of the anti-aircraft shells fired by our forces falling back to the ground. According to her, that was the reason that we had found shelter in the doorway in the first place. "Nasty to get hit by the falling debris," she quipped. When the guns stopped firing, even before the all clear sounded, she said, "Let's go."

We proceeded to her apartment where I met her female roommate. The greeting by her female friend left no doubt that I was in the wrong place that evening. I had never seen two women kiss on the lips as these ladies did. They were apparently lovers and I was not welcome. I left to find a taxi back to my quarters.

When I talked to the guys the next morning, I described the air raid experience and thought that they would be interested, but their only remark was, did you strike out again? A resounding, "yes" preceded the relating of my night's experience and new awareness of a lesbian relationship. I guess that my "lady of the evening" just wanted an escort home. My buddies howled!

Joe and I had one more trip together before we left for home. It was either to Ipswitch or Norwitch, or somewhere in that area of Britain. On our way back to London, I saw an attractive young female British Naval officer sitting by herself on the rail coach. I told Joe that I was going to "hit" on her and try to get a date that night in London. He smiled his usual "good luck Loo-tenant." I sat by her and started talking to the young woman, who I found to be very pleasant and easy to converse with. She was on her way from her home back to London for duty.

We talked about our hometowns and about our countries in general. She asked me if I was going into London for a few days vacation. I said "yes" and she asked where in England I was stationed. I told her that I was a B-17 pilot and that I was stationed at the airbase that I had just left. (I was forbidden to tell anyone that I was attached to 63 Brook St). I hoped that she was not familiar with the town or village that was near the airbase, because I certainly wasn't. She then asked why I wasn't wearing an 8th AF shoulder patch. I was taken back a bit by this question but quickly recovered and said that I had just picked up this new "battle" jacket and hadn't had time to have a tailor sew one on. I told her that I would find a tailor shop and get it done in London. She accepted this story.

I had found a tailor in London who had a 15th AF patch and I had it sewn on my regular blouse but hadn't, as yet, had one put on my "battle" jacket. She asked me how many missions I had flown and I said, truthfully, 21. I asked her what she did in London and she was evasive so I didn't press it, as I thought that she must have been involved in some type of sensitive work.

She may have been my age or a year older. She had been in college before becoming an officer. I proposed a date that evening and told her that I had heard of a pub where we could get a steak dinner. She quickly accepted and gave me her name and the address of the quarters where she was staying, and I arranged to pick her up at 1830 that evening.

She was ready for our date when I arrived. We went to the pub, and in the entry way there was a sign advertising "steak night" and in bold letters below was the word "Cheval." We proceeded to order a gin and tonic and both ordered the steak dinner. When it came it was large, thick, and delicious. I ordered another round of drinks as we continued to enjoy our dinner. She said several times, "I didn't know one could get a steak dinner anywhere in London at this time." Much too flippantly I said, "I'm sure you know that this is horse meat," which was of course, a terrible mistake. She dropped her knife and fork and wouldn't eat another bite. The atmosphere got extremely "chilly" and finally she asked me to take her home. I left the remainder of my steak, paid the check, hailed a taxi, and took her back to her quarters. We didn't speak on the ride to her lodgings - what was there to say? I was only sorry that I had told her of what I thought she already knew - "cheval" was horse. I asked her if I could see her to her door and she emphatically said, "Never mind."

The next day when I saw Joe, he asked, "How did it go Loo-tenant?" I said, "Not good," and left it at that. I didn't want to go into details. When I told Paul Packer and Earl Wolf the tale they had a good laugh at my expense.

We began to ask when we were going to go home. The reply was always "soon." It was expensive in London and I was constantly running out of money. The per-diem I received for my trips out of London was about the only spending money that I had left. I had gotten my flying time in for April, and was looking forward to the next payday on the 15th.

On April 7th, Joe remarked that a lot had happened in the last 40 days, I said, "Yes, there sure has but how do you know it has been 40 days?" He said, "You remember the night we left the apartment in Perpignon, that was the night before Ash Wednesday, Mardi Grau. Today is "Good Friday" and it's been 40 days." I said, "How do you know that Joe?" He said, "Trust me Loo-tenant, it's been 40 days." I trusted Joe!

I went to the paymaster to see if I could get an advance on my April 15th pay. He said that with my departure orders I could receive the advance because I would be on leave in the United States on my next payday. I was grateful for this because I was "flat broke," except for cigarette money. I was definitely ready to leave. I picked up my pay, packed my bag, and was ready to travel, hopefully by air. When Joe and I left 63 Brook St., we had a chance to say goodbye to the staff and to thank them for tolerating us for so long.

We departed London by air early on the 8th of April, en-route to Iceland. The airplane was a C-54 (like a commercial DC-4) four-engine transport and was piloted by a TWA airline crew in TWA uniforms. Lt. Paul Packer and Joe were in our group of airmen departing London for the States that day. We arrived in Iceland's Keflivik airport in the daylight and it looked much different than I had expected. I envisioned ice and snow, but was pleasantly surprised to see a lot of green pastures and rock fences. It was very similar to what I had experienced when I was in the RCAF in Eastern Canada.

It had been almost dark when we left Iceland, and it seemed to be an awfully long night before we were on the approach to either Goose Bay or Gander airport in Newfoundland. A long trip, but the airplane was equipped with regular airline seats and it was much more comfortable than the flight from Gibraltar to London. . Dark and snowy skies awaited our approach for the landing in Newfoundland.

The pilot of the C-54 had to make a circling approach to the airport as he missed being lined up with the runway on the first approach. I could barely see the lights of the runway as we pulled up in the missed approach procedure. We climbed out and started another approach and this time we were able to land. I said a short prayer as we started our go-round, and it was obviously answered.

We were taken by bus to a "chow hall" to eat while they were re-fueling the airplane, and then were off to somewhere in the U.S.; I think it was Bangor, Maine. Another re-fueling and we then were en-route to New York City. We arrived in New York on the morning of the 10th of April, and were taken by military bus to an office building in the city, where we were given our orders for our transportation to our hometown; we also received a leave of absence. I was to report to Miami Beach for re-assignment on May 9th.

I said goodbye to Joe Kinnane in front of the building, as he was going to another train station for the short ride to his home in Bayonne, New Jersey. It was a fond goodbye; we had been through a lot together. We expected to see each other in Miami Beach, but somehow we never did connect up and that was the last time that I was ever to see this true friend.

Before Paul Packer and I boarded a train to Chicago, I sent a telegram to my parents saying that I was back in "God's Country" and would be home on Tuesday the 11th. We were on a sleeper Pullman car, and after dinner and a drink in the "smoker," we retired to a full night's sleep. In the morning, we arrived in Chicago to a joyful greeting by Paul Packer's family - mother, father, and aunts and uncles. It was quite a greeting; even a photographer from The Chicago Tribune was on hand to record the greeting that Paul received from his family. (I still have that clipping from the newspaper).

CHAPTER 15

HOME AT LAST

I called my parents and told them what time I would arrive in Aurora, Illinois on the inter-urban train, and asked if they could please pick me up. I arrived around noon in Aurora and it was a joyful and tearful greeting from my mother and my Aunt Mabel. My dad and my uncle were happy to see me as they forestalled the normal handshakes for long-awaited hugs. It was wonderful to be with my family again. We talked non-stop on the ride home and it was so nice to drive into *my* small hometown once more.

It was a town where everyone knew that I had been MIA, and many came to our house to say hello, give me a hug, a pat on the shoulder, and a welcoming and lengthy shake of my hand.

On the car ride home, I learned what their reaction was to receiving the two telegrams from England on the same day that they were sent. Since they were relayed from New York, Pat Kroh, the station agent/telegrapher, didn't know where they had originated. My parents thought that I had rejoined my unit in Italy after the first telegram. Later that day they were completely mystified with the 2nd telegram saying that I was spending time in London with Ambrose. They knew that the telegram was authentic because it was signed "Wes." The telegrams were both transferred through New York but they now knew that I was in London, England.

STARDUST FALLING

I was fortunate that in the list of phrases that could be sent through the censor that there was one that said who I was visiting and where. I sent this particular message on purpose to let them know for sure that I *was* in London. This second telegram, of course, totally confounded them. How could I be flying out of Italy and shot down somewhere in the south of France and end up visiting Amby Moore in London? They certainly were elated that I was safe, but there were far more questions than easy answers.

They wondered why the War Department hadn't advised them of the fact that I was no longer missing in action. Exactly one week after my two messages from England were received, a telegram did arrive from the War Department stating that I was no longer MIA and would return to my unit for duty. Bureaucracy in action….then as now.

My mother's imagination "ran wild," for she had made up her mind that I must have been seriously wounded and that I had been flown to England for treatment. She could see no other answer as to how I had gotten to England.

Late in the afternoon of the day I arrived home, I was in the bedroom changing clothes when my mother knocked on the door and came in. I was barefooted, with just my pants on. She demanded that I take my pants off and that I show her where I had been wounded. I had told all of them repeatedly on the ride home that I hadn't been injured but she wanted to see for herself, just to be certain. After she had inspected me, she said for me to get dressed and that supper would be ready shortly. This was my mother; *bless her heart…*

I had a wonderful leave before reporting to Miami Beach. I turned 21 while I was home and I had a great birthday party. Dionne and I spent the first weekend at my house and we really enjoyed being together again. She was working now and we only had the weekends to be together. Gasoline was rationed and I really couldn't use my parent's ration stamps to go back and forth to where she worked. She roomed with my younger sister Norma when she was visiting us. My

HOME AT LAST

older sister Audrey, who was Dionne's age, was in Cadet Nurse training and was not living at home at this time.

I was asked to speak at several veterans' organizations meetings in nearby towns and these were fun. I wasn't allowed to make any remarks, or answer any questions, about where, when and how I escaped. The known fact was that I had spent time behind the enemy lines and was now talking to them. Of course I couldn't buy a drink as someone always wanted to pay for mine.

At one of these meetings, my dad was with me and when someone bought me a drink, of course my father was included. He usually had a coke, as I had never seen him drink hard liquor. Finally, after some coaxing, someone suggested a sloe gin fizz and he said he would try one. Soon he had another and another and I realized that I had better take him home. The unfamiliar liquor really hit him hard and he was soon sound asleep in the car with me. When we got home, he whispered to me to be quiet and not wake my mother. Their bedroom was on the first floor and we had to pass it to get to the kitchen.

My dad had decided that he wanted to have a fried egg sandwich before going to bed. He picked up a large iron skillet and let it bang down on the stove with a noise that shook the whole house. My mother came charging out of their bedroom and quickly sensed that *both* of us had a little too much of the "sauce." She proceeded to cook the eggs and make the sandwiches but was boiling mad. I thought she would take it out on me for leading my dad astray, but while she didn't say much to me, she really let him have it.

The poor guy - it was probably the first time in his life that he drank "hard" liquor. He always said that he didn't drink because it didn't agree with him. Well, this time it did agree with him until he caught hell from his wife for the pleasure.

I spent a couple of days with the Paul Packer family in Chicago and thoroughly enjoyed it. They were a loving, close family and they made me most welcome. After spending the last couple of days of my leave with Dionne, I boarded a train for Miami Beach. As I was leaving home, my mother asked me to promise that I wouldn't volunteer for combat again and I readily agreed. I really thought then that I had paid my "dues" and didn't want any more combat.

When I arrived at Miami along with Paul Packer, we were quizzed and evaluated, given a physical exam, and then told to enjoy the sand while they sorted out our papers and decided where to assign us.

My friend Lt. Earl Wolf had arrived a day or two before us, bringing along his new bride, Dorothy. I remembered that he had told me that his airplane was named after his sweetheart, "DOTTIE I." I was now to meet her in person and I enjoyed having lunch with them. We had a very nice visit, reliving our adventures in England. He embarrassed me by recited the story of the night that I was caught in the bombing raid in England, and how I struck out when I took my *date* home and found out that she wasn't really the "date" that I had expected.

The time in Miami Beach went fairly fast, although I was there longer than the others because all of my papers were still in Italy. This included my military official logbook (Form 5). It was hard to assign me without a full set of papers. They had to take my word for a lot of it, such as my experience and flight time. Also, I had to certify that I had indeed flown the required number of hours to receive flight pay for April. I had the aircraft numbers and flight time written on a paper, but that was the only record available of those flights.

In due time, I was assigned to the B-17 pilot training school at Sebring, Florida, as an instructor. I enjoyed this and was later sent to the flight instructor's school at Lockbourne, Ohio. I went through the instrument flight training school while continuing to instruct pilots transitioning to the B-17 in Sebring, Florida.

While I was based at Sebring, I had the occasion to take my first vacation back home to Paw Paw. In the meantime, my belongings had arrived from Italy. I happily found my RCAF logbook which had all

HOME AT LAST

of my military flight time in it. There was little else except summer clothes and socks and underwear. My camera and pictures were gone and my Shady Lady had also disappeared. I sifted through the summer clothing that apparently no one had any use for, as it had been winter in Italy when the box was packed. I decided that they perhaps had kept my Shady Lady to also keep them warm. In my haste and impatience to see what else had come, I dumped the remaining contents out onto the carpeting in the middle of the living room floor. I was now surrounded by my parents, sister, aunt and uncle. To my surprise and complete embarrassment, out poured pack after pack of condoms. They had been on the very bottom but now were stacked on top of the heap.

My dad and Uncle Cloyd slid slightly down in their seats and covered their smirks with their hands while mother and Aunt Mable quickly pulled my fifteen year old sister Norma into the kitchen. I tried explaining our use of the condoms as urine bags in combat but I could tell that my dad and uncle didn't believe a word of it. I later hoped that my dad told mother my story and I know that *she* would have believed me.

I began to get restless and wished that I hadn't promised my mother that I wouldn't volunteer for combat again. A list was posted for B-29 training and I signed up. I had visions of getting a shiny new "aluminum tube with wings and four engines" that I could name "Shady Lady," and a new combat crew. I was ready to go to combat in the Pacific. I was excited about the B-29; a new and larger airplane has always excited me. It was a big step up from the B-17 and I loved it. I graduated from the B-29 school at Maxwell Field, Montgomery, Alabama, and I was looking forward to being sent to combat phase school to be ready to go back to combat.

I knew that I could get Alice (Eakle) Marks to make me another "Shady Lady" window shade to replace the one that remained in Italy. It was with mixed emotions, and some disappointment, when I found out that I was to be an instructor in the B-29 pilot training school at Maxwell Field. I had to settle for this and was eventually promoted to Captain. I had been a 1st Lt. for a long time. I fully believe that if the war had lasted a few months longer however, I would have gotten my wish to fly off in a new "Shady Lady" B-29.

One forenoon, I was instructing two students on takeoffs and landings at my base at Maxwell Field, the tower operator called me and asked if my students had both been "soloed." I replied in the affirmative and he told me that I was to report to the base adjutant as soon as possible. I had the students stop the airplane on the ramp, and I got out and proceeded to the adjutant's office in my flight suit.

When I arrived, I saluted and he said, "Captain, do you want to stay in the Air Corps or do you want out?" I asked how soon I had to make the decision and he replied that I had till 1330 that afternoon. I left his office tying to figure out what to do. I changed into my uniform and went to lunch still trying to figure it all out. I was pretty sure that if I stayed in, I would have a desk job and my flying would be limited. All I had ever wanted to do was to fly airplanes. I reported back at 1330 and told the adjutant that I wanted to get out, and he said that orders would be issued. I was to report back to his office to pick up the travel orders at 1600 that same afternoon.

I left the B-29, Maxwell Field, and the military in that fashion that very evening. My travel orders allowed me to have a chance to stop off and visit a lady friend and her parents in Anniston, Alabama, enroute to my final destination of Chicago. I celebrated V-J Day night with my young lady friend. Her father gave us a bottle of bourbon and told us to have a good time, whereupon we joined the people of Anniston in a joyous celebration in the town square. The next day, I proceeded to Chicago and to Ft. Sheridan, Illinois, to be formally discharged. That was the end of my active duty in the military for the time being. I had flown about 2500 hours in my four years of active duty in WWII. It was now time to move on. I was 22, and like millions of other young men, I was looking for a job, preferably a flying job.

THE END

EPILOGUE

I would like to give the reader the information that I have gathered on my crewmembers when they returned to civilian life after WWII. This data is as accurate as I have found possible.

With the exception of Flight/Engineer, Staff/Sergeant *Edward T. Madigan*, who replaced Staff/Sergeant *Frank Rogers* on the crew, all survived the crash of Stardust. Lt. *Robert W. Johnson,* Lt. *Ernest Jenkins, and* Lt. *Walter M. Amundsen* spent the remainder of the war as POW's in Stalag Luft #1 on the Baltic. Sergeants *Henderson, Hoskins, Najarian, and Rice* spent the remainder of the war in Stalag Luft #4 POW camp. Only *Joe ("Mike") Kinnane* and I escaped capture by the Germans. (All of my sergeants who were POW'S were promoted to Staff/Sergeants upon their release from the POW camp).

After the war, Lt. *Robert W. Johnson*, Co-Pilot, left the Air Corps for a short time, only to rejoin the newly re-named Air Force for a total of 21 years. He then retired as a Lt. Col., USAF, and worked as an inspector for the Department of Defense for another 23 years. On January 24, 2005, just short of his 85th birthday, Bob passed away in northern Illinois, leaving his wife Irene of 53 years, three daughters, and one son.

Lt. *Ernest Jenkins*, bombardier/right front gun, returned to his hometown, Charlotte, South Carolina, after the war and was the personnel manager for International Aircraft. He left that position to be the regional manager of personnel for the state of South Carolina. He and his wife, Sarah, now live in quiet retirement. "Ernie" stayed active in the Air Force Reserve and retired as a Lt. Colonel. I often communicated with Ernie, when I wanted to check my data, as he has a most remarkable memory of the events of our adventure together.

Lt. *Walter M. Amundsen*, navigator/left front gun, returned to Minnesota, and possibly to his old job as a newspaper reporter. I am unable to confirm this, but I am sure that our "super scrounger" was very good at whatever he did. Walt passed away in the late 1990's.

I have tried to find information on S/Sgt *Edward Madigan* (who was killed in the crash) for years. I know that he was from Wisconsin and I believe near the city of Madison. I found a letter from his mother to my mother written while we were all MIA. The letter was from the Madison area. Fortunately the letter contained the only photo that I have of Ed Madigan and it is in the picture section of the book. We had him on our crew only a short time and I was not well acquainted with him.

Sergeant *Harold B. Rice*, ball turret gunner. Unfortunately, I have not been able to obtain any information on Harold. He was a good-looking kid with blond hair and an infectious smile. He was a delight to the entire crew.

S/Sergeant *Joe "Mike" Kinnane,* waist gunner, became a combat gunnery instructor at an airbase in Florida for the remainder of the war. He was promoted to Staff Sergeant during his tour as a gunnery instructor. After his discharge from the service, he went back to his original job at the General Motors factory near his home in Bayonne, New Jersey. Health problems plagued him after he retired, and Joe died at age 65 from a sudden heart attack. His family had always known him as "Mike" and I have had several fine conversations with his only daughter, Diane Levinson, who lives in New Jersey. I have also corresponded with his brother, John, who sent me the photograph of Joe "Mike" for the picture section.

S/Sergeant *Ascamie ("Arky") Najarian*, radio operator and upper rear gun, lives with his wife in Rhode Island. "Arky" pursued a lifetime job as a mailman after he was discharged from the service. I have spoken with him on the phone and we have re-lived the events of our combat experiences. His daughter Janice Kavjian, of Massachusetts, and I have also had several good phone conversations about her father, and I am indebted to her for sending me her father's picture.

EPILOGUE

S/Sergeant *James P. Hoskins*, tail gunner and sometimes waist gunner, lives in retirement with his wife *Juanita* in Tennessee. They have three sons. I have enjoyed visiting with both of them by phone. He worked for the Eastman Kodak Company in his area for his entire working career.

S/Sergeant *Clifford E. Henderson* was our waist gunner and also our armorer. Cliff has been reported as deceased, but I cannot confirm this. Occasionally, with my permission, Jim Hoskins and Cliff Henderson changed crew positions on our missions in Stardust. On the final mission, they had exchanged positions once again and Hoskins was at the waist gun position, with Cliff Henderson in the tail gun position.

I have no information on our former flight/engineer S/Sergeant *Frank Rogers*. He was not on the mission on Jan 27th, 1944.

My original radio operator, Sergeant *Parks,* was ill when we were ready to depart Grand Island, Nebraska, and was left behind. He was replaced by S/Sergeant *Najarian*.

I have no doubt that each of these men could write their own account of this time spent with equally fervent recollections. I am ever grateful for their presence in my life's story.

Through the early years after the war, I corresponded several times with my French friend and benefactor Jean Juvenile and his family. He wrote to me in French and I wrote to him in English. I would have to find someone who could translate French to English to read his letters to me. In one letter, he told me that *Pierre Dudet* and a friend were stopped by the Gestapo on the street and asked for their identification papers. The friend panicked and pulled out his gun rather than his perfectly good identification papers. The Gestapo shot both of them immediately and their bodies were left in the street for four hours as a warning to all of the Resistance workers. This happened two weeks before the Allied invasion of southern France.

(Pierre had been very active in the Resistance movement and was #2 in command to Jean Juvenile.) His death at the hands of the Gestapo was very sad for me - Pierre and his family was the host for my bombardier, Ernie Jenkins, while we were in Aix-en-Provence. I saw Pierre almost nightly at the Juvenile home dinner table.

I have tried unsuccessfully to find any information on our Perpignon hostess, *Simone Pasquet.* I would really like to learn whether she made good her escape from Perpignon, and survived the war. I did find that she is listed as one of the members (helpers) of the "Burgundy" escape route. I am still trying to find her. (Thanks to e-mail and the Internet, it is my hope that this may still be possible as well as locating others through this publication.)

My lifelong friend Capt. Tommy Boyle retired from airline piloting in 1986, after 35 years of flying for UAL. He lost his beloved wife Margaret this past summer and continues to live in northern Illinois. Tom and I have enjoyed many fishing trips together through the years, and I know that Tom is the best salmon fisherman that I have ever known. We stay in touch regularly by telephone.

My teenage girlfriend, *Dionne,* married and has one child, a beautiful daughter, living near them in northern Illinois. Dionne owned and managed a beauty shop for years and her husband was a plumber. They are both retired and have remained in that area.

Alice (Eakle) Marks still lives in her little red house on the boundary of the Rochelle airport in northern Illinois. She started her life in the early days of aviation, helping her father light the flares at the emergency landing field at Waterman Illinois. She has lived on or near an airport all of her life. She is one of a select group of pioneering, air-minded people, who have been involved in aviation for a lifetime. Alice enchanted the imaginations of more than 40 soldiers, sailors and airmen with her "Shady Lady" drawings, expertly done on window shades so that they could be rolled up conveniently. Her

EPILOGUE

husband, "*Hank*, was a B-17 pilot in WWII, and after the war he was a crop-duster pilot and aircraft mechanic in the northern Illinois area. He also worked in De Kalb, Illinois for the GE Company for over 30 years. Hank held the rank of 1st Lt. when he left military service in 1945. Their son Mike was killed in a tragic aircraft accident. Their two daughters, Heather and Melissa live in Washington State and northern Illinois, respectively.

I am indebted to Melissa (Marks) Van Drew for some of the pictures that appear in the photo section. Nancy (Eakle) Coss, Alice's sister, who lives in the state of Washington, sent me the beautiful picture of the "Shady Lady" shown in the picture section, thank you both. I was able to glean some of the information on the Eakle family from the John A. Eakle's book, "The Eakle Family of Progress Corner." I received this fine book from Heather Marks and her husband Cliff Sanderlin. It was also a privilege to receive a written record of how the "Shady Lady" started her life in WWII and all of her adventures thereafter. Alice (Eakle) Marks wrote all of this down in 1945 and it is a most interesting read. I had no idea that her pin up's were so well received, and how they had traveled around the world.

Major Harry Reed (USMC) survived WWII after two complete combat tours in the Pacific; his "Shady Lady" airplanes were shot out from under him twice. Harry went on to manage the Downtown Airpark in Oklahoma City. He had gotten in the good graces of the FAA and now held all of the necessary pilot licenses to operate a successful airport venture. I had a chance to visit with him in Oklahoma City and to fly his "Howard DGA" airplane, which was indeed quite a thrill.

Harry was the Commander of the Marine Reserve Air Squadron in Dallas and commuted to Dallas for his scheduled military duties. His squadron was recalled to active duty during the Korean War and he led his unit of F4U's into combat. Harry was a Lt. Col. at the time and was on a low-altitude strafing mission when he was involved in a mid-air collision with one of his comrade pilots.

Harry was able to bail out of the stricken airplane only to land in the middle of a nest of the North Korean enemy. He decided to fight his way out with only his 45-caliber side-arm. This Marine hero would rather fight to the end than be captured. He was killed in his effort. His squadron circled overhead and could do little to help or protect their leader. I was able to get this description of Harry Reed's heroic death in Korea from a retired Marine Major General, who served with Harry in both WWII and Korea. It was only 12 short years after my first flying lesson that my instructor, mentor and friend was killed in combat. On July 30, 1951 a Marine legend was born. "Fate" is truly the "hunter".

Spencer Mack and his wife *Joyce* lived out their lives in their home in Waterman, Illinois. "Spence" passed away in 2003, and his wife Joyce preceded him by several years. I kept in contact with Spence until he passed away. He was indeed a fine man and a good friend. I was notified of his passing by his son Spencer Jr.

My good friend *Capt. John Fannin*, from the Roswell days and Continental Airlines, died of a heart attack at age 59 after a 33 year airline career. I was honored to be one of the pallbearers at his funeral. His wife *Jane* has remarried and lives in Texas.

Capt. Gene Hersche left the service as a Captain at the end of the war, and went to work for Continental Airlines as a pilot in the spring of 1946. He completed his Continental Airline career at age 60 and retired to west Texas. Sadly, he suffered a severe stroke several years ago and is cared for by his daughter, Alison, in the San Diego area.

Capt. Harold Spores and his wife Jean, my good friends from the Roswell and Continental Airlines days, live in happy retirement in west Texas. Through frequent e-mails we stay in contact.

My own career after the war went like this:

On May 10, 1946, I was hired by Continental Airlines as a co-pilot. Over my 37-year airline career with Continental I was privileged to fly, as a pilot, in most of the airplanes that Continental operated. The

EPILOGUE

Boeing 747-100 was the largest airplane that I had the pleasure of flying as the captain. I retired in 1983, after flying the DC10-30 (long range) airplane on the South Pacific run from Los Angeles to Sydney, Australia.

I was recalled to active military duty during the Korean War (1951-1953) and flew the C97 Strato-cruiser. The C-97 was a double-decked cargo and personnel carrier. I was attached to the Pacific Division of MATS (Military Air Transport Service) and was based in Honolulu, Hawaii. Most of my flights were from Honolulu to Wake Island to Tokyo, and the return flights were through Midway Island to Honolulu and then on to San Francisco (Travis Air Force Base). We often carried the most severely wounded of the Korean War back home in the pressurized, high-altitude C-97.

During the time that I was based in Honolulu, I was assigned to ferry a YC-97 from the Boeing factory in Seattle, Washington to Frankfort, Germany. The YC-97 was the prototype airplane for the C-97. It was closely associated with the Boeing B-29 in most respects other than the cargo fuselage. The YC was a bit smaller than the familiar C-97. The C-97 was the military version of the Boeing 377 "Strato-Cruiser." All of these airplanes were pressurized for high-altitude flight. I believe that all of the YC-97s were based in Honolulu, and only 9 were built. It was one of the YC-97s from Hickam Field Honolulu that was chosen by the Air Force to be modified into a photo reconnaissance configuration, and was to be ferried to Frankfort, Germany by my Honolulu-based crew.

My first sight of this airplane in the hangar at Boeing Field was bewildering, to say the least. The nose and cockpit section were completely severed from the airframe and wheeled aside. In the front of the remaining airframe, a huge camera had been installed. The cargo floor had been cut away in the camera area so that the monster camera completely filled the airplane from top to bottom. The camera and mount weighed 7,000 lbs. (3.5 tons). This was the largest airborne camera ever built (and the *only* one of its kind) and is now on display at the Air Force Museum in Dayton, Ohio.

I was to ferry this nose-heavy monster from Seattle to Frankfort, Germany. It took some sharp calculations to determine how much weight to put in the rear of the airplane to allow it to fly in a normal manner. Of course, it could no longer be pressurized, and I had no intention of ever flying it through a thunderstorm.

The ferry flight to Germany went smoothly, with only one emergency landing en-route (engine fire), and I had fully expected to be returned to Honolulu after completing the task of delivering the airplane. This was not to be.

I was "shanghaied" into remaining in Germany with the airplane and was to fly it on photo-recon spy missions from its base in Frankfort for four months. (This was during a time prior to the U-2 and other spy planes.) We were able to photograph much of the Russian operations in the Baltic Sea area, as well as along the air corridor from Frankfort to Berlin. This unarmed spy plane duty was in some ways as dangerous as flying in combat in WWII. My part, as pilot of the airplane on the "Daisy Mae" project is another story for another day.

I had been in the Air Force Reserve in El Paso, Texas, and had gratefully taken the reserve duty pay, plus I had the opportunity to fly many great military airplanes including the P-51, AT-6, B-29, and B-50. It was now dues-paying time and I paid mine, and perhaps in some small way helped my country remain free of the Soviet threat.

I was to return to Continental Airlines and completed the next 30 years as a flight captain, stationed in El Paso, Texas until 1963. I then transferred to Los Angeles and to the jet airplanes, until I retired.

My last flight as a Continental Airlines captain was April 29, 1983 (…that antiquated age sixty rule…). My farewell flight was a DC10-30 flight from Honolulu to Los Angeles, completing a round trip from LA to Sidney, Australia. It was a bitter-sweet graduation day indeed.

For the last 13 months of my career, I enjoyed the number-one pilot seniority position at Continental. Not being cooped up in a POW

EPILOGUE

camp for the duration of WWII probably gave me the extra flight hours that enabled me to enter a commercial airline pilot career ten days after my 23rd birthday, than otherwise would have been possible. At least one perk came out of those months after being shot down over France!

After my retirement from Continental I pursued a second career as a commercial fisherman. I soon decided that it was a young man's job and gave it up to enjoy cruising up and down the southern California coast with my "first mate" Annette. These were truly the "Golden Years."

My beloved wife of 38 years, *Annette (Carson) Coss,* and I have loved and lived on the Palos Verdes Peninsula of southern California, overlooking the beautiful Pacific Ocean and Catalina Island. Annette is an accomplished artist who is not only recognized for her oil and watercolor work but is greatly thanked for her expertise with the cover of this book. It was Annette who also suggested the book title, "Stardust Falling."

Together, we have enjoyed years of cruising the Pacific on both our earlier sailboat and our powerboat, "Sea Whiskers," with many, many memorable trips.

I began sailing with my close friend, Continental Airlines Captain, *Sam Bickford* soon after I moved to Los Angeles. I bought a sailboat, and the years of sailing boats was exciting, as I often entered regattas and sailed against other boats of my class. My daughter, Nancy, was sometimes my only crewmember on these race events. After I tired of smaller sailboats, my wife Annette and I purchased an Islander 33' sailboat and thoroughly enjoyed cruising the blue Pacific.

Before my retirement from airline flying, we purchased a 42' "twin diesel" powerboat. This was the boat that I used alternately as a pleasure yacht and as a commercial fishing boat.

My friend *Sam Bickford* passed away in early 1991. Annette and I and Sam's wife *Ruth,* had the sad duty of scattering the "Captain's"

381

ashes in the Pacific, from the stern of "Sea Whiskers" at a spot that *Sam* had earlier chosen.

My former wife *Dee (Fuhrmann) Coss* (deceased*)* and I had two wonderful children, each inheriting the love of flight gene. My son *Casey* is currently a part owner, with his uncle Jerry, in the Cessna 172 "Sky-Hawk" and holds his commercial pilot license and is instrument flight rated. While making flying an avocation, he has owned two extremely successful entrepreneurial businesses in California. My daughter, *Nancy (Coss) Pohlig,* and her husband *Mike* have given me my only granddaughter, my cherished *Katie*, who is a fourth-year student in architecture here in California.

My daughter Nancy is an accomplished glider pilot in the southern California area, and at one time held the women's high-altitude sailplane record (30,000 ft.) in the state of Nevada. Nancy's husband Mike soloed a glider at age 14 and holds licenses in both power and sail planes. Mike works as a senior aeronautical engineer at the fabled Lockheed "Skunk Works" in Palmdale, California.

Until the summer of 2007, all of my three siblings and their spouses were each well, although scattered from coast to coast. We remain in touch by phone and e-mail.

My brother *Jerry* retired from a career as a Captain with United Airlines as well as continuing to enjoy over 34 years of private piloting his Cessna "Hawk" 172 with the colorful and distinctive cat on the tail. Jerry came to flying in his early thirties, retiring from UAL in 1995. I proudly rode in the cockpit jump seat on *his* last flight as Captain, just as he had ridden on mine – a privilege very few flying brothers are able to experience. He currently lives with his wife, Jaculine, in Denver, Colorado. Three step-children have now joined the family.

Jerry and his former wife, *Donna (Ackland) Coss*, have a daughter and two sons - both holding their private pilot licenses, with one working in the aviation field and their daughter owning a thriving

EPILOGUE

photography business in northern Illinois. Jerry's son-in-law holds a pilots license, owns, instructs and sells ultra-light aircraft in the midwest area. A granddaughter is currently studying in California to become a federal air traffic controller, continuing aviation into the next generation.

My sister *Audrey* lives in Florida. Her husband *Dick (Richard) Bell*, passed away in late June of this year (2007) and is missed greatly. Dick was a very successful businessman and community leader in the Clearwater area. They had one son (deceased) and three daughters, one of whom is employed with the FAA. They all live in the vicinity of their parents.

My sister *Norma* and her husband *"Gene" (Robert) Keller*, own and reside on a large tree farm in Florida, where they have lived for many years. They have three delightful daughters. One of the daughters lives near them in Florida, and the other two live in Texas.

Each of my nieces and nephews has been extremely successful in their chosen careers and have made their parents and their uncle quite proud.

I was blessed with a wonderful family that surrounded me with love and values that have carried me through the best and worst of times. I knew my own worth from an early age and was encouraged to dream and go forth with those dreams. My parents believed that hard work built character, tendered by love and discipline.

The last of my mother's siblings passed away in 2005 - Aunt Olive, at 100 and one-half. I still enjoy returning to my roots, Paw Paw, Illinois, to attend as many of the annual Labor Day town reunions as I can arrange. Visiting with cousins and school friends mean, and has always meant, a great deal to me.

People -- my family and my friends have always been important and necessary throughout my life and they have given me far more than I could possibly return. I am a blessed man that still enjoys the love and closeness of each of my siblings, their spouses and their children, and now, grandchildren and great-grandchildren.

I want to finish this epilogue with a tribute to my sister-in-law, *Jaculine Harrier-Coss*, my brothers' wife. She was kind to write the introduction to this book and with her considerable organizational, editing, and writing skills, she has been enormously helpful in completing this biography. I am very grateful to her - many, many thanks Jaculine! (I kiddingly sometimes refer to her as my loveable "Allez Vite #3)." My brother Jerry worked for many weeks on the procurement, and the layout of the pictorial section of the book. He and his wife Jaculine were particularly helpful in organizing the entire book into CD's so that it could be printed and published - thank you both very much. I also want to thank his grand-daughter Tara and daughter Jody, and her Hillside Studio staff in northern Illinois, for their expert help in producing the photography sections of this book.

The Lord kept me safe during frightening and dangerous times. Annette and I share our tremendous love of our Lord Jesus Christ and the many blessings bestowed upon us. My parents began that journey and He continues to guide me daily.

Now, at 84 years of age, I am comfortable with having lived and seen a great deal of the best that life has to offer.

I lived my dream – I flew for enjoyment, I flew to serve my country, and I flew for a living. What more could any one ask? I continue to be a very lucky man. I've said it once and I'll say it again, "All I ever wanted to do was to fly."   -WES COSS-

EPILOGUE

Post Script:

My friend, John Sevens, a retired professor of military history from the University of Indiana, has been working on a book for which I have contributed some of my experiences. John is a true "word-smith" and I highly recommend his book when it is published.

2007

The author's daughter Nancy Pohlig and son Casey with the Cessna 172 Sky-Hawk owned by Casey and his Uncle Jerry Coss

Casey and Nancy shown with the tail-art of the "Hawk"

Granddaughter Katie (right) ready to take a sailplane flight with her mother Nancy Pohlig

Granddaughter Kate Pohlig after viewing the cockpit of a B-17 like her Grandfather flew in WWII

2007

The author and his wife Annette in their home in Palos Verdes, CA overlooking the blue Pacific Ocean